The Way of the House Husband

KOUSUKE OONO

7

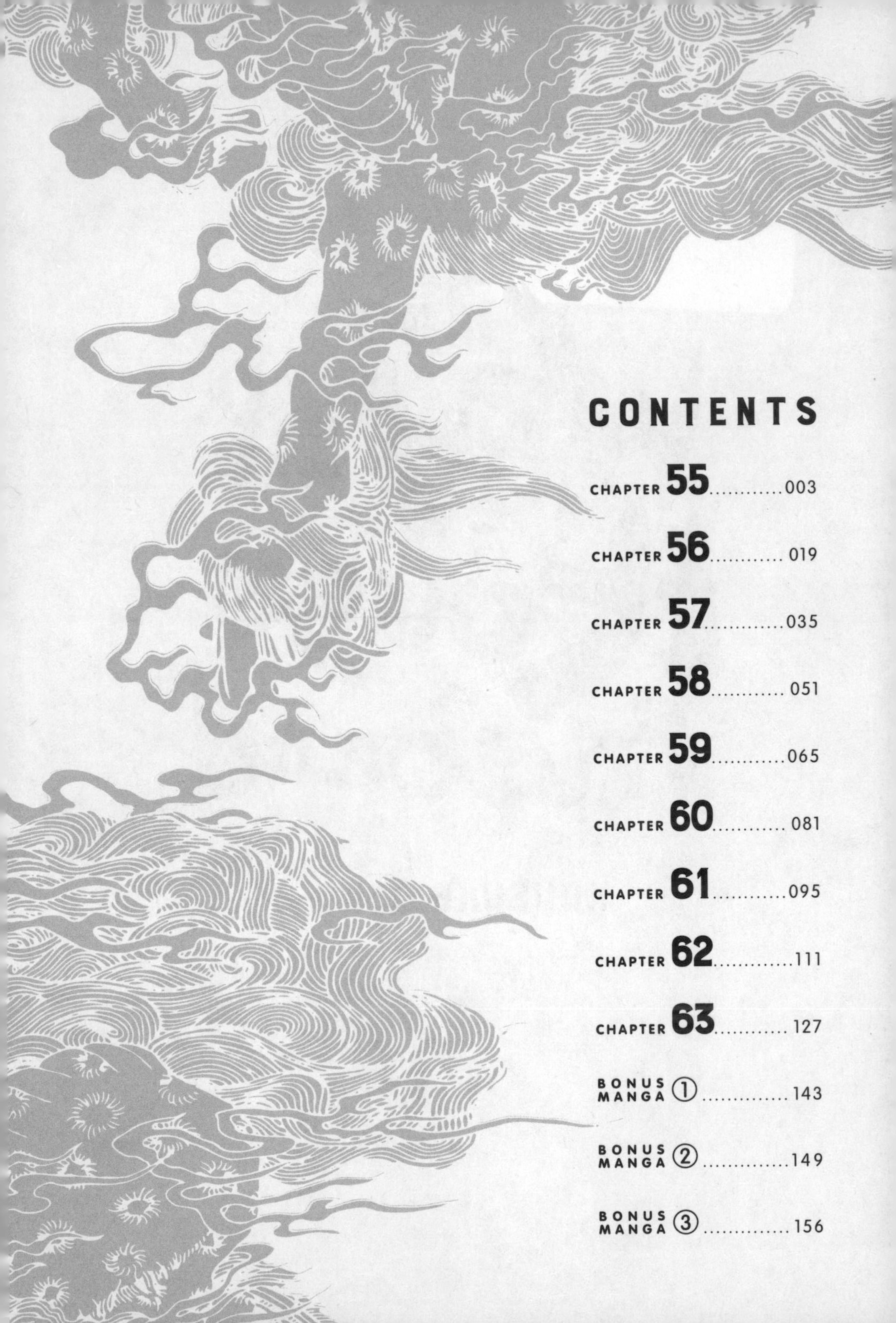

CONTENTS

CHAPTER 55

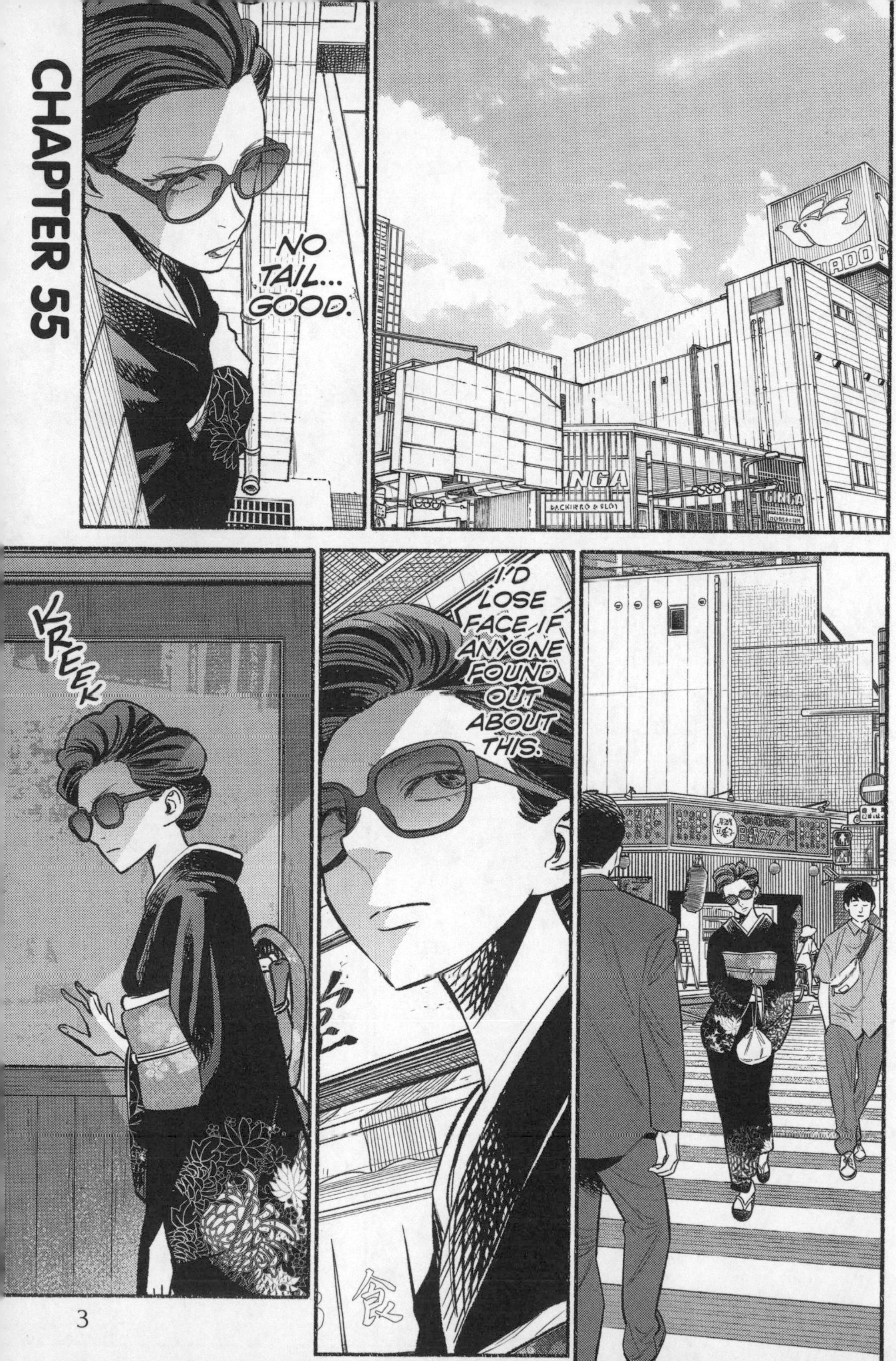
NO TAIL... GOOD.
I'D LOSE FACE IF ANYONE FOUND OUT ABOUT THIS.
KREEK

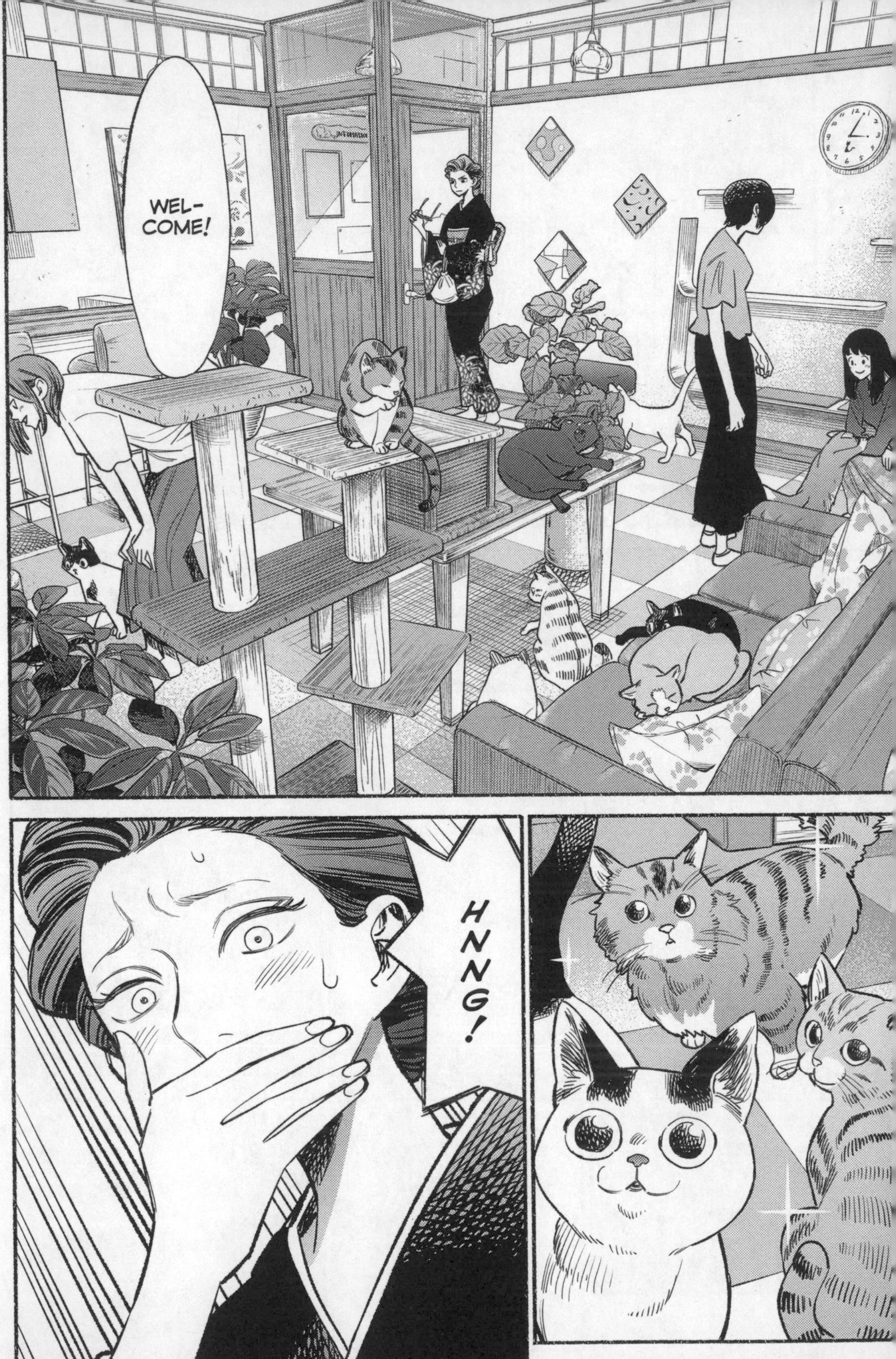
WEL-
COME!
HNNG!

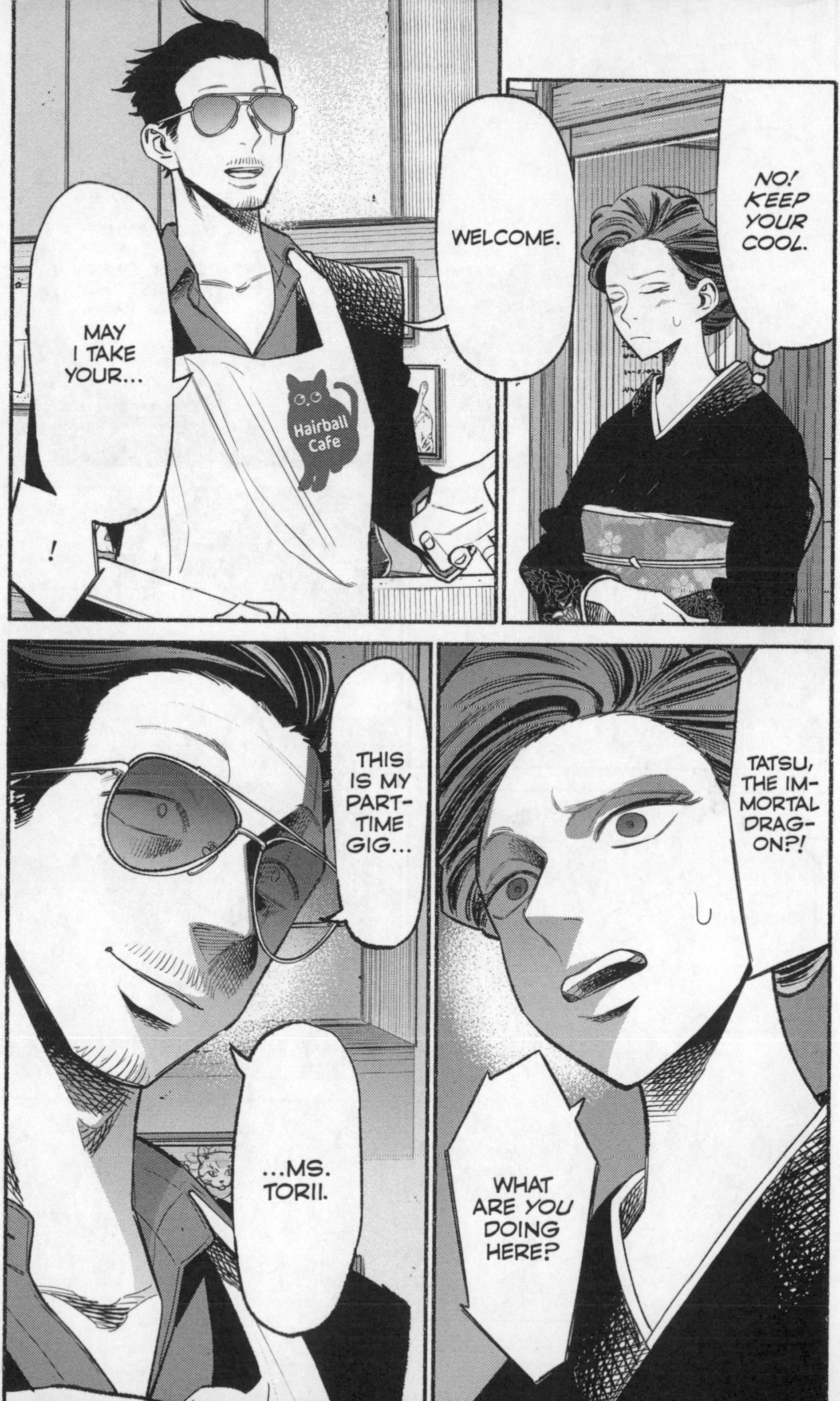
NO! KEEP YOUR COOL.
WELCOME.
Hairball Cafe
MAY I TAKE YOUR...
!
TATSU, THE IMMORTAL DRAGON?!
WHAT ARE YOU DOING HERE?
THIS IS MY PART-TIME GIG...
...MS. TORII.

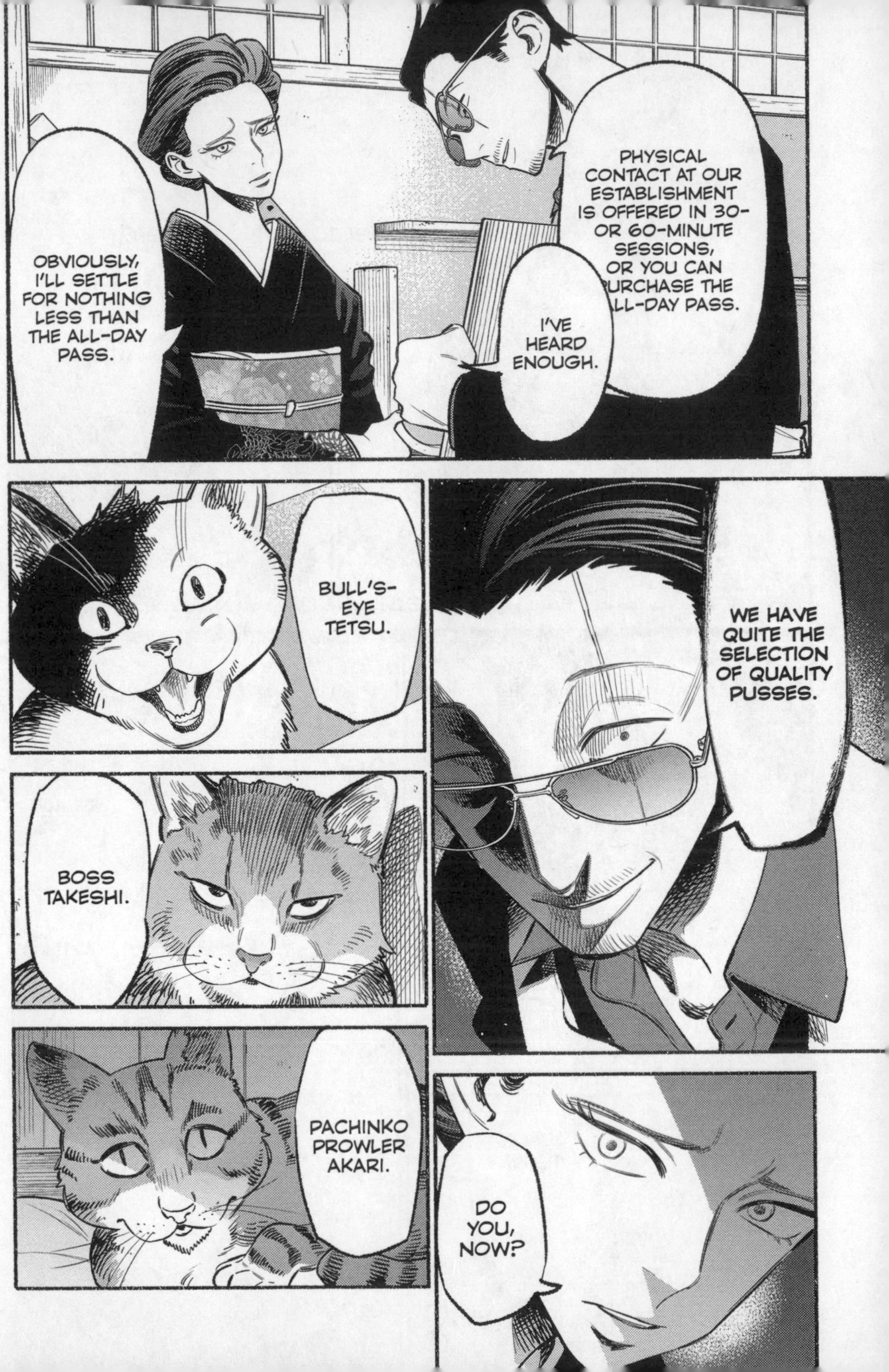
PHYSICAL CONTACT AT OUR ESTABLISHMENT IS OFFERED IN 30- OR 60-MINUTE SESSIONS, OR YOU CAN URCHASE THE LL-DAY PASS.
I'VE HEARD ENOUGH.
OBVIOUSLY, I'LL SETTLE FOR NOTHING LESS THAN THE ALL-DAY PASS.
WE HAVE QUITE THE SELECTION OF QUALITY PUSSES.
BULL'S-EYE TETSU.
BOSS TAKESHI.
DO YOU, NOW?
PACHINKO PROWLER AKARI.

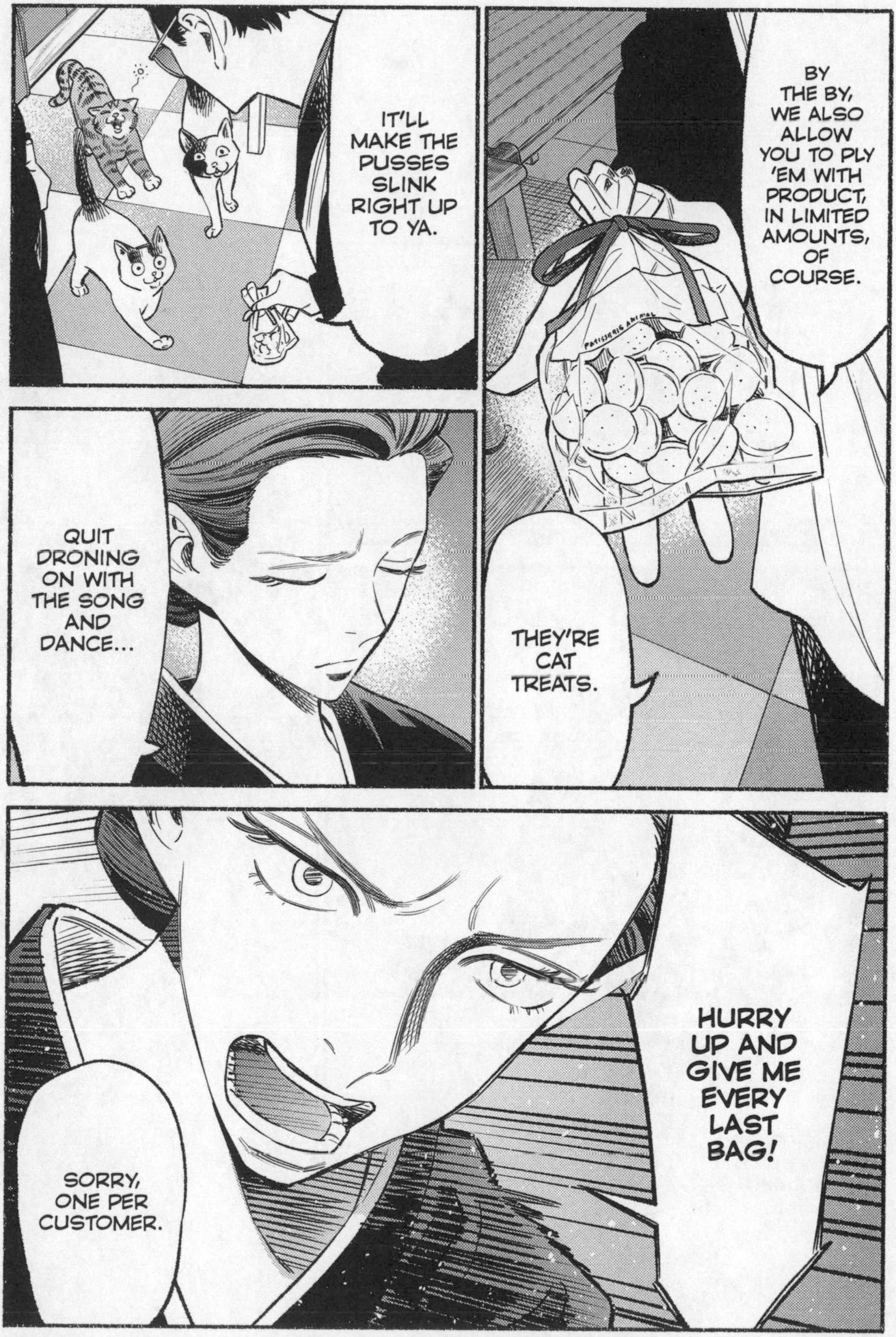
BY THE BY, WE ALSO ALLOW YOU TO PLY 'EM WITH PRODUCT, IN LIMITED AMOUNTS, OF COURSE.
THEY'RE CAT TREATS.
IT'LL MAKE THE PUSSES SLINK RIGHT UP TO YA.
QUIT DRONING ON WITH THE SONG AND DANCE...
HURRY UP AND GIVE ME EVERY LAST BAG!
SORRY, ONE PER CUSTOMER.

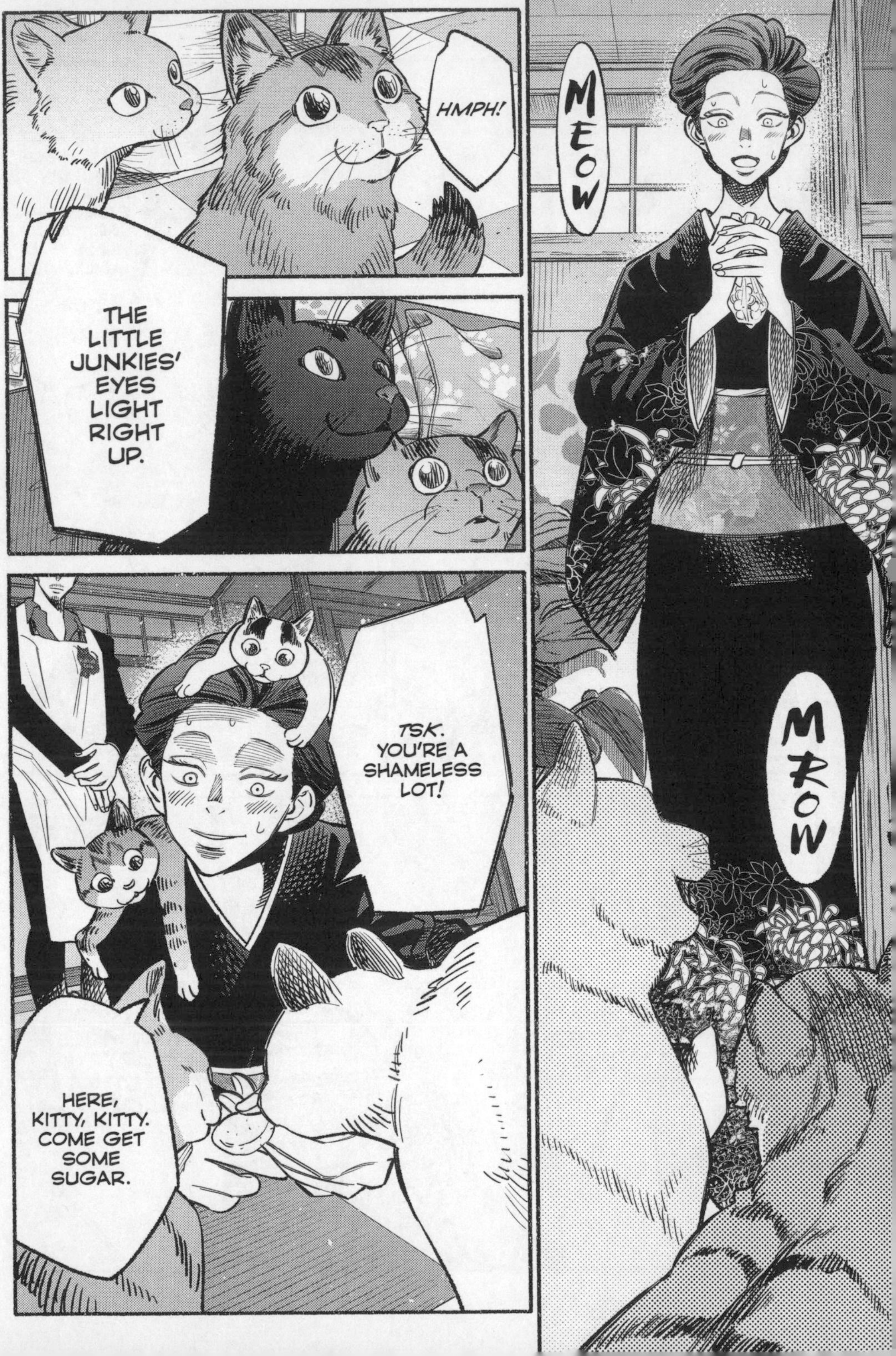
MEOW
MROW
HMPH!
THE LITTLE JUNKIES' EYES LIGHT RIGHT UP.
TSK. YOU'RE A SHAMELESS LOT!
HERE, KITTY, KITTY. COME GET SOME SUGAR.

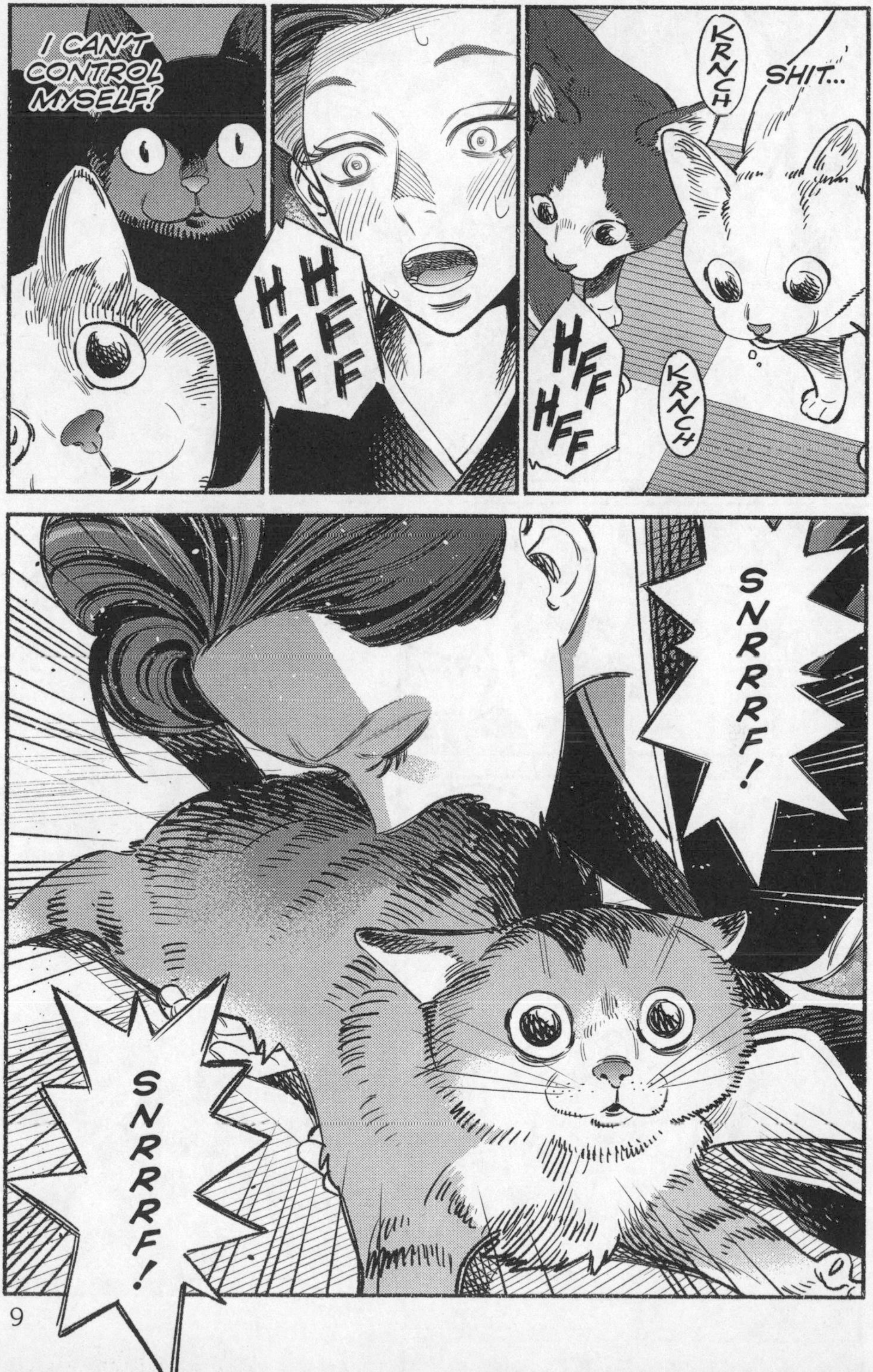
SHIT...
KRNCH
KRNCH
HFF HFF
I CAN'T CONTROL MYSELF!
HHFFFFFF
SNRRRF!
SNRRRF!

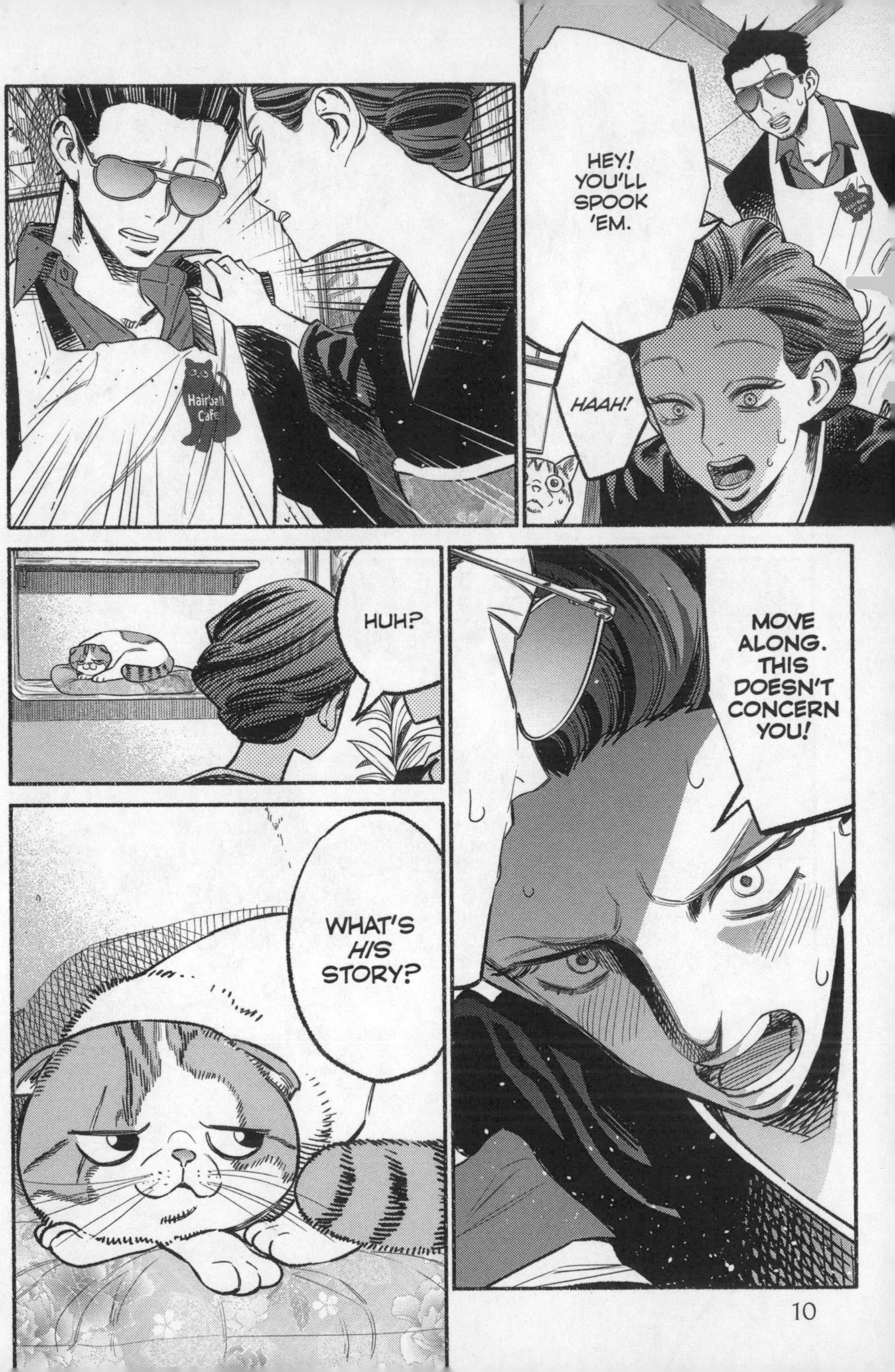
HEY! YOU'LL SPOOK 'EM.
HAAH!
MOVE ALONG. THIS DOESN'T CONCERN YOU!
HUH?
WHAT'S HIS STORY?

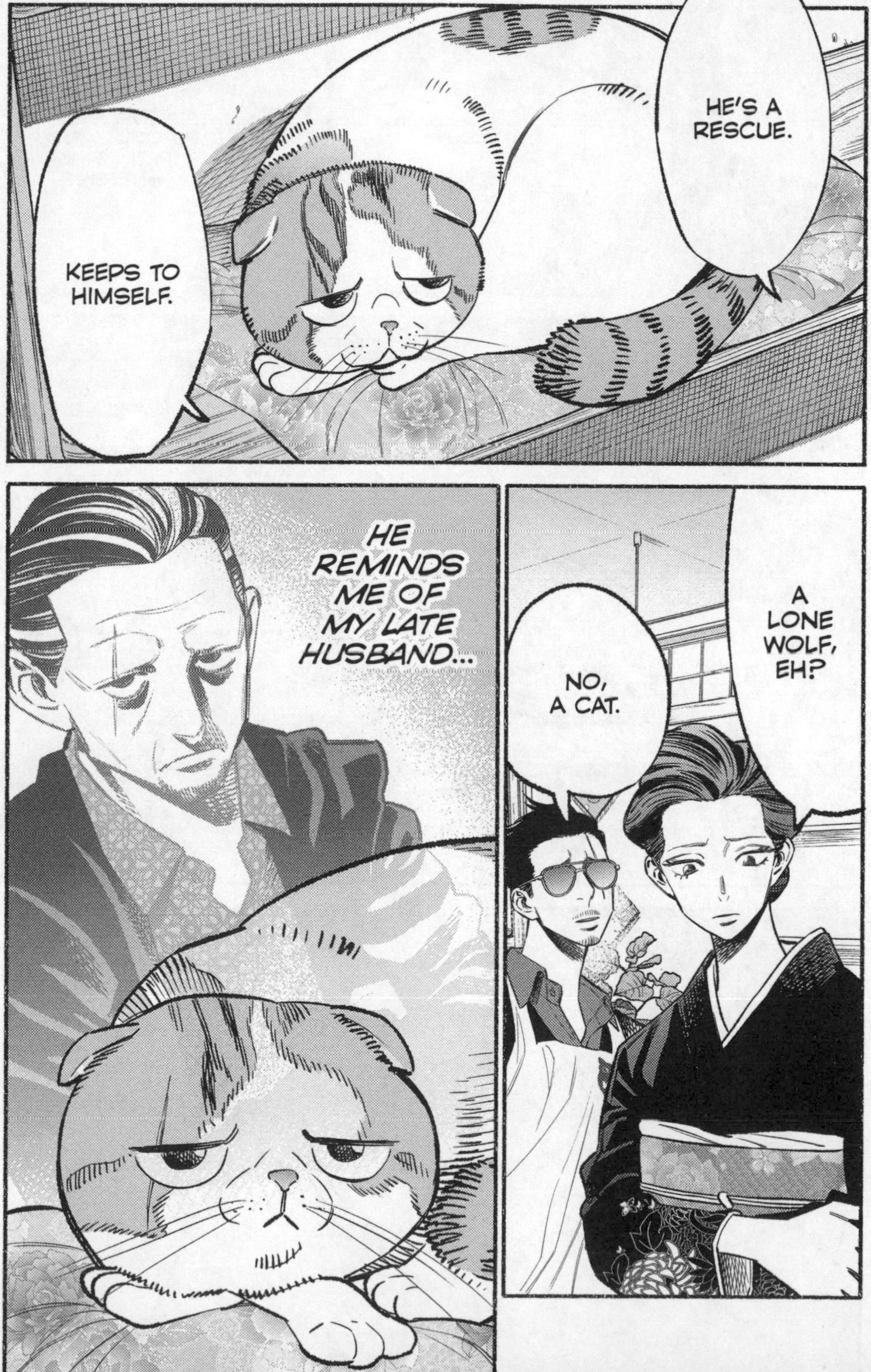
HE'S A RESCUE.
KEEPS TO HIMSELF.
A LONE WOLF, EH?
NO, A CAT.
HE REMINDS ME OF MY LATE HUSBAND...

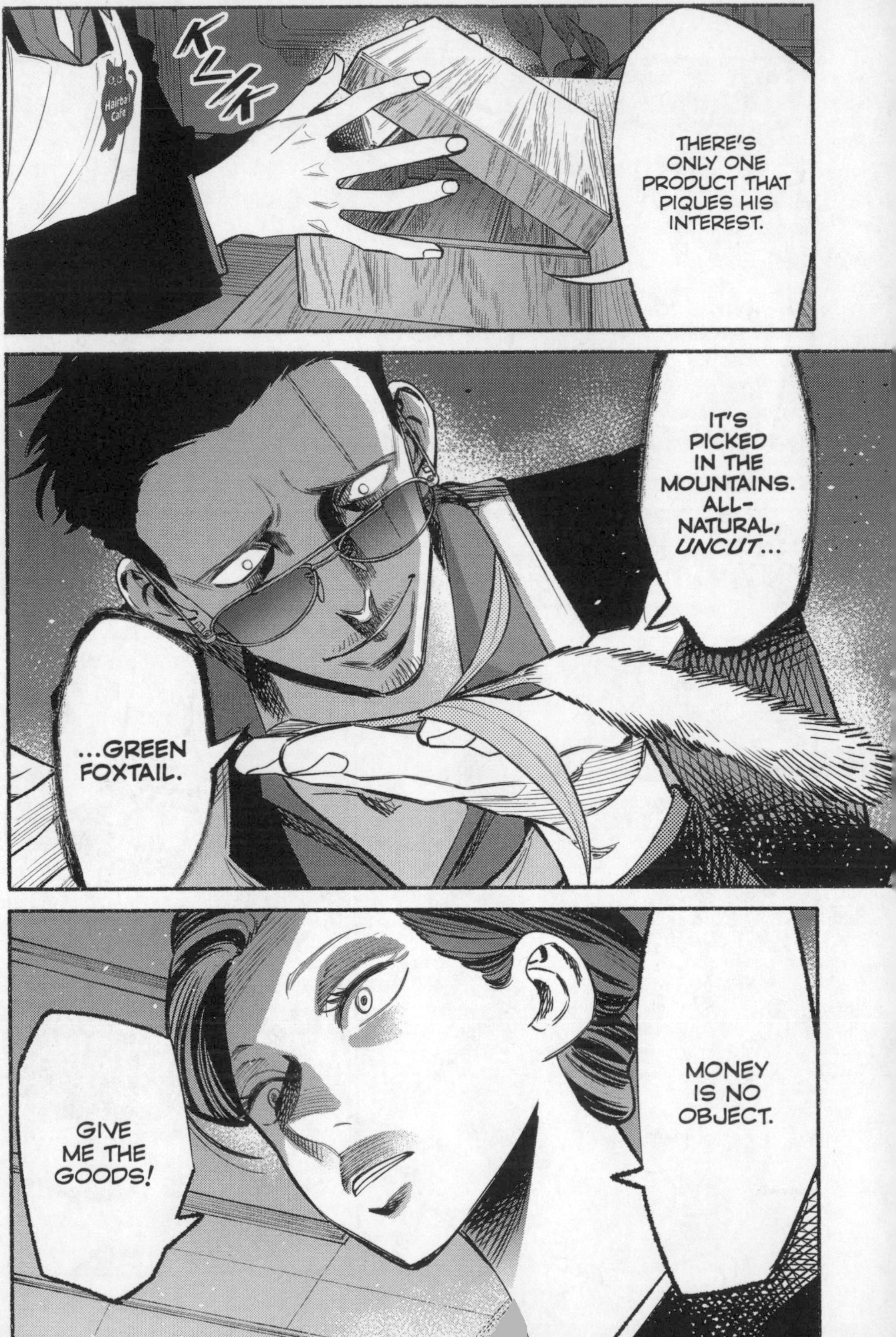
THERE'S ONLY ONE PRODUCT THAT PIQUES HIS INTEREST.
KLIK
Hairball Cafe
IT'S PICKED IN THE MOUNTAINS. ALL-NATURAL, *UNCUT*...
...GREEN FOXTAIL.
MONEY IS NO OBJECT.
GIVE ME THE GOODS!

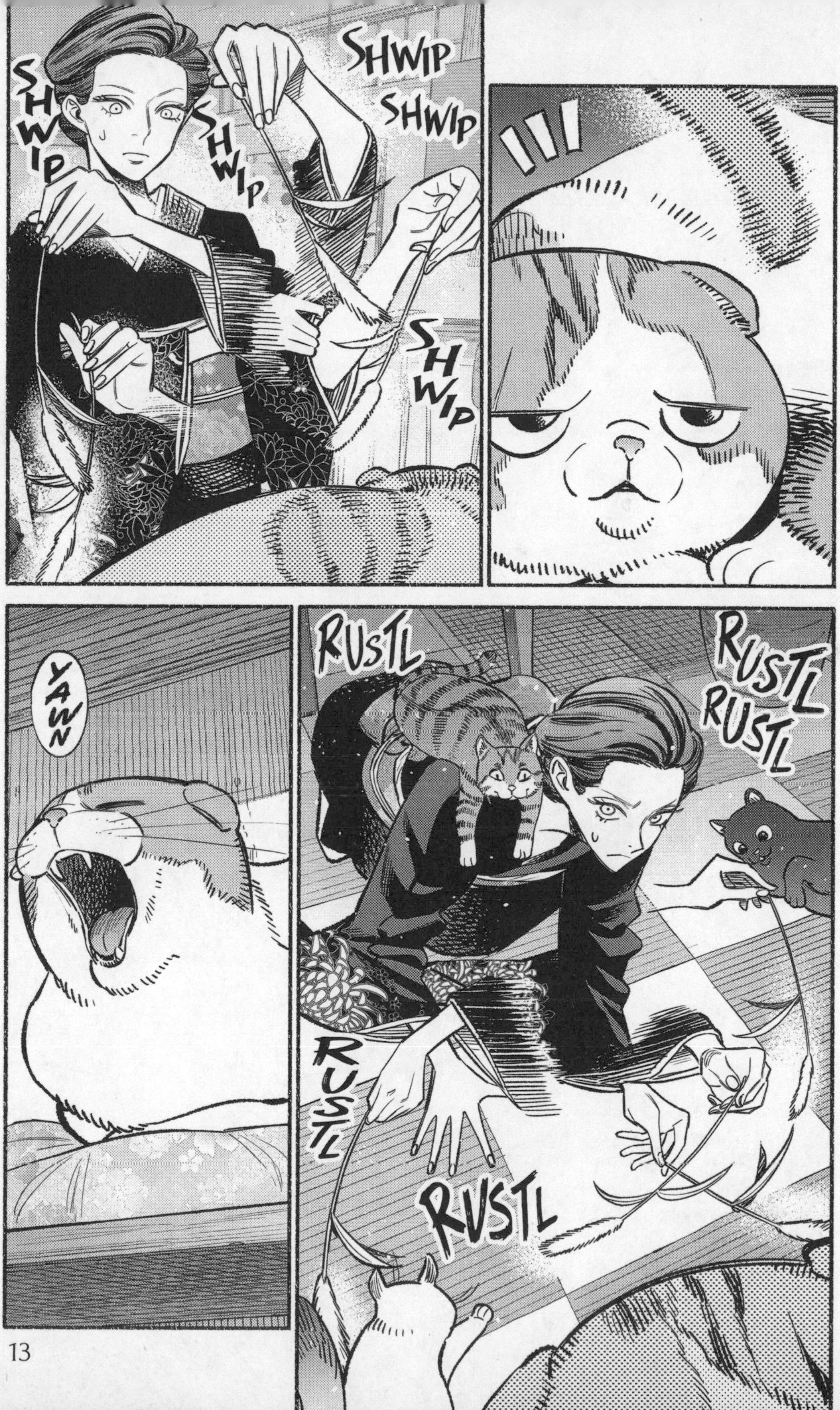
SHWIP
SHWIP
SHWIP
SHWIP
SHWIP
RUSTL
RUSTL
RUSTL
RUSTL
RUSTL
YAWN

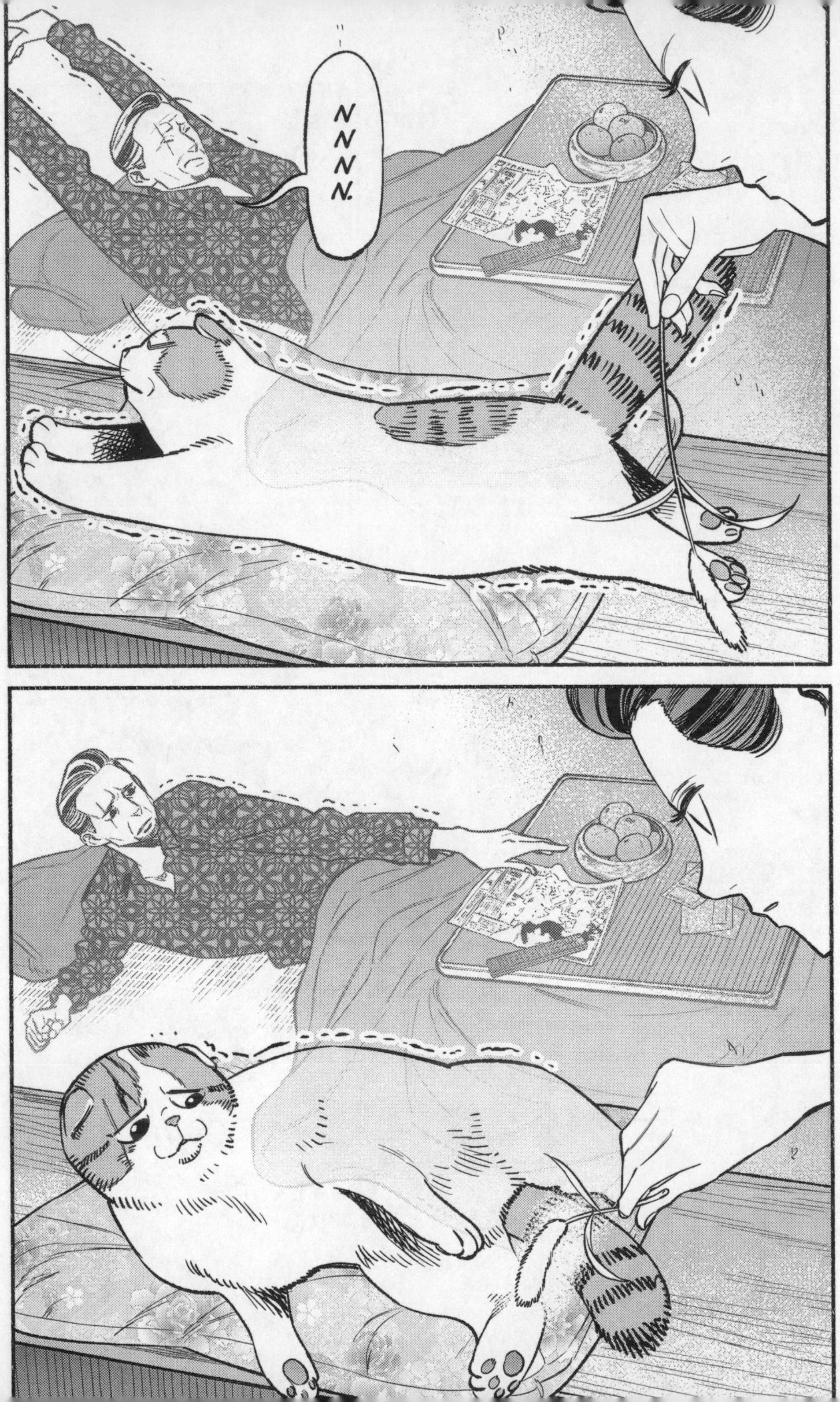
NNNN.

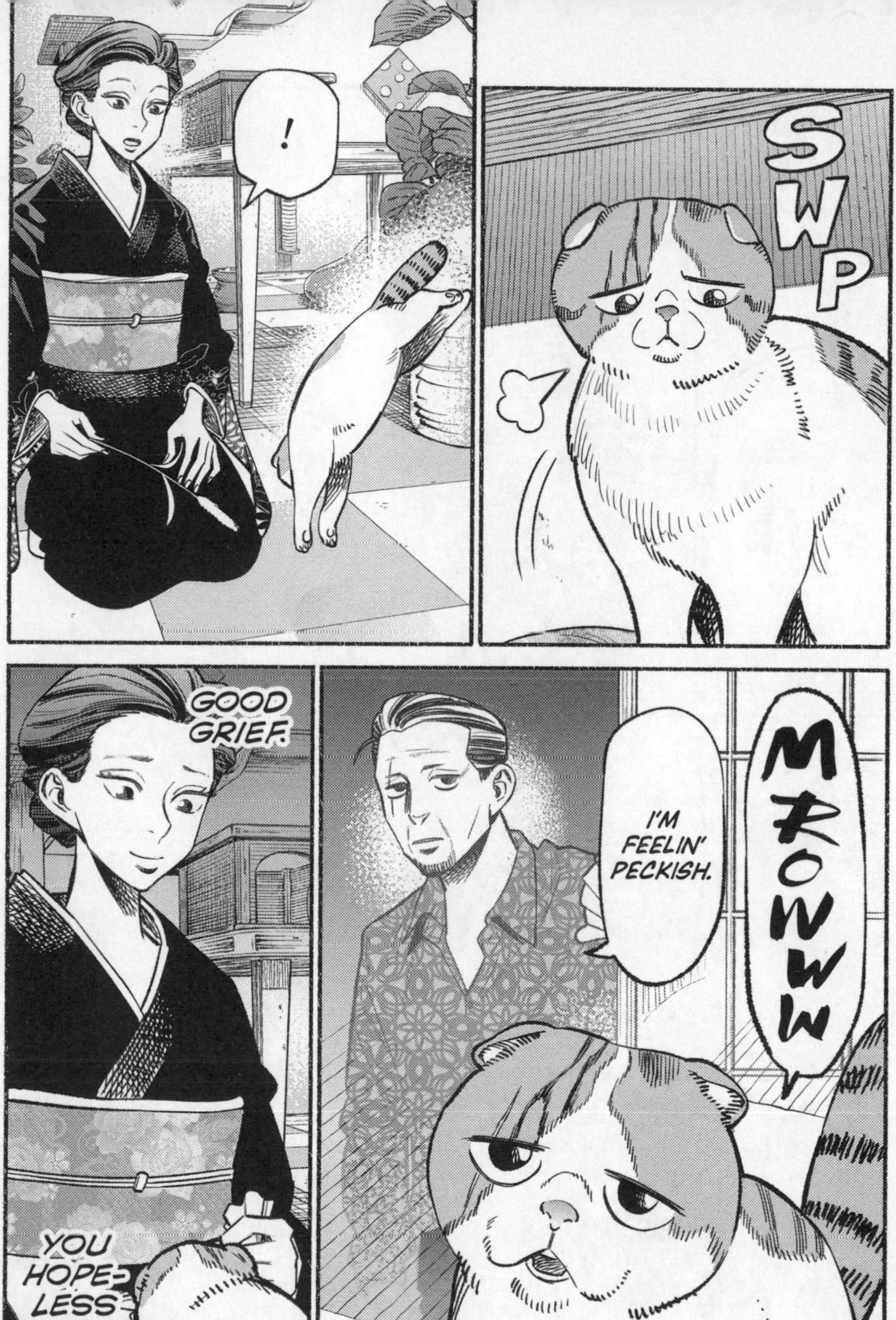
SWP
!
MROWWW
I'M FEELIN' PECKISH.
GOOD GRIEF.
YOU HOPE-LESS OLD COOT.

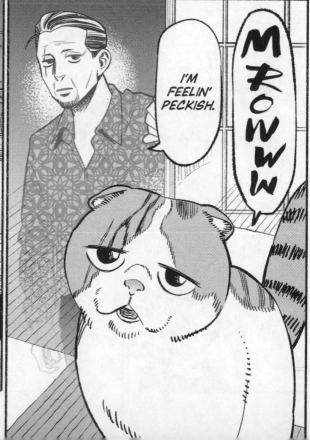

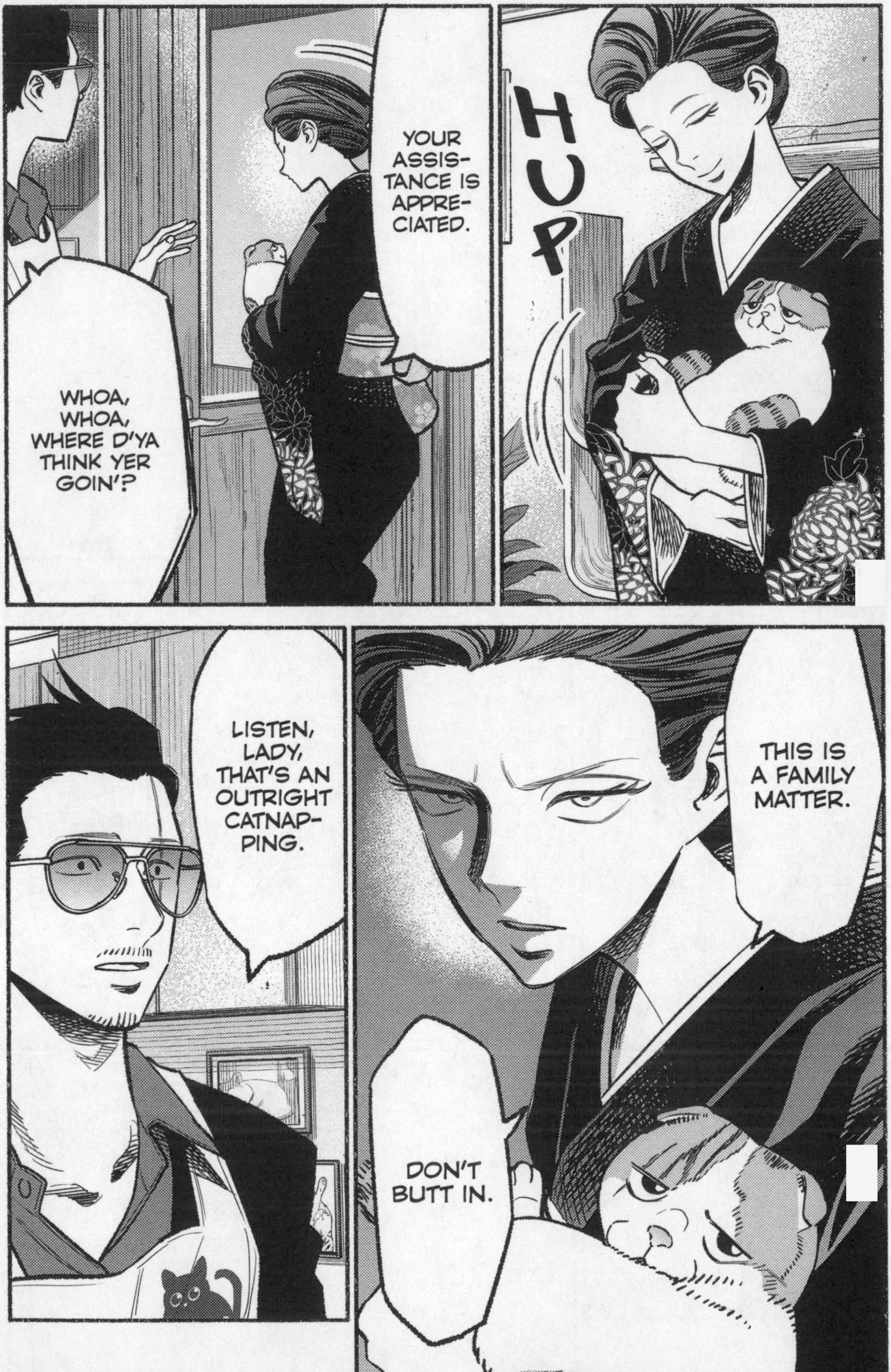
HUP
YOUR ASSISTANCE IS APPRECIATED.
WHOA, WHOA, WHERE D'YA THINK YER GOIN'?
THIS IS A FAMILY MATTER.
DON'T BUTT IN.
LISTEN, LADY, THAT'S AN OUTRIGHT CATNAPPING.

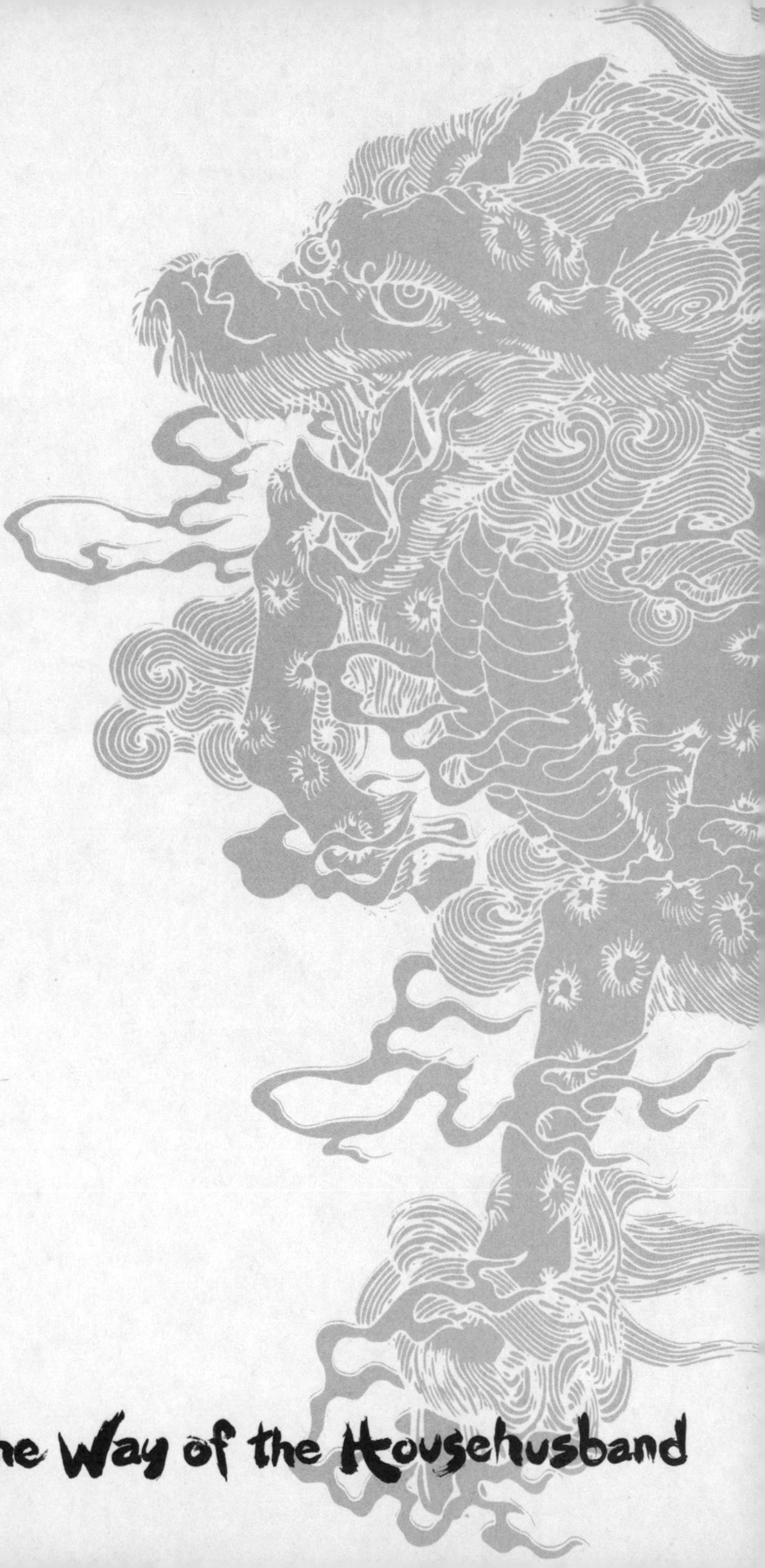

The Way of the Househusband

CHAPTER 56

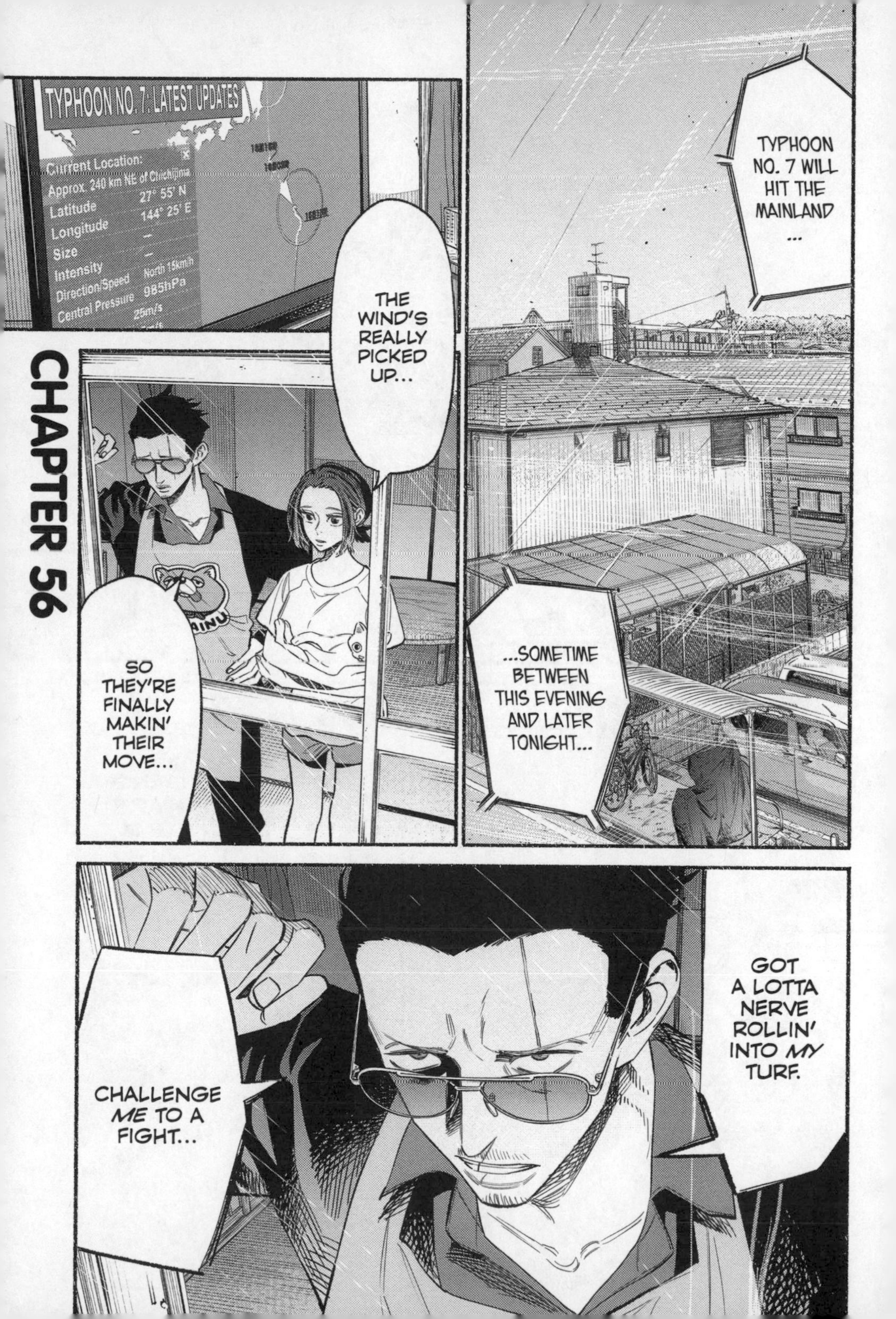
TYPHOON NO. 7 WILL HIT THE MAINLAND ...
...SOMETIME BETWEEN THIS EVENING AND LATER TONIGHT...
TYPHOON NO. 7: LATEST UPDATES
Current Location:
Approx. 240 km NE of Chichijima
Latitude 27° 55' N
Longitude 144° 25' E
Size –
Intensity –
Direction/Speed North 15km/h
Central Pressure 985hPa
25m/s
THE WIND'S REALLY PICKED UP...
SO THEY'RE FINALLY MAKIN' THEIR MOVE...
GOT A LOTTA NERVE ROLLIN' INTO *MY* TURF.
CHALLENGE *ME* TO A FIGHT...

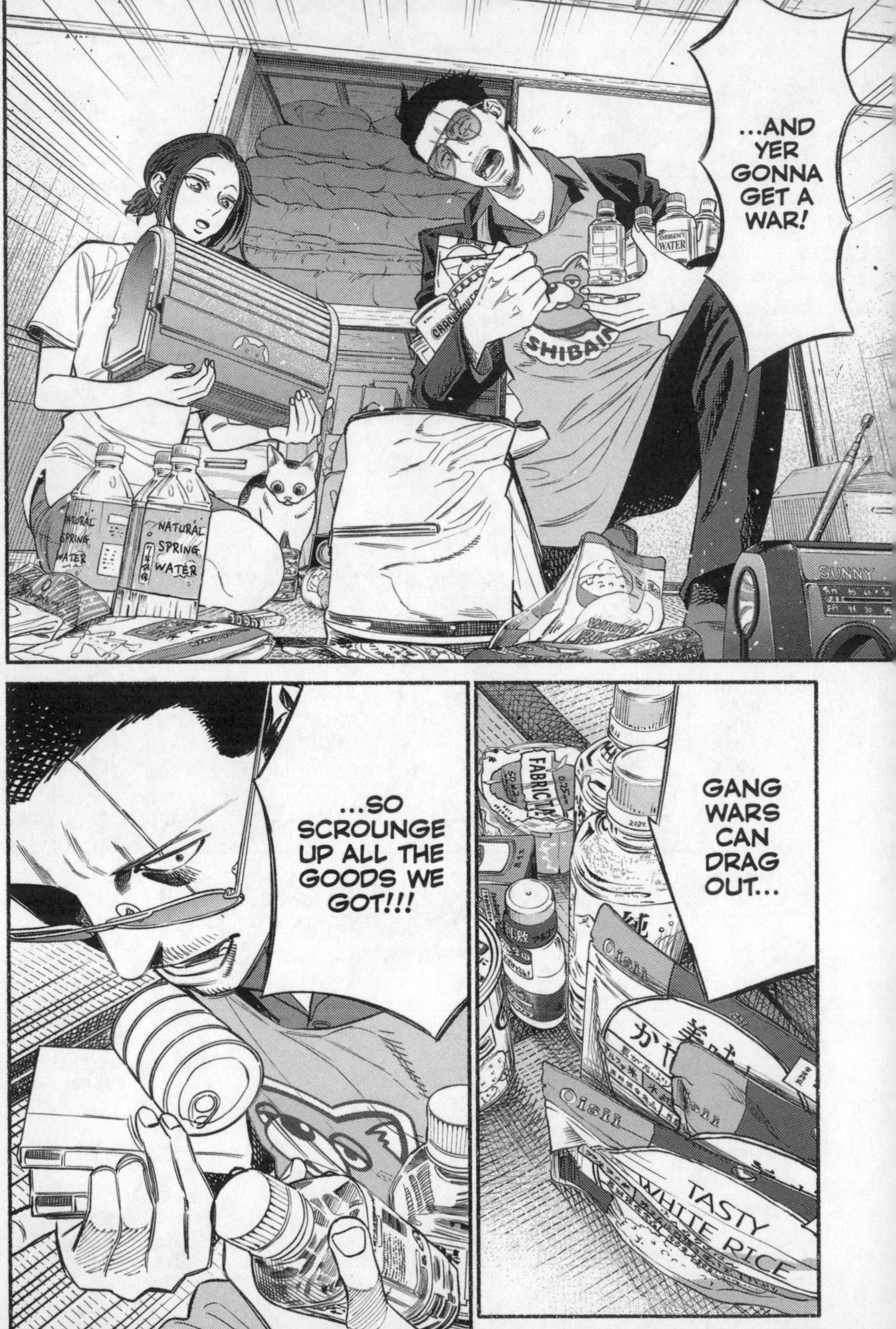
...AND YER GONNA GET A WAR!
EMERGENCY WATER
NATURAL SPRING WATER
NATURAL SPRING WATER
SUNNY
GANG WARS CAN DRAG OUT...
TASTY WHITE RICE
...SO SCROUNGE UP ALL THE GOODS WE GOT!!!

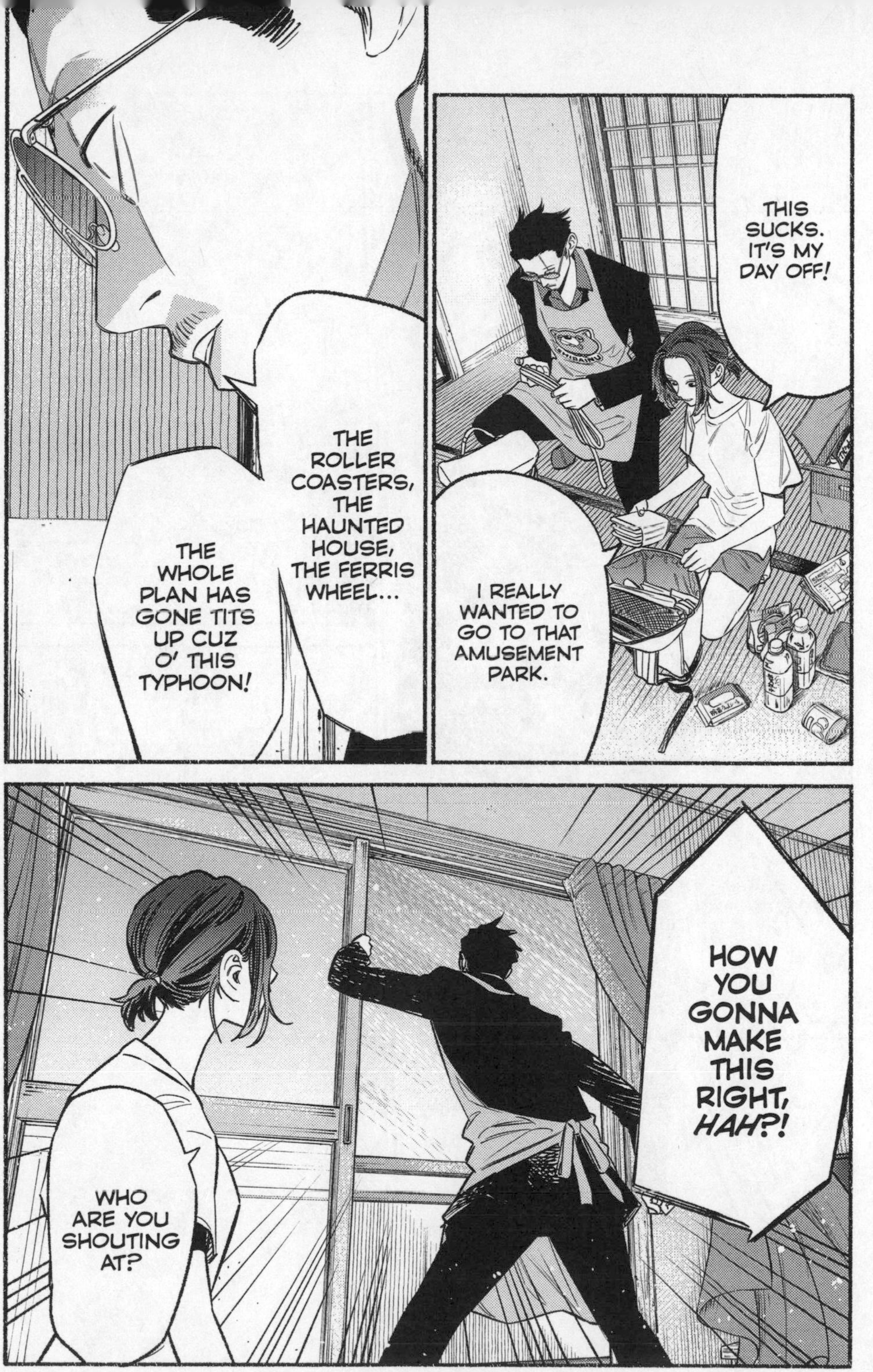
THIS SUCKS. IT'S MY DAY OFF!
I REALLY WANTED TO GO TO THAT AMUSEMENT PARK.
THE ROLLER COASTERS, THE HAUNTED HOUSE, THE FERRIS WHEEL...
THE WHOLE PLAN HAS GONE TITS UP CUZ O' THIS TYPHOON!
HOW YOU GONNA MAKE THIS RIGHT, *HAH?!*
WHO ARE YOU SHOUTING AT?

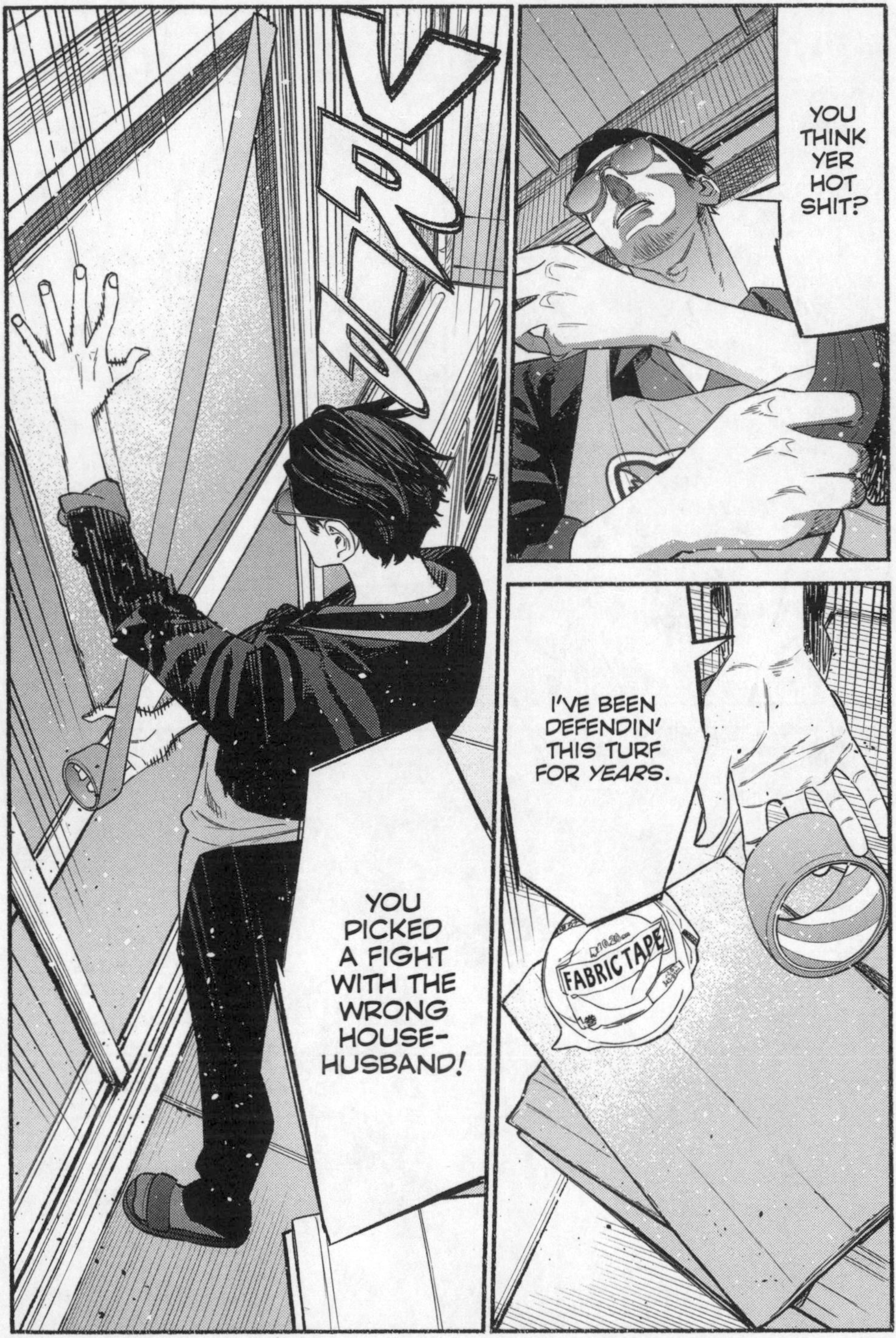
YOU THINK YER HOT SHIT?
I'VE BEEN DEFENDIN' THIS TURF FOR *YEARS*.
FABRIC TAPE
YOU PICKED A FIGHT WITH THE WRONG HOUSE-HUSBAND!

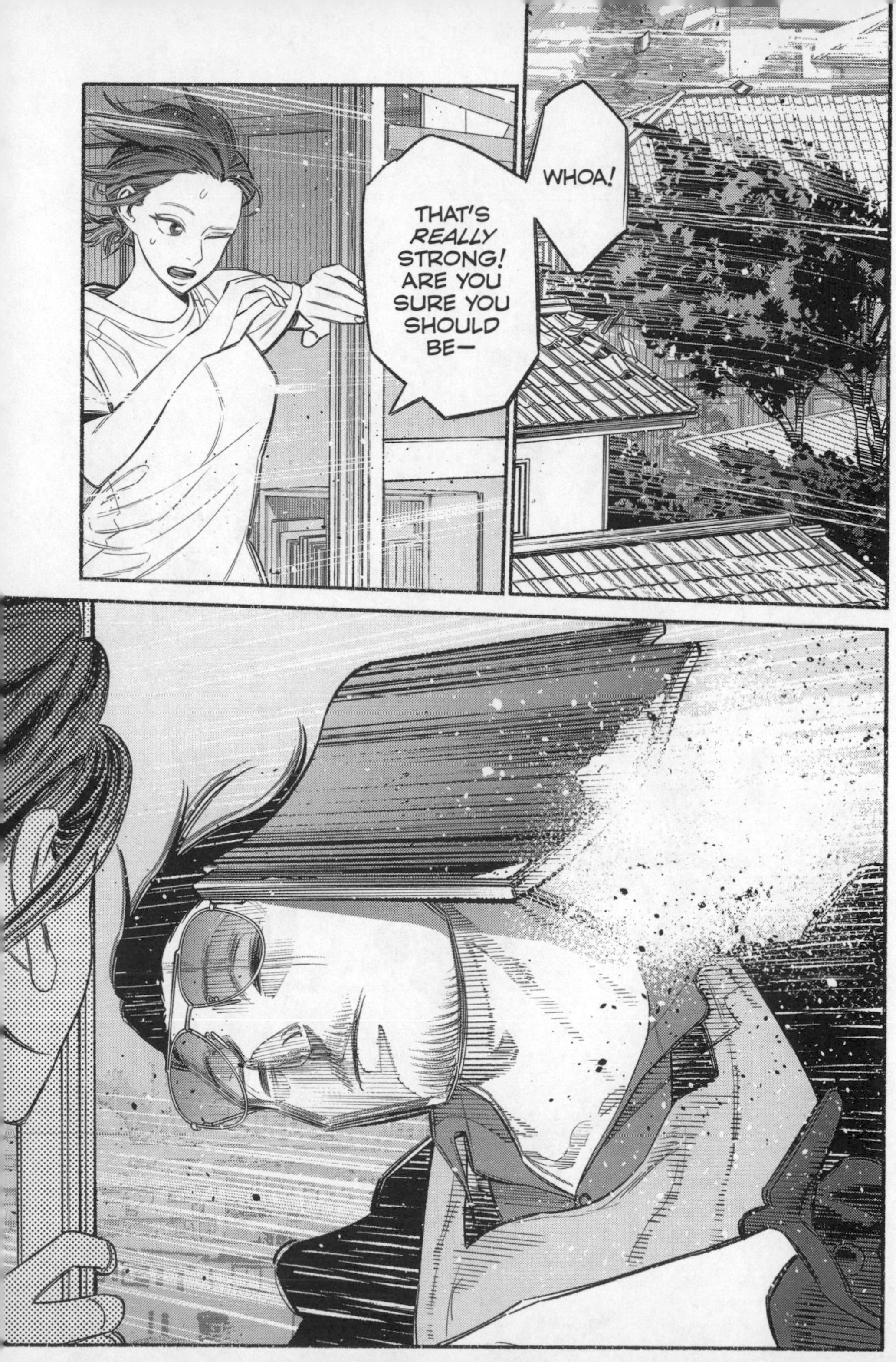
WHOA!
THAT'S *REALLY* STRONG! ARE YOU SURE YOU SHOULD BE—

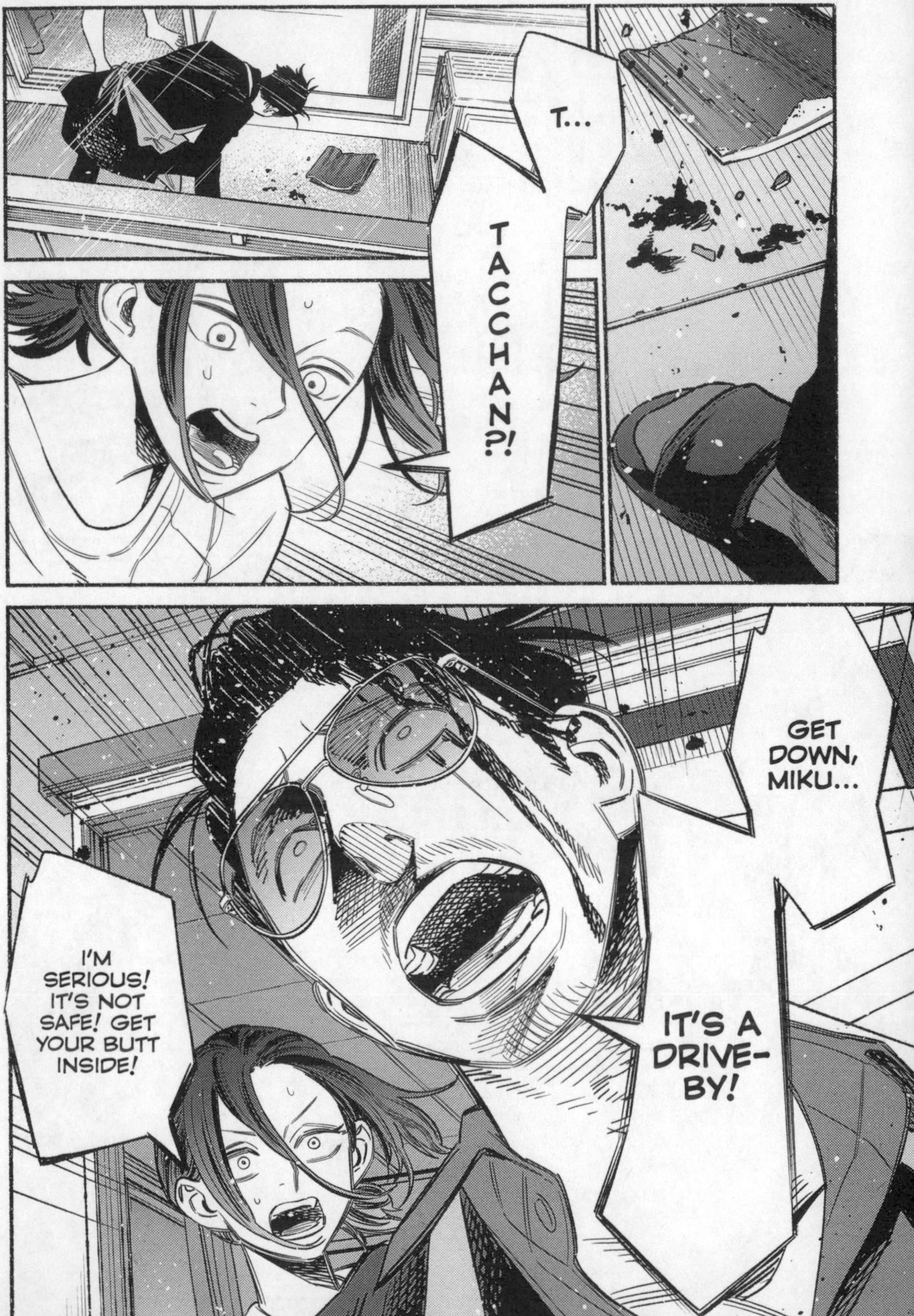
T...
TACCHAN?!
GET DOWN, MIKU...
IT'S A DRIVE-BY!
I'M SERIOUS! IT'S NOT SAFE! GET YOUR BUTT INSIDE!

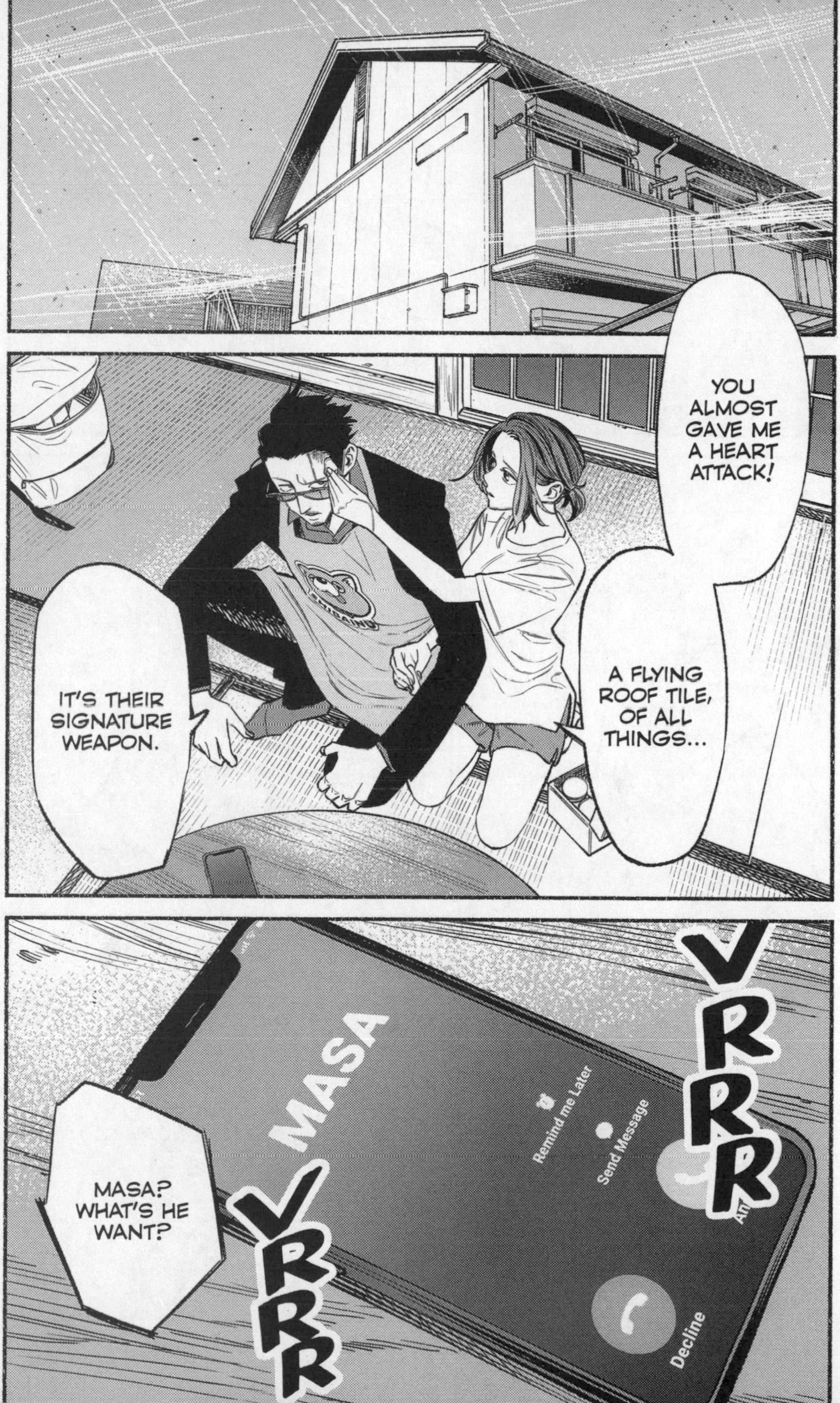
YOU ALMOST GAVE ME A HEART ATTACK!
A FLYING ROOF TILE, OF ALL THINGS...
IT'S THEIR SIGNATURE WEAPON.
VRRR
MASA
Remind me Later
Send Message
MASA? WHAT'S HE WANT?
VRRR
Decline

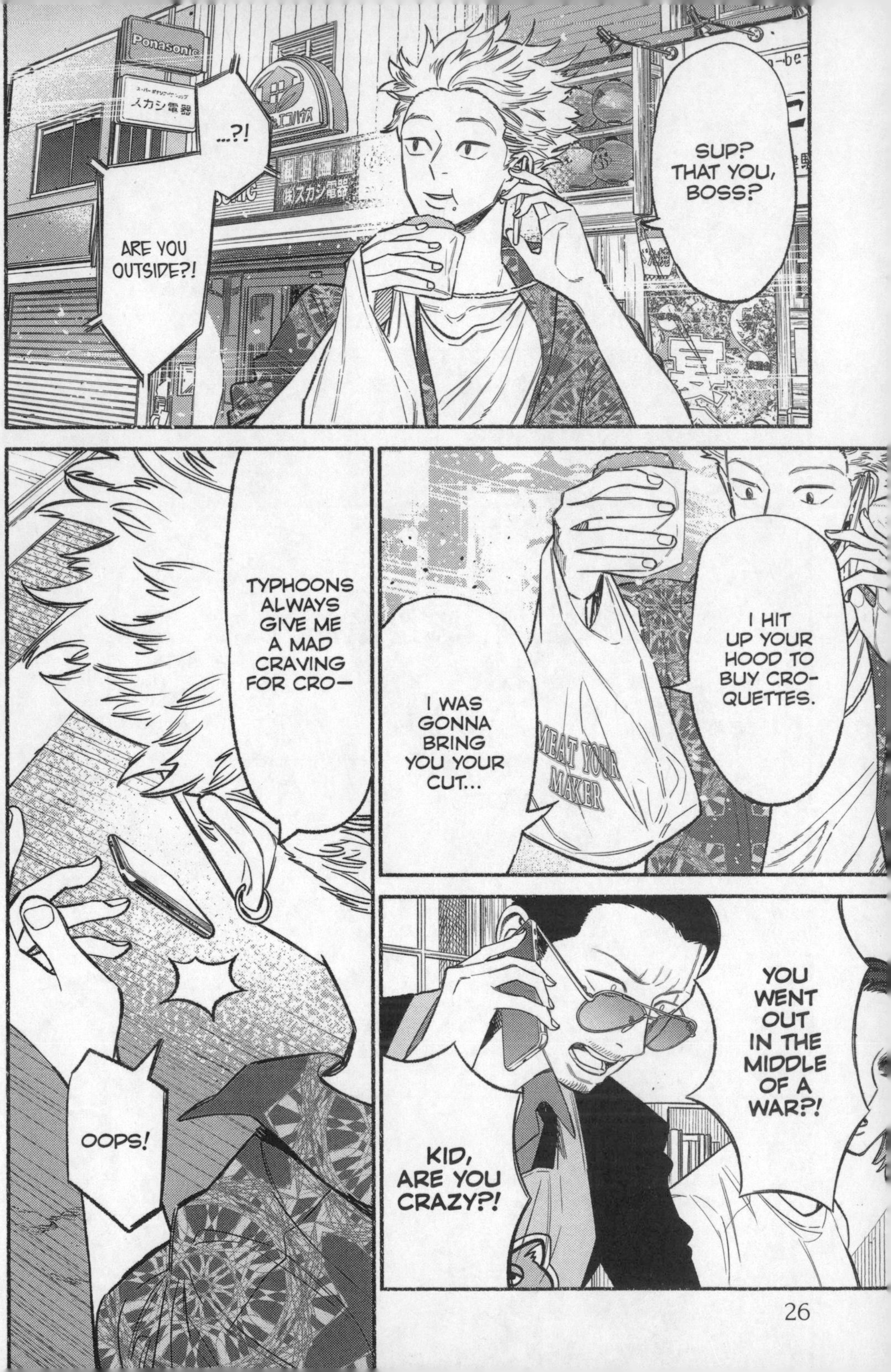
Ponasonic
スカシ電器
SUP? THAT YOU, BOSS?
...?!
ARE YOU OUTSIDE?!
I HIT UP YOUR HOOD TO BUY CRO-QUETTES.
I WAS GONNA BRING YOU YOUR CUT...
MEAT YOUR MAKER
YOU WENT OUT IN THE MIDDLE OF A WAR?!
KID, ARE YOU CRAZY?!
TYPHOONS ALWAYS GIVE ME A MAD CRAVING FOR CRO—
OOPS!

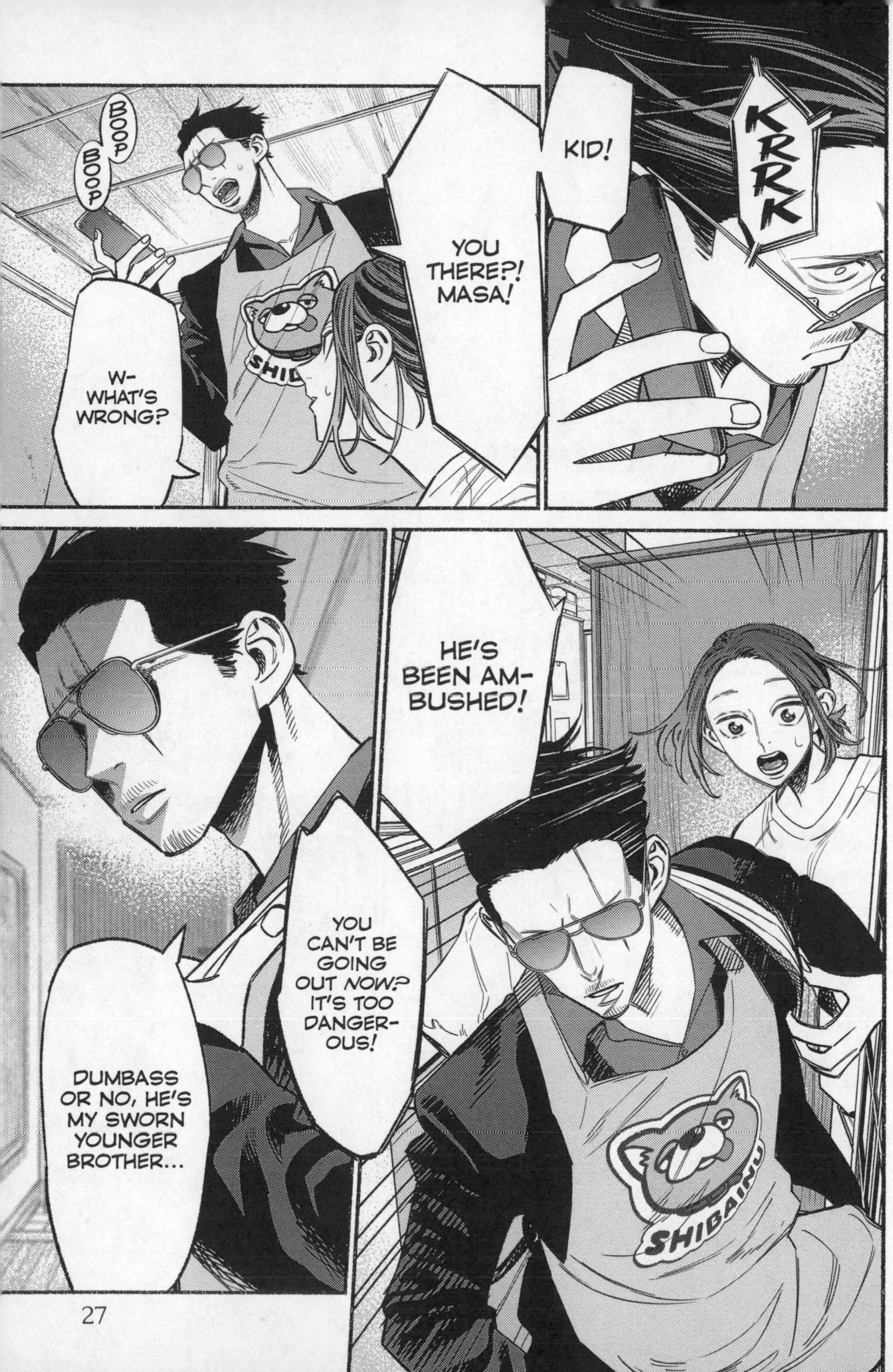
KRRK
KID! YOU THERE?! MASA!
BOOP BOOP
W- WHAT'S WRONG?
HE'S BEEN AM-BUSHED!
YOU CAN'T BE GOING OUT *NOW*? IT'S TOO DANGER-OUS!
DUMBASS OR NO, HE'S MY SWORN YOUNGER BROTHER...

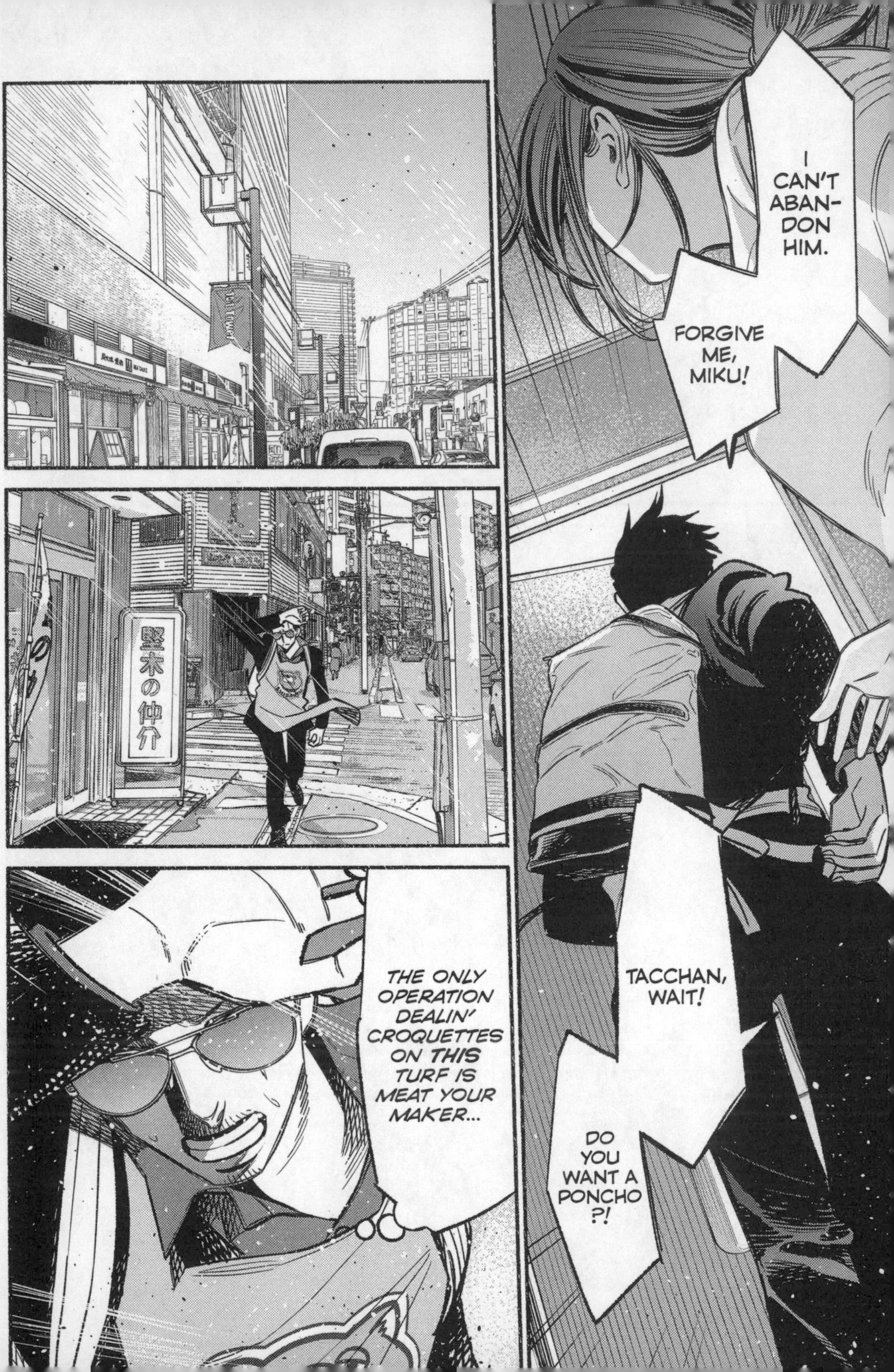
I CAN'T ABANDON HIM.
FORGIVE ME, MIKU!
TACCHAN, WAIT!
DO YOU WANT A PONCHO?!
堅木の仲介
THE ONLY OPERATION DEALIN' CROQUETTES ON THIS TURF IS MEAT YOUR MAKER...

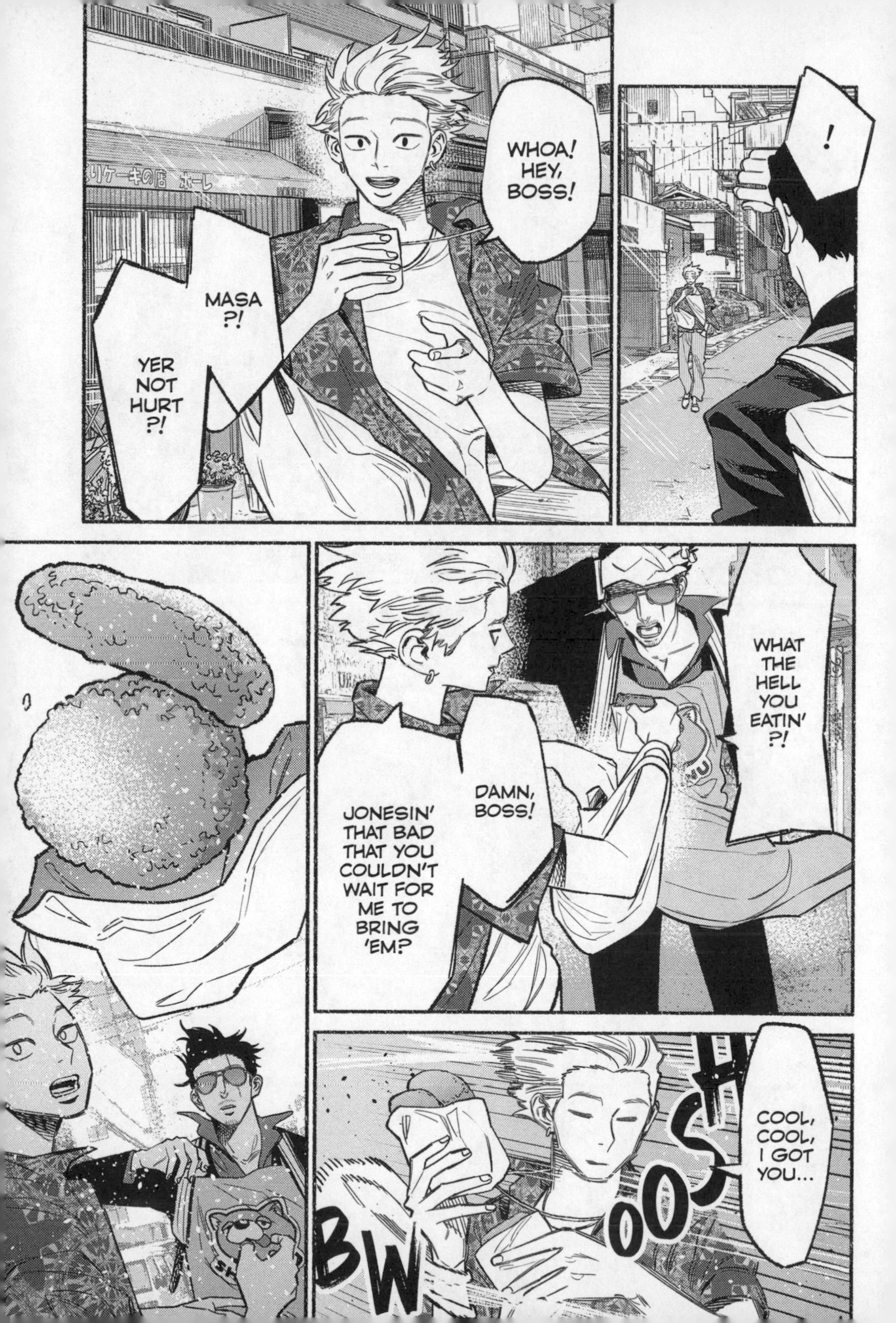
!
WHOA! HEY, BOSS!
MASA?!
YER NOT HURT?!
WHAT THE HELL YOU EATIN'?!
DAMN, BOSS!
JONESIN' THAT BAD THAT YOU COULDN'T WAIT FOR ME TO BRING 'EM?
COOL, COOL, I GOT YOU...
BWOOSH

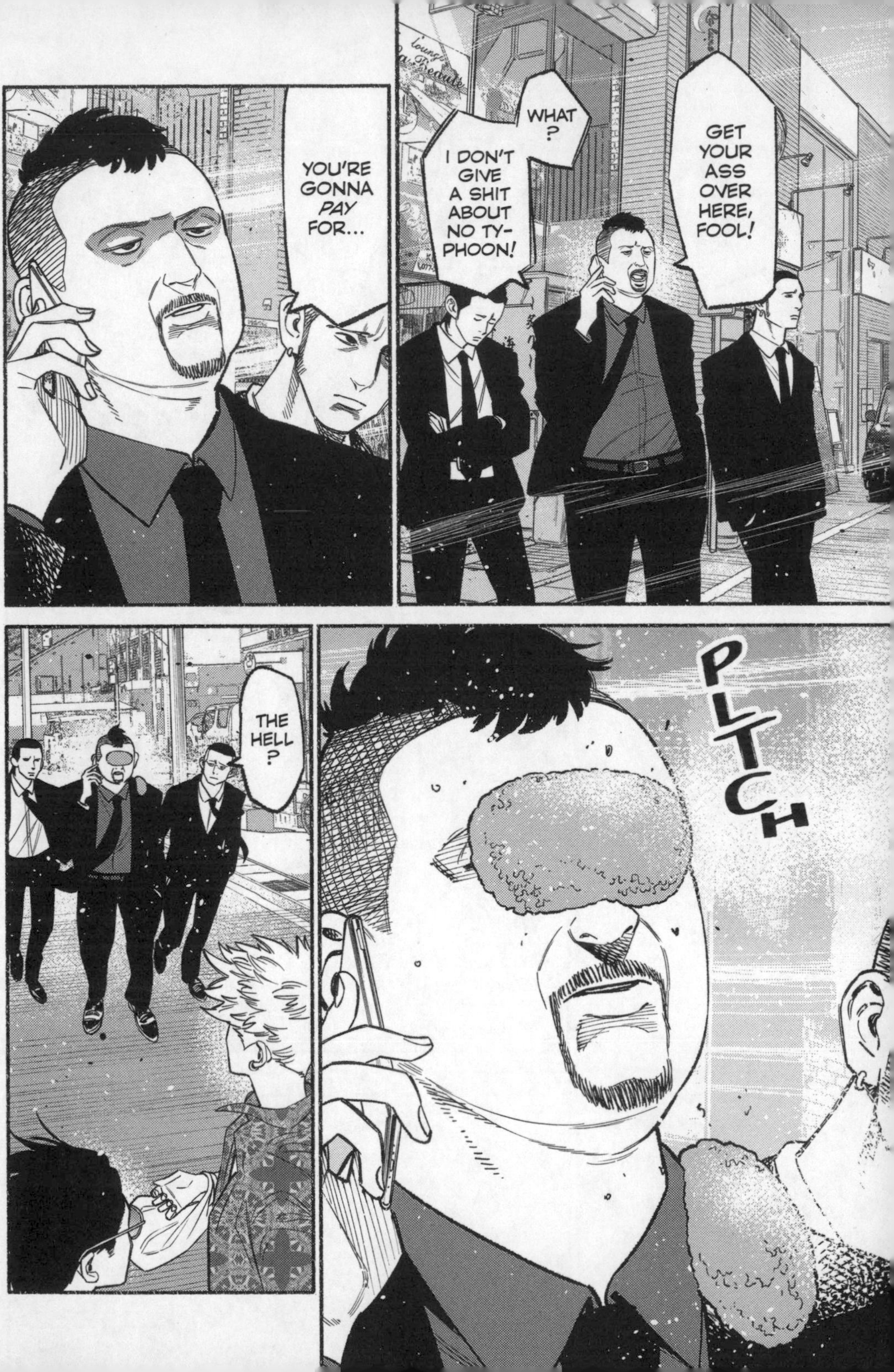
GET YOUR ASS OVER HERE, FOOL!
WHAT? I DON'T GIVE A SHIT ABOUT NO TY-PHOON!
YOU'RE GONNA *PAY* FOR...
PLTCH
THE HELL?

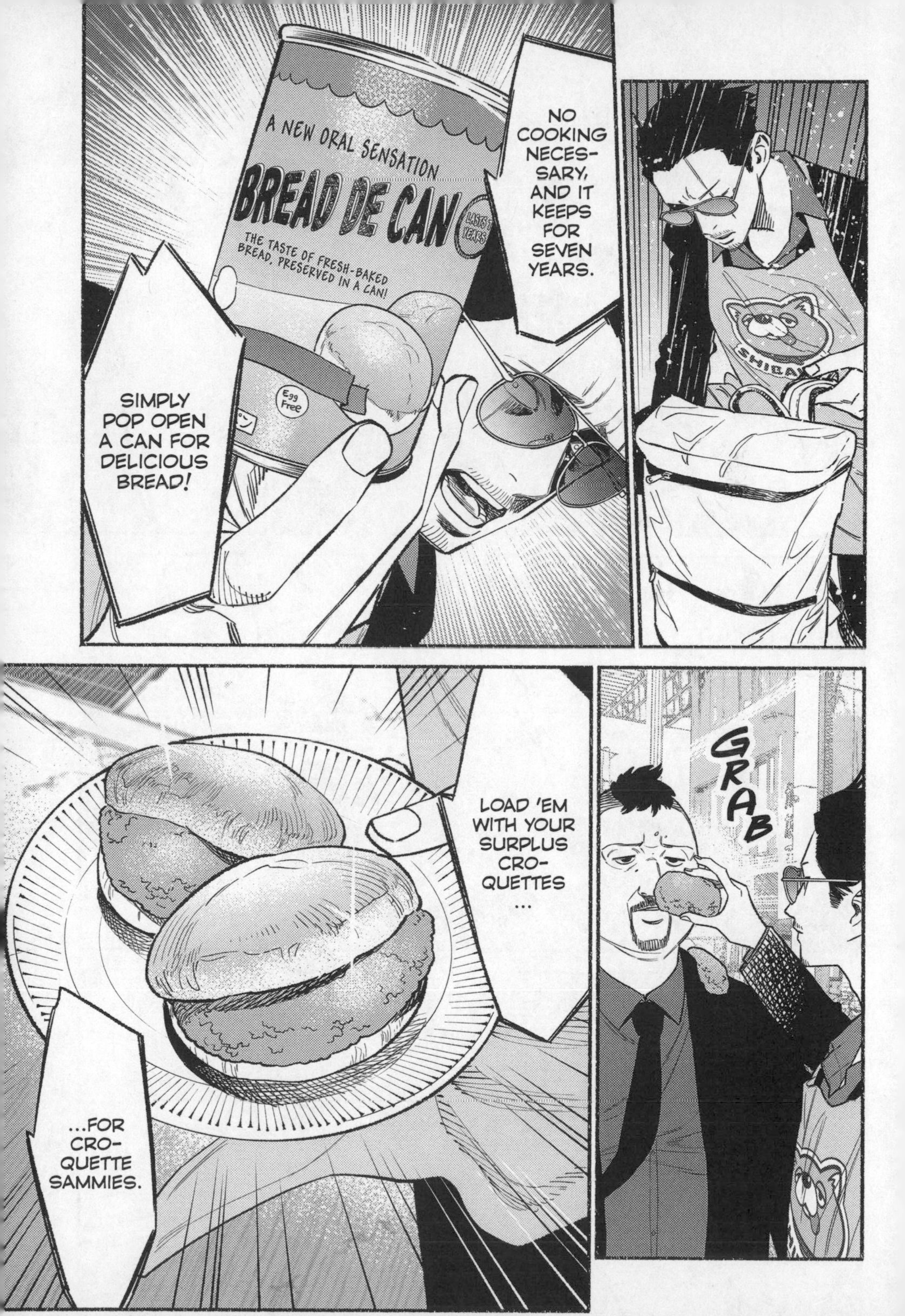
NO COOKING NECES-SARY, AND IT KEEPS FOR SEVEN YEARS.
A NEW ORAL SENSATION
BREAD DE CAN
THE TASTE OF FRESH-BAKED BREAD, PRESERVED IN A CAN!
Egg Free
SIMPLY POP OPEN A CAN FOR DELICIOUS BREAD!
GRAB
LOAD 'EM WITH YOUR SURPLUS CRO-QUETTES ...
...FOR CRO-QUETTE SAMMIES.

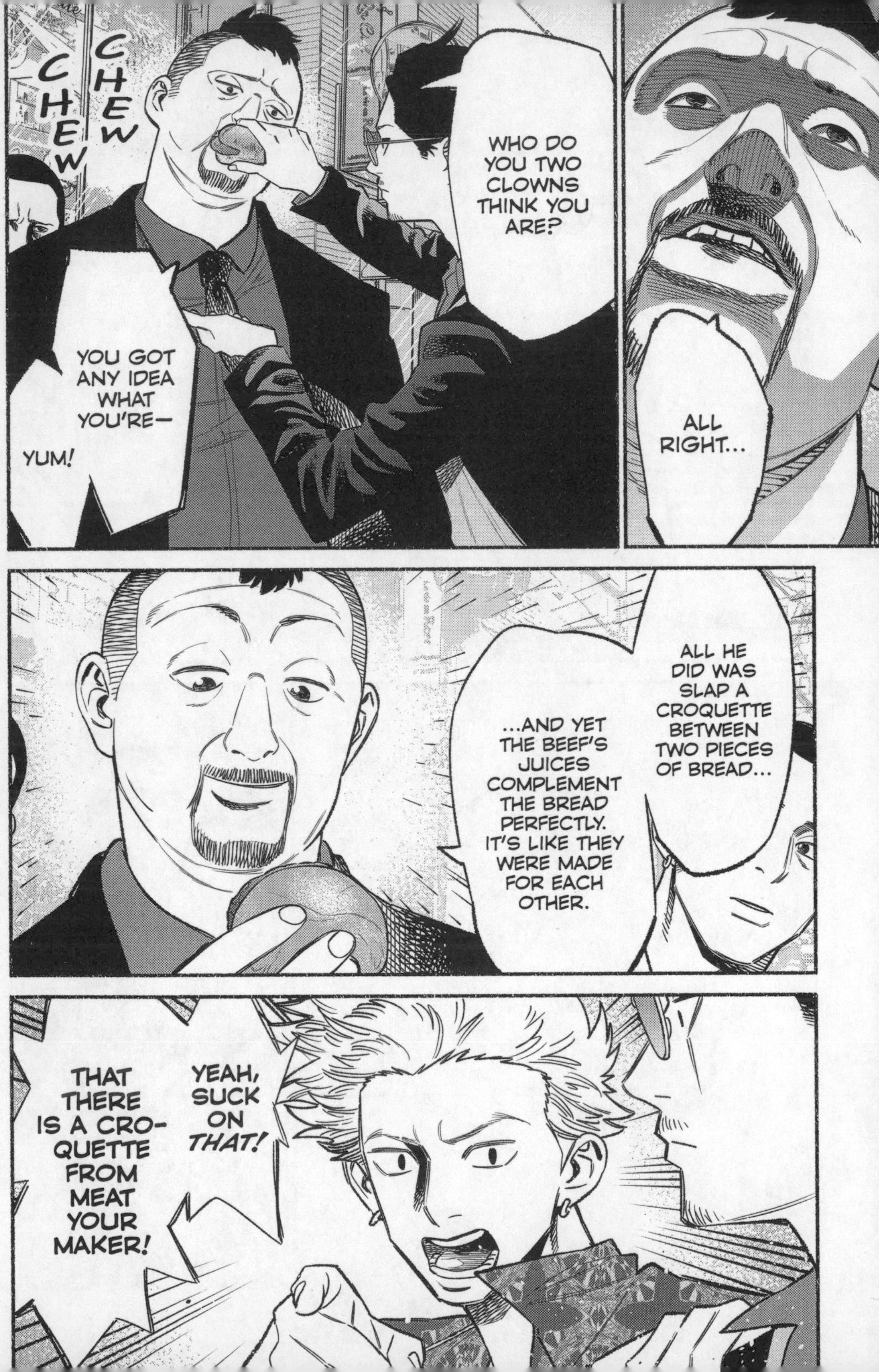

ALL RIGHT...
WHO DO YOU TWO CLOWNS THINK YOU ARE?
CHEW CHEW
YOU GOT ANY IDEA WHAT YOU'RE—
YUM!
ALL HE DID WAS SLAP A CROQUETTE BETWEEN TWO PIECES OF BREAD...
...AND YET THE BEEF'S JUICES COMPLEMENT THE BREAD PERFECTLY. IT'S LIKE THEY WERE MADE FOR EACH OTHER.
YEAH, SUCK ON *THAT!*
THAT THERE IS A CRO-QUETTE FROM MEAT YOUR MAKER!

YOUR

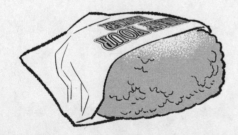

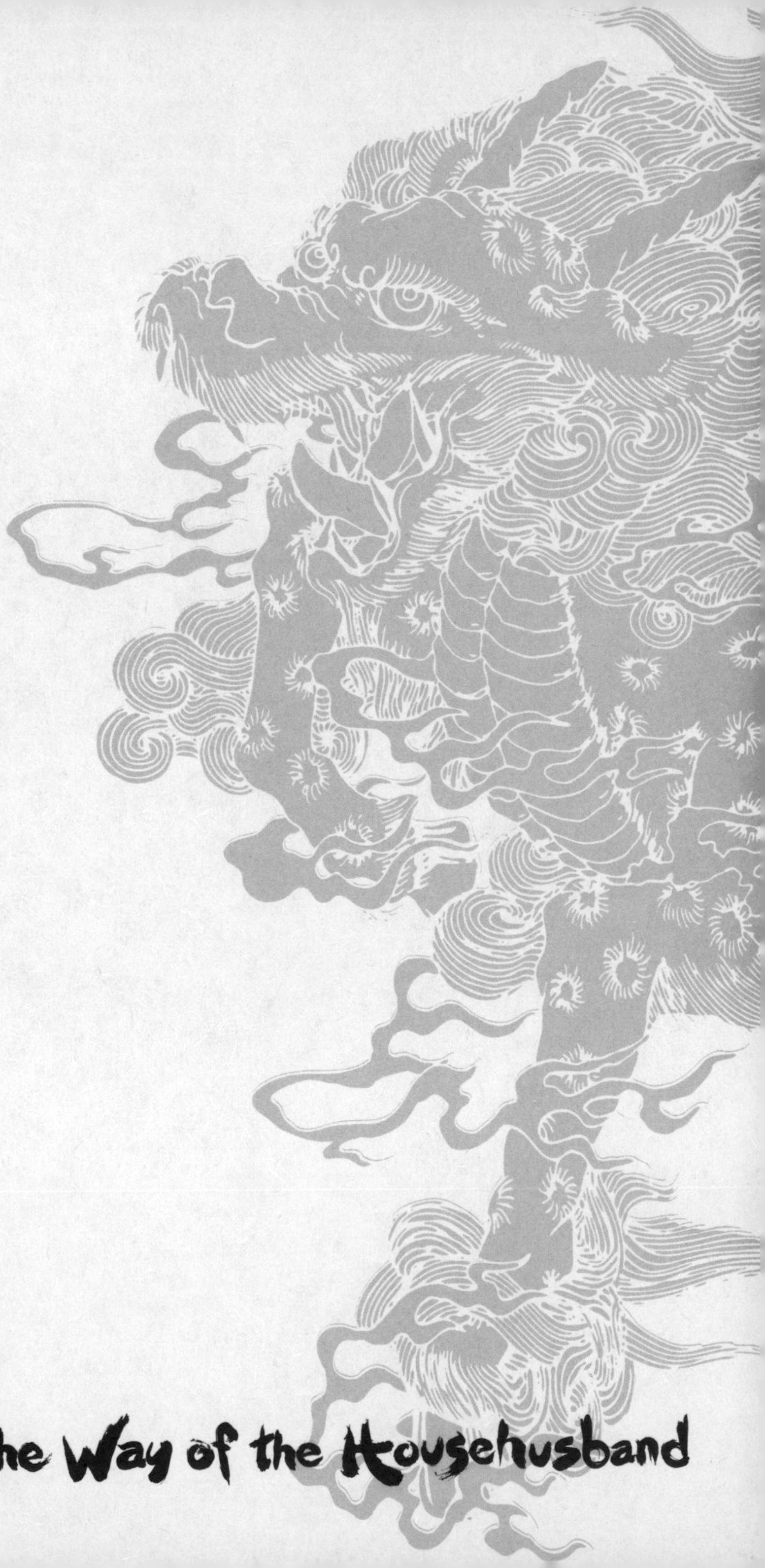

The Way of the Househusband

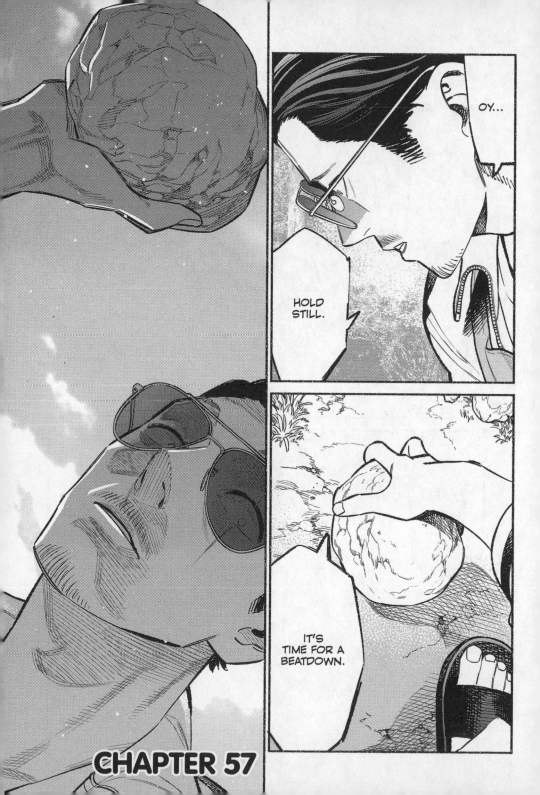

OY...

HOLD STILL.

IT'S TIME FOR A BEATDOWN.

CHAPTER 57

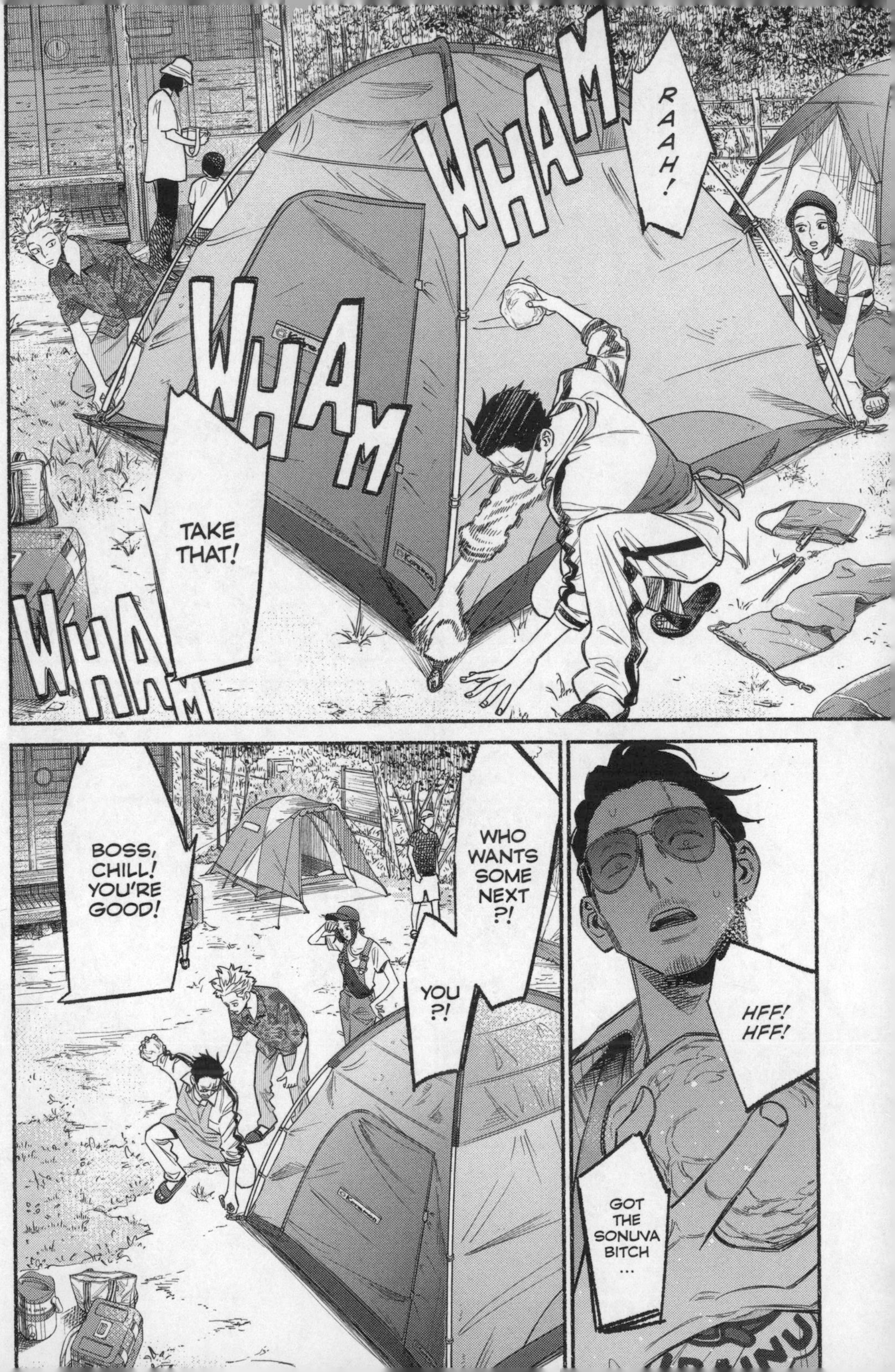
RAAH!
WHAM
WHAM
TAKE THAT!
WHAM
HFF! HFF!
GOT THE SONUVA BITCH ...
WHO WANTS SOME NEXT ?!
BOSS, CHILL! YOU'RE GOOD!
YOU ?!

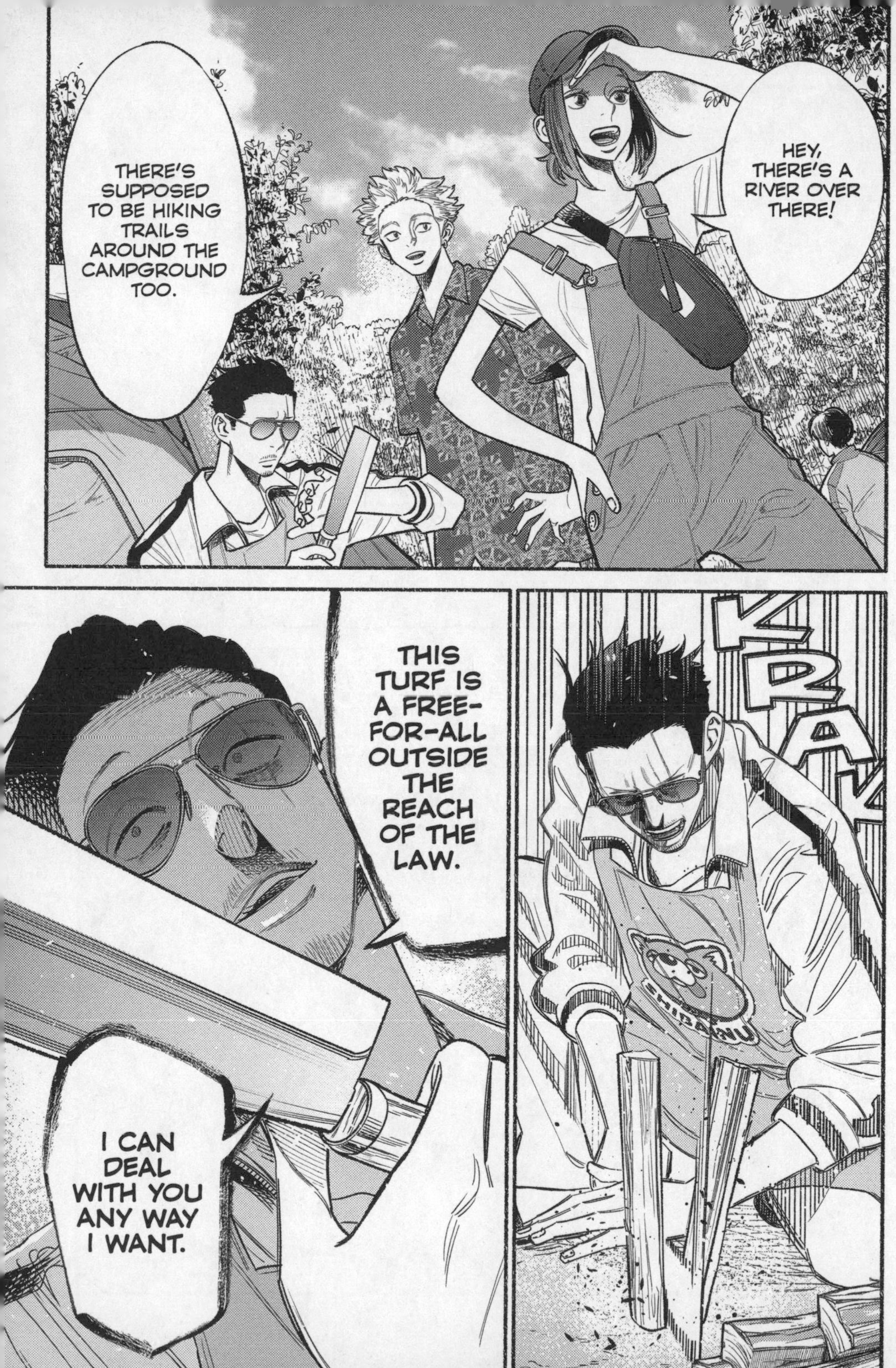
HEY, THERE'S A RIVER OVER THERE!
THERE'S SUPPOSED TO BE HIKING TRAILS AROUND THE CAMPGROUND TOO.
KRA
THIS TURF IS A FREE-FOR-ALL OUTSIDE THE REACH OF THE LAW.
I CAN DEAL WITH YOU ANY WAY I WANT.

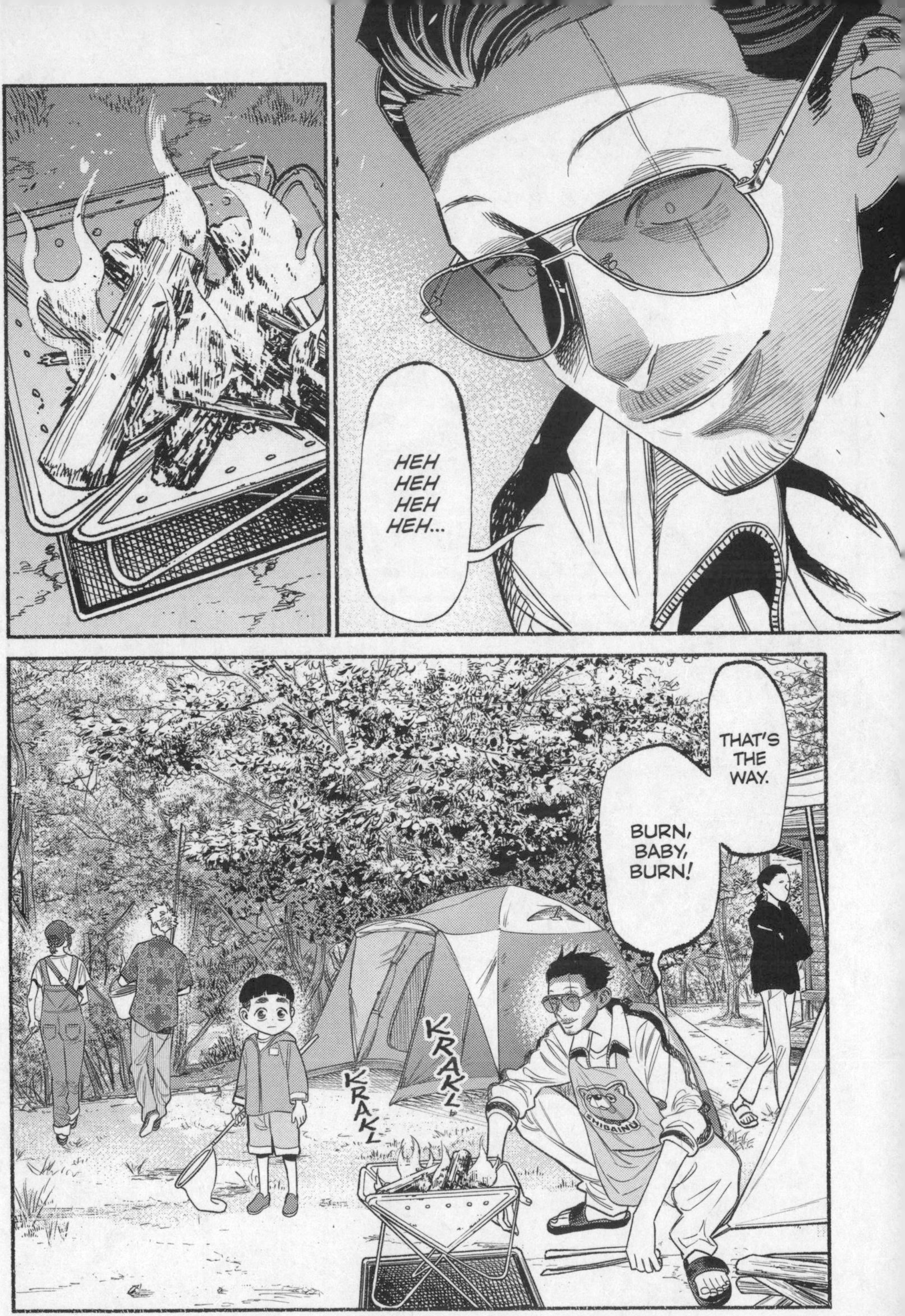
HEH HEH HEH HEH...
THAT'S THE WAY.
BURN, BABY, BURN!
KRAKL
KRAKL

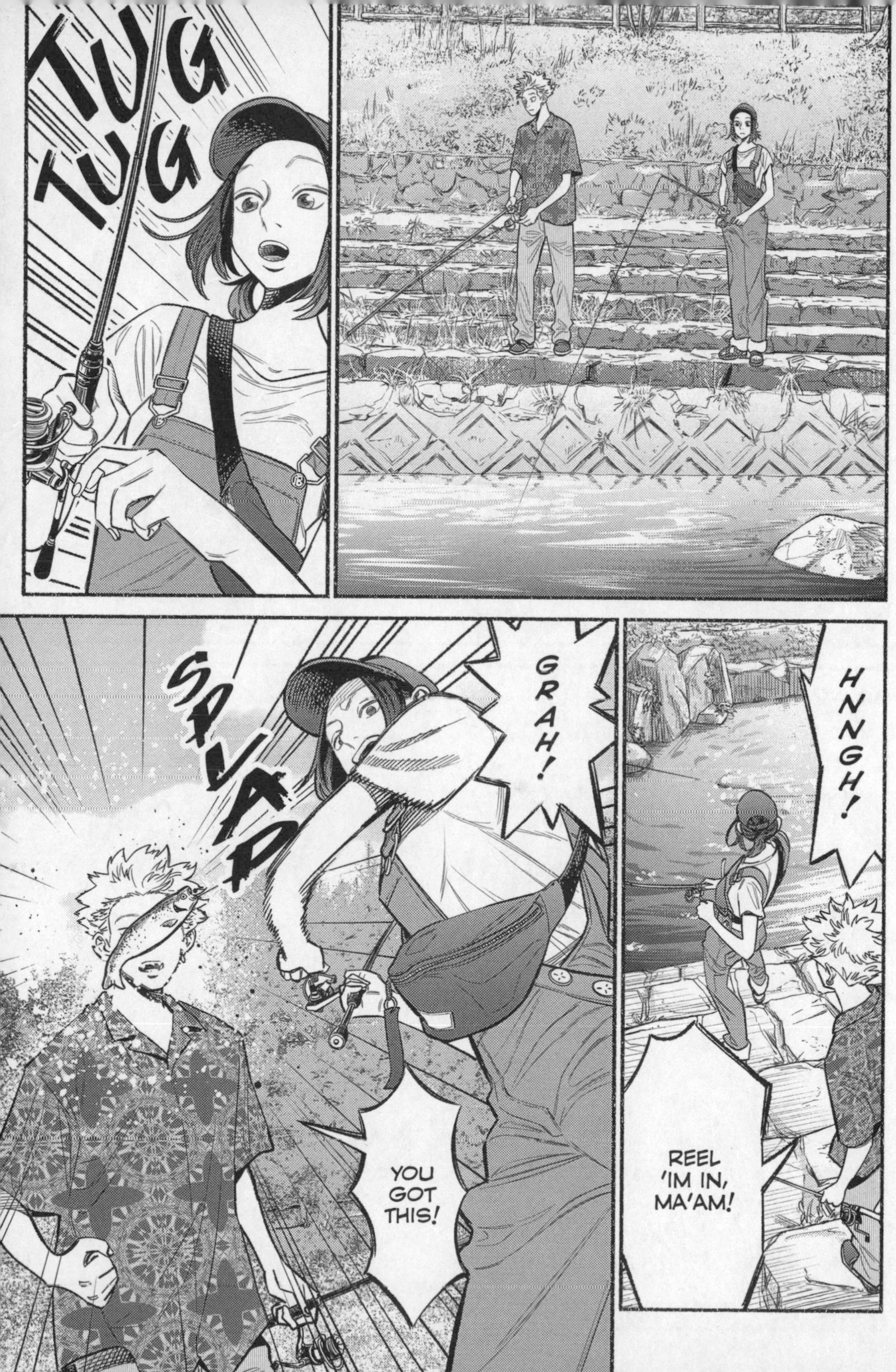
TUG
TUG
HNNGH!
REEL 'IM IN, MA'AM!
GRAH!
SPLAP
YOU GOT THIS!

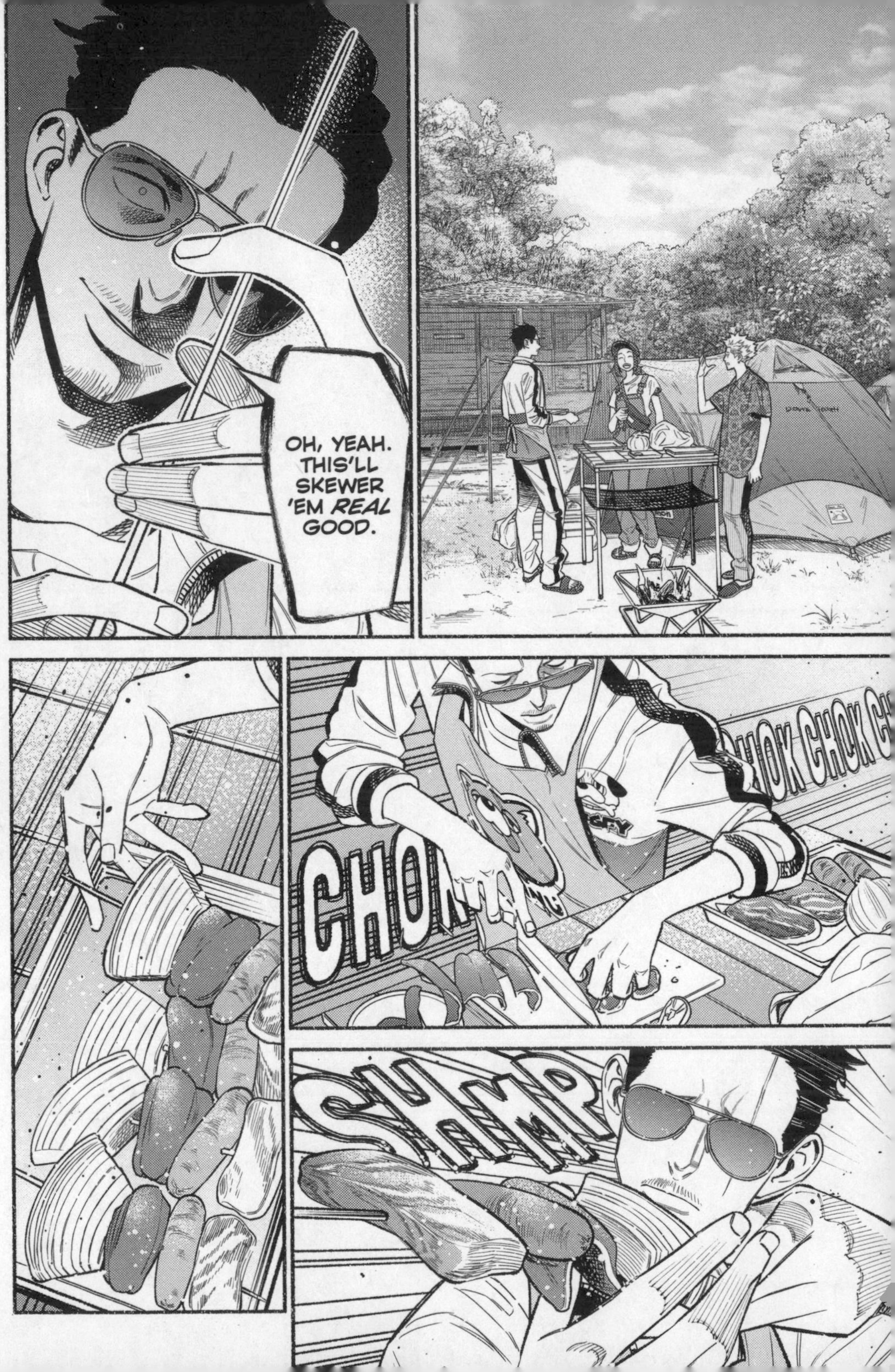
OH, YEAH. THIS'LL SKEWER 'EM *REAL* GOOD.
CHOK CHOK

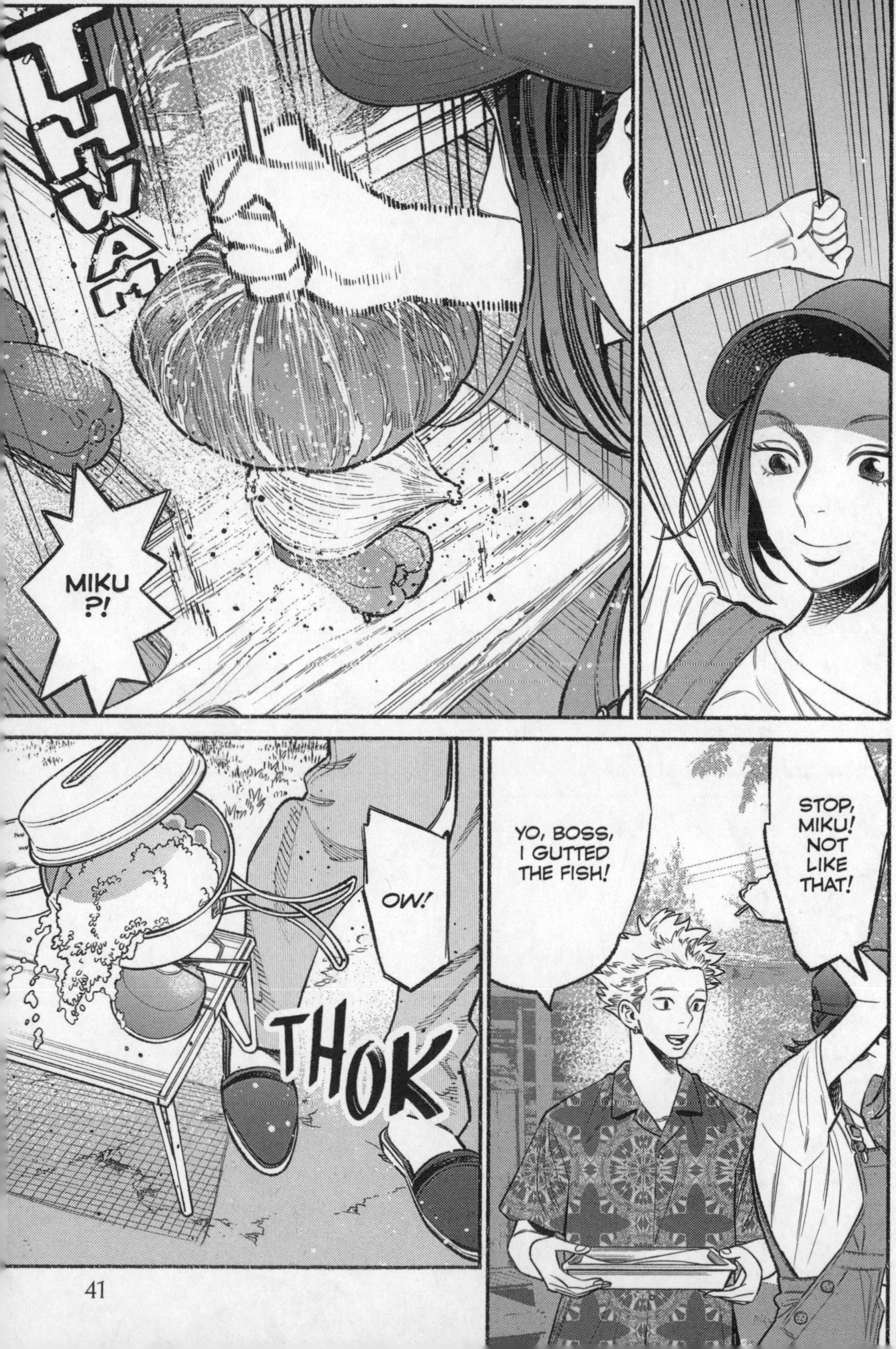
THWAM
MIKU ?!
STOP, MIKU! NOT LIKE THAT!
YO, BOSS, I GUTTED THE FISH!
OW!
THOK

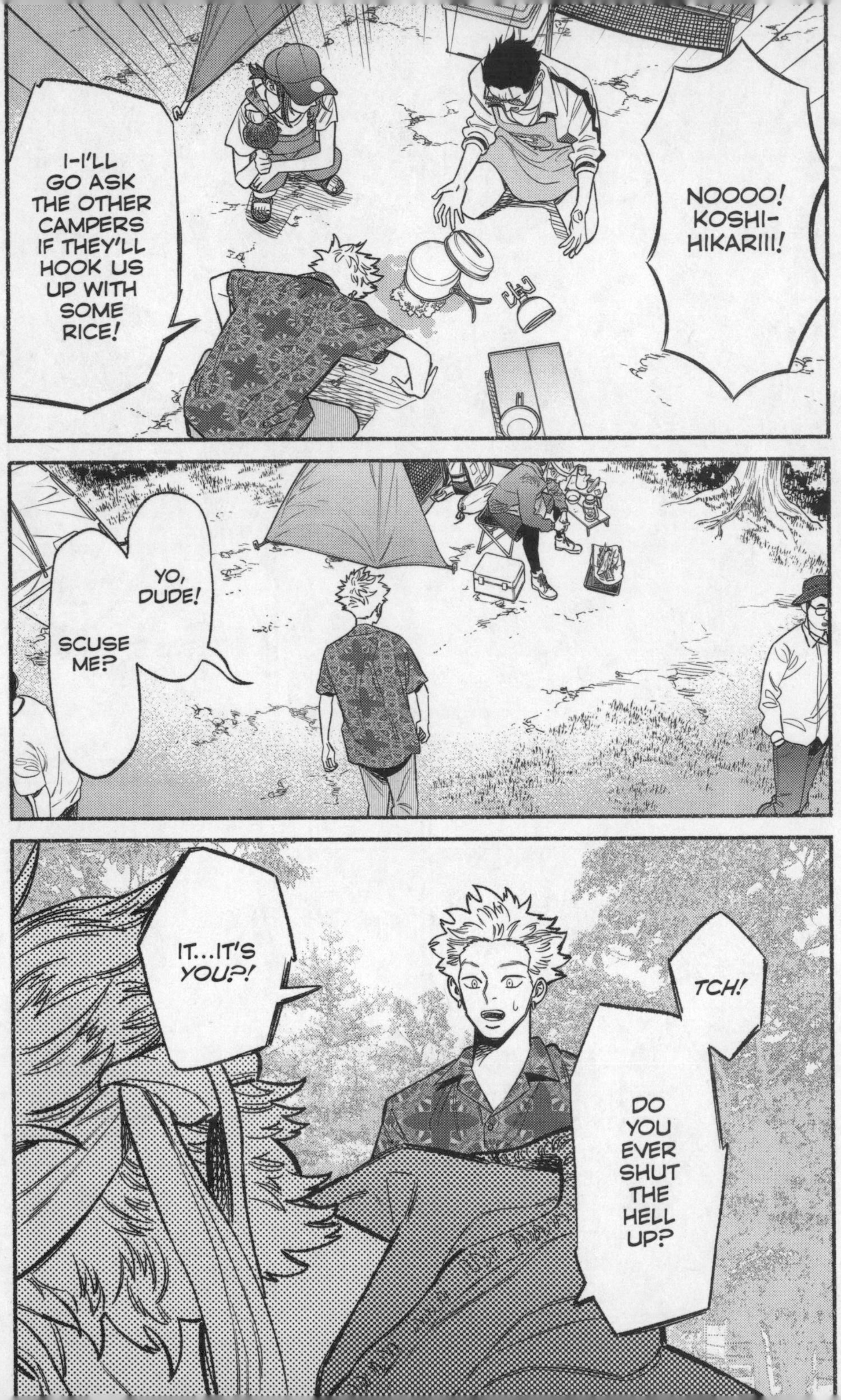
NOOOO! KOSHI-HIKARIII!
I-I'LL GO ASK THE OTHER CAMPERS IF THEY'LL HOOK US UP WITH SOME RICE!
YO, DUDE!
SCUSE ME?
IT...IT'S *YOU?!*
TCH!
DO YOU EVER SHUT THE HELL UP?

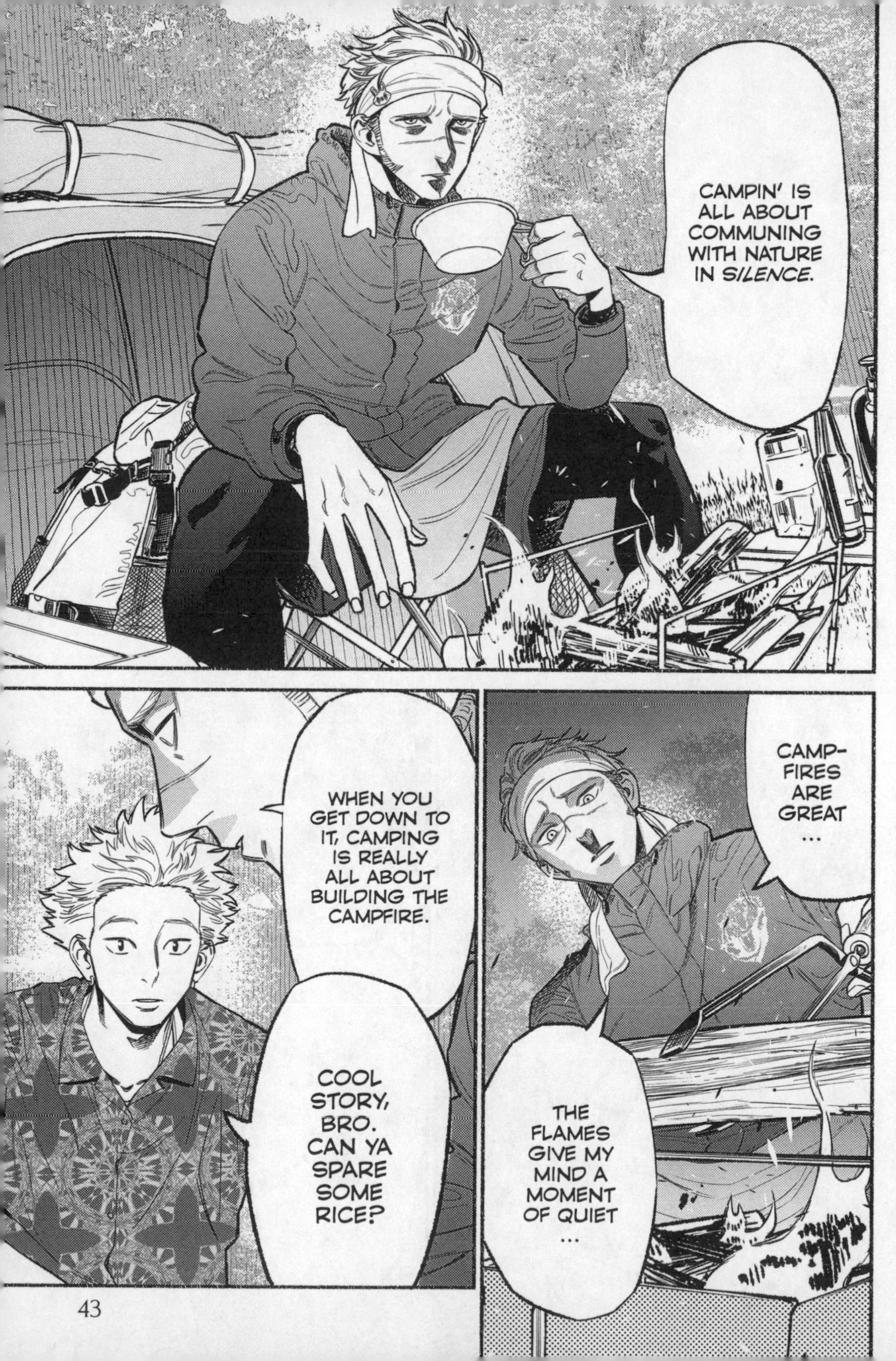
CAMPIN' IS ALL ABOUT COMMUNING WITH NATURE IN *SILENCE*.
CAMP-FIRES ARE GREAT ...
THE FLAMES GIVE MY MIND A MOMENT OF QUIET ...
WHEN YOU GET DOWN TO IT, CAMPING IS REALLY ALL ABOUT BUILDING THE CAMPFIRE.
COOL STORY, BRO. CAN YA SPARE SOME RICE?

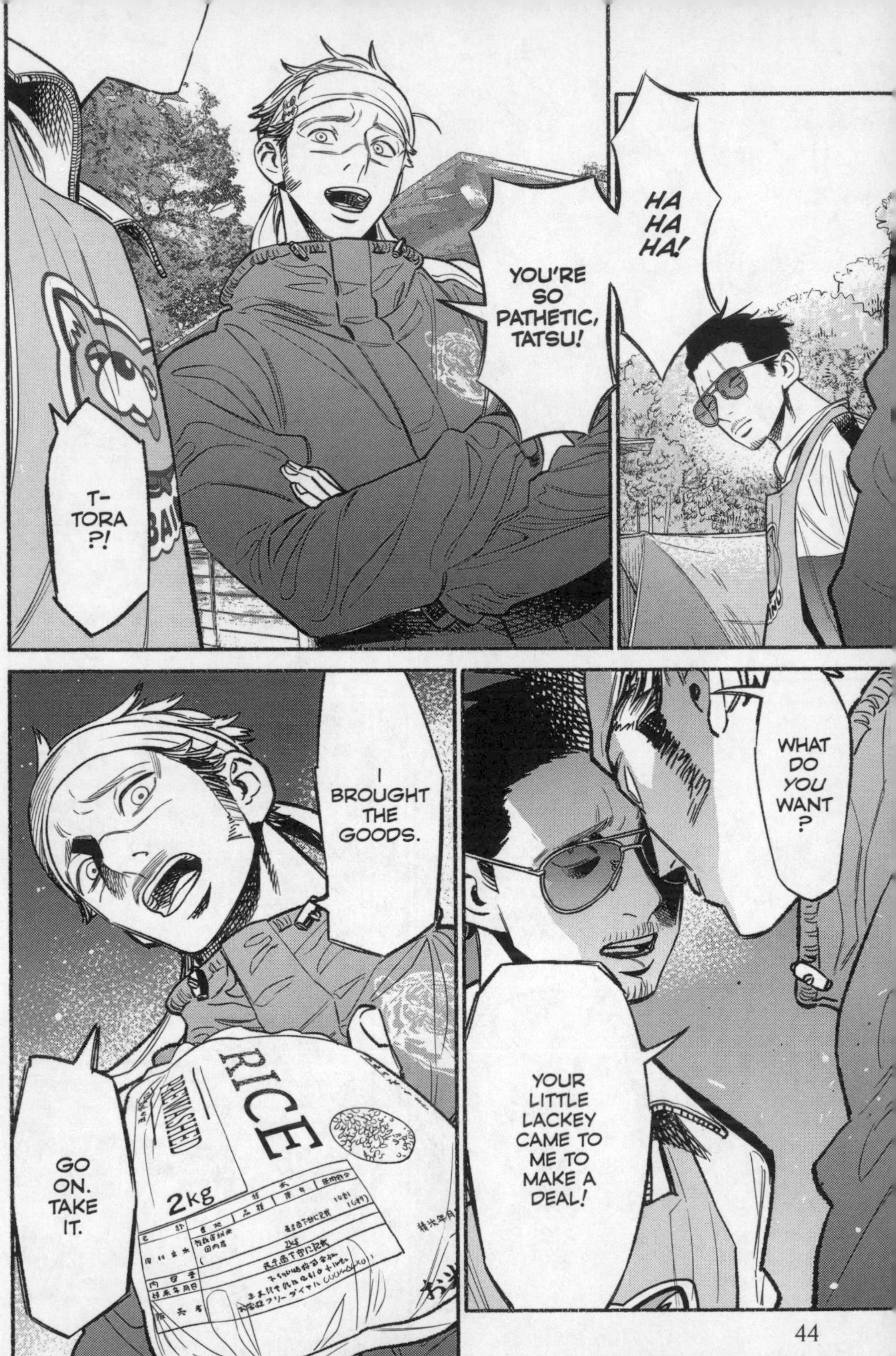
HA HA HA!
YOU'RE SO PATHETIC, TATSU!
T-TORA ?!
WHAT DO YOU WANT ?
YOUR LITTLE LACKEY CAME TO ME TO MAKE A DEAL!
I BROUGHT THE GOODS.
RICE
PREWASHED
2kg
GO ON. TAKE IT.

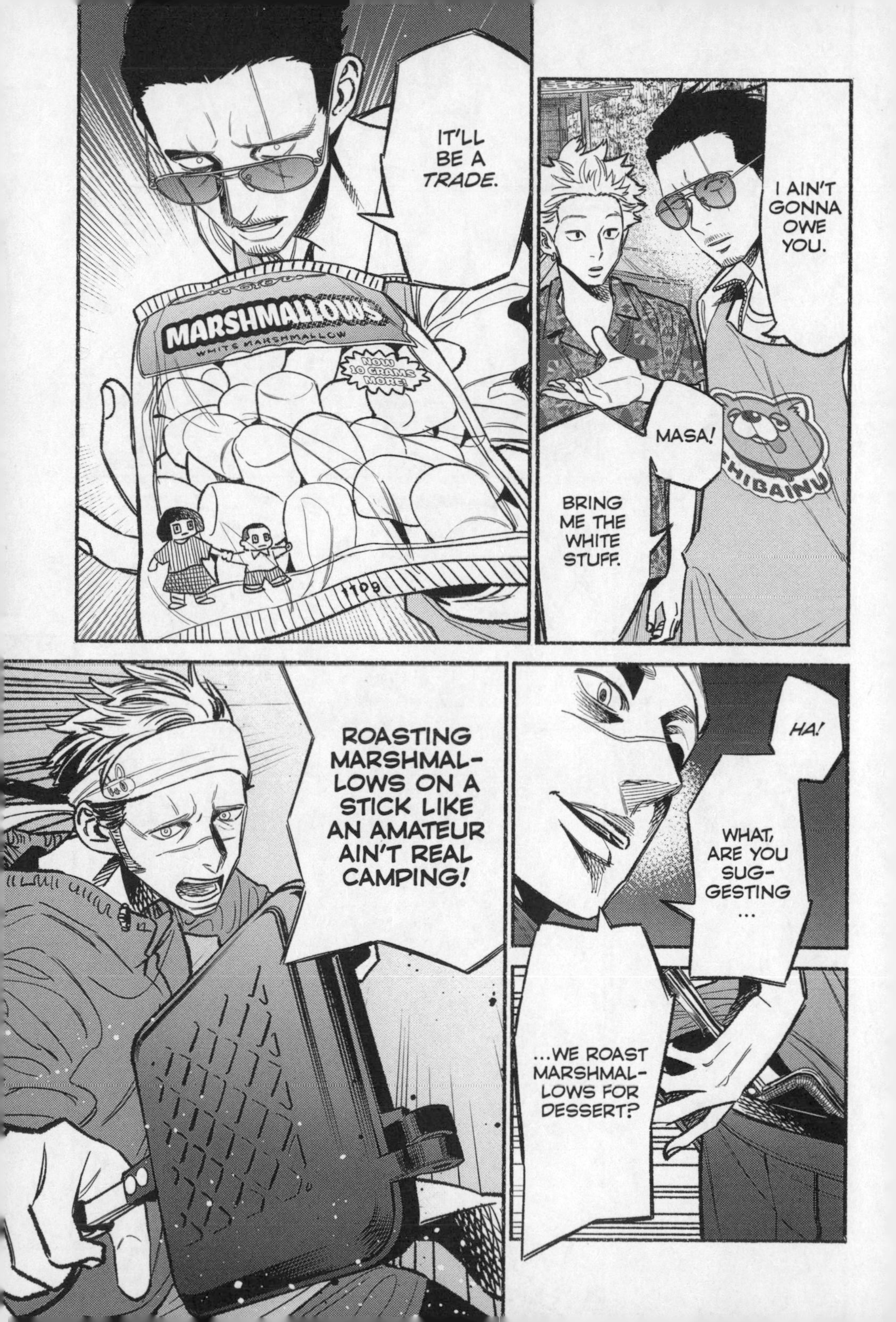
I AIN'T GONNA OWE YOU.
MASA!
BRING ME THE WHITE STUFF.
IT'LL BE A *TRADE*.
MARSHMALLOWS
WHITE MARSHMALLOW
NOW 10 GRAMS MORE!
110g
HA!
WHAT, ARE YOU SUGGESTING ...
...WE ROAST MARSHMALLOWS FOR DESSERT?
ROASTING MARSHMALLOWS ON A STICK LIKE AN AMATEUR AIN'T REAL CAMPING!

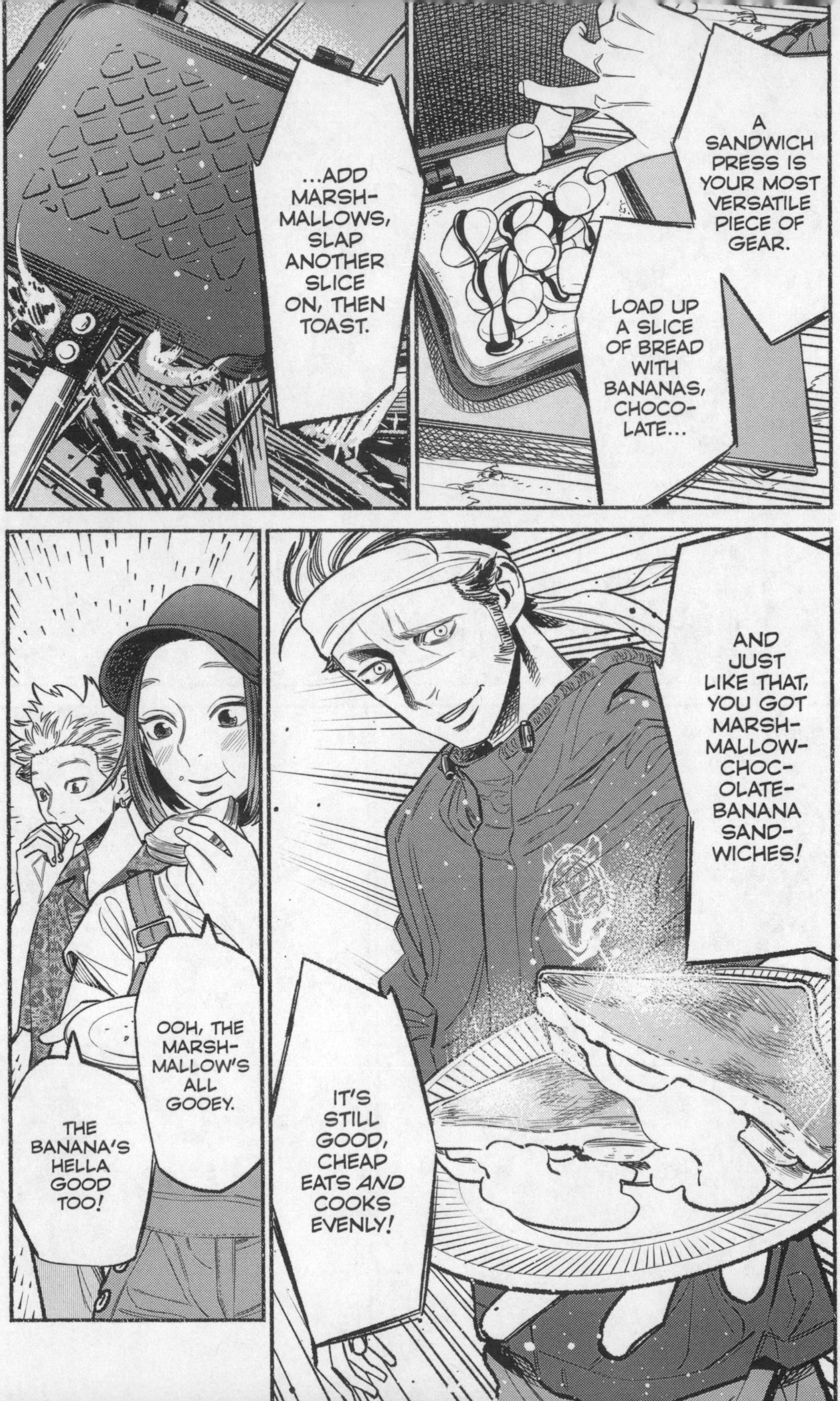
A SANDWICH PRESS IS YOUR MOST VERSATILE PIECE OF GEAR.
LOAD UP A SLICE OF BREAD WITH BANANAS, CHOCOLATE...
...ADD MARSHMALLOWS, SLAP ANOTHER SLICE ON, THEN TOAST.
AND JUST LIKE THAT, YOU GOT MARSHMALLOW-CHOCOLATE-BANANA SANDWICHES!
IT'S STILL GOOD, CHEAP EATS *AND* COOKS EVENLY!
OOH, THE MARSHMALLOW'S ALL GOOEY.
THE BANANA'S HELLA GOOD TOO!

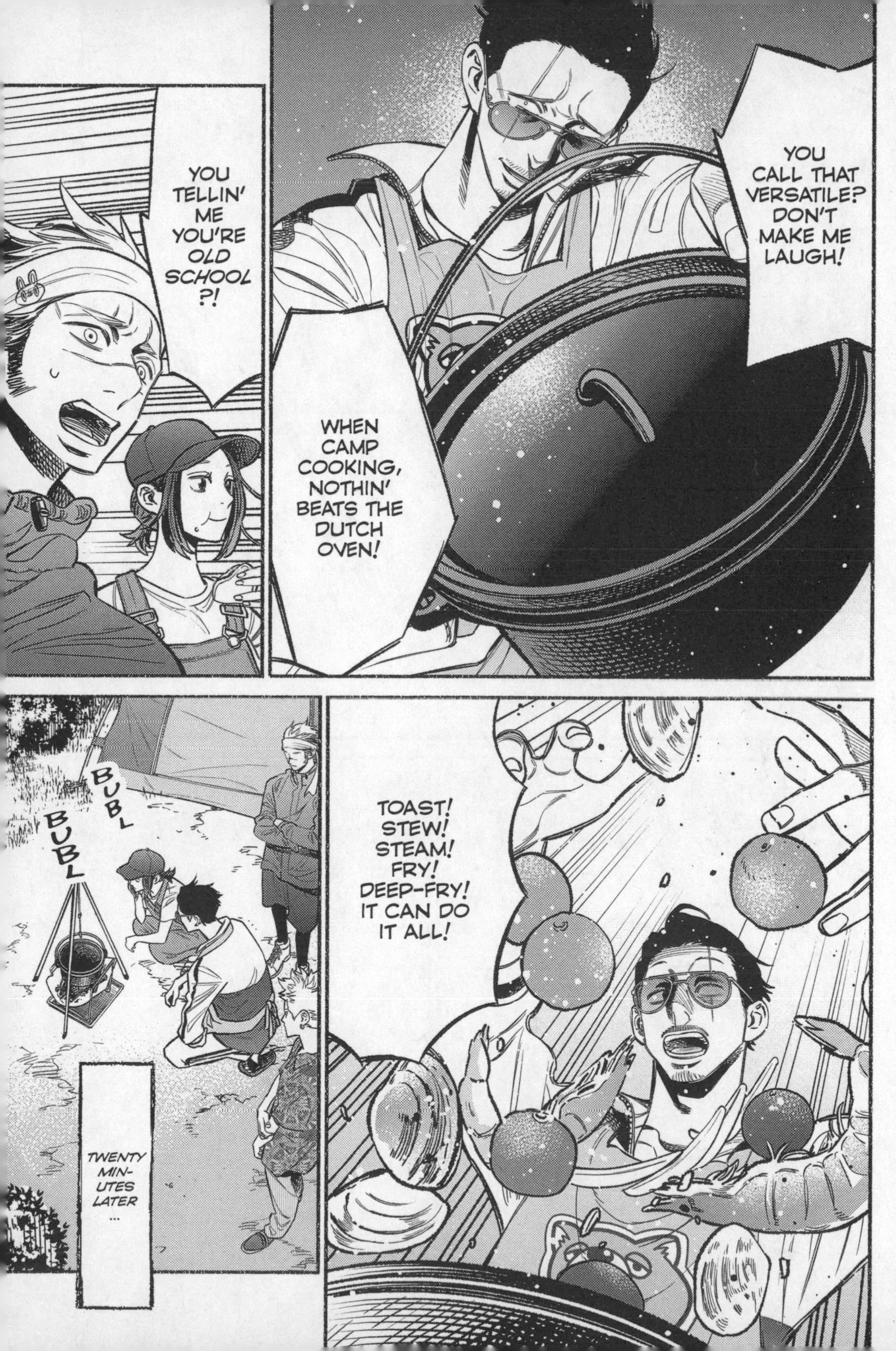
YOU CALL THAT VERSATILE? DON'T MAKE ME LAUGH!
WHEN CAMP COOKING, NOTHIN' BEATS THE DUTCH OVEN!
YOU TELLIN' ME YOU'RE *OLD SCHOOL*?!
TOAST! STEW! STEAM! FRY! DEEP-FRY! IT CAN DO IT ALL!
BUBL
BUBL
TWENTY MIN-UTES LATER ...

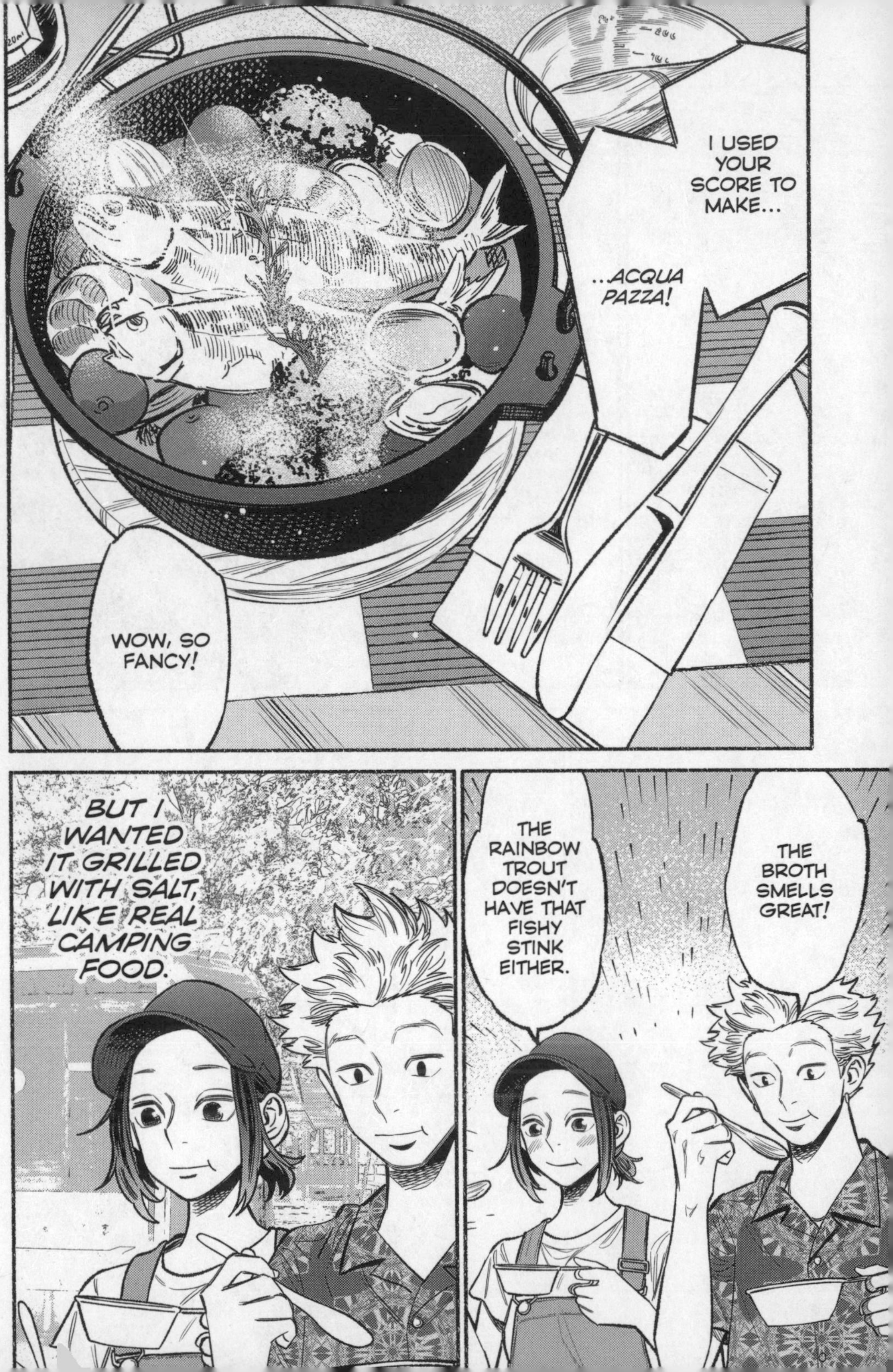
I USED YOUR SCORE TO MAKE...
...ACQUA PAZZA!
WOW, SO FANCY!
THE BROTH SMELLS GREAT!
THE RAINBOW TROUT DOESN'T HAVE THAT FISHY STINK EITHER.
BUT I WANTED IT GRILLED WITH SALT, LIKE REAL CAMPING FOOD.

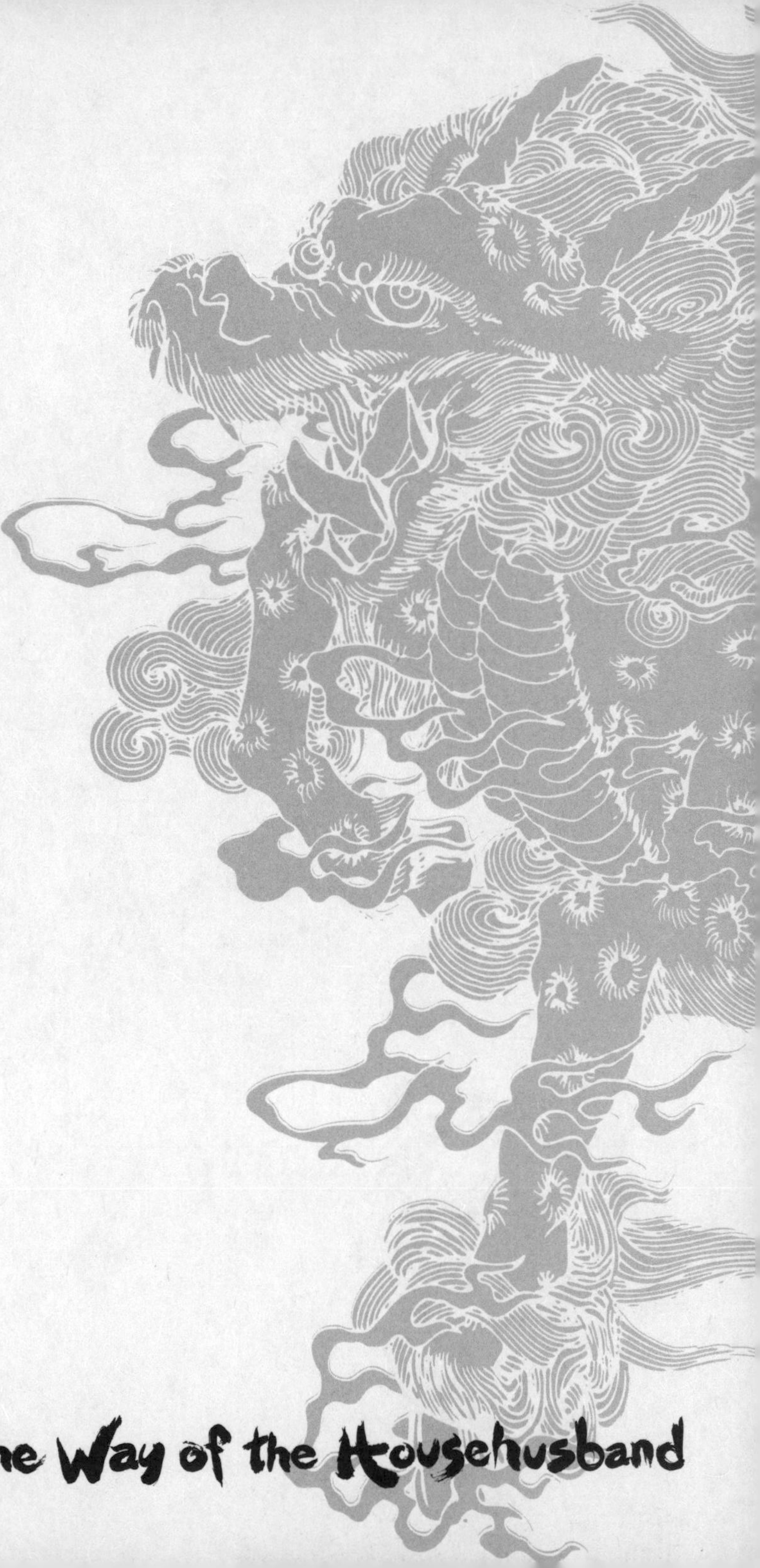

The Way of the Househusband

CHAPTER 58

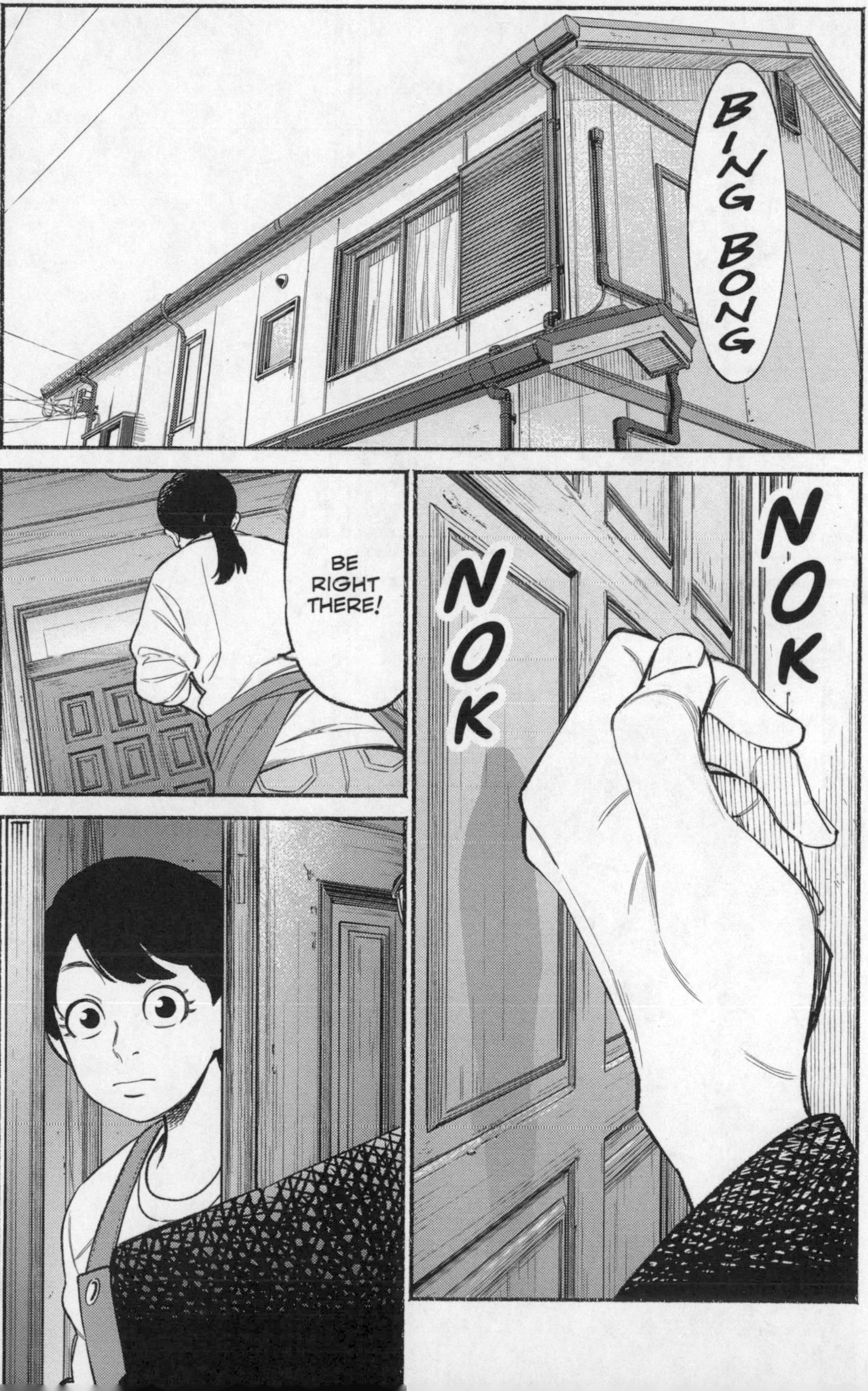
BING BONG
NOK NOK
BE RIGHT THERE!

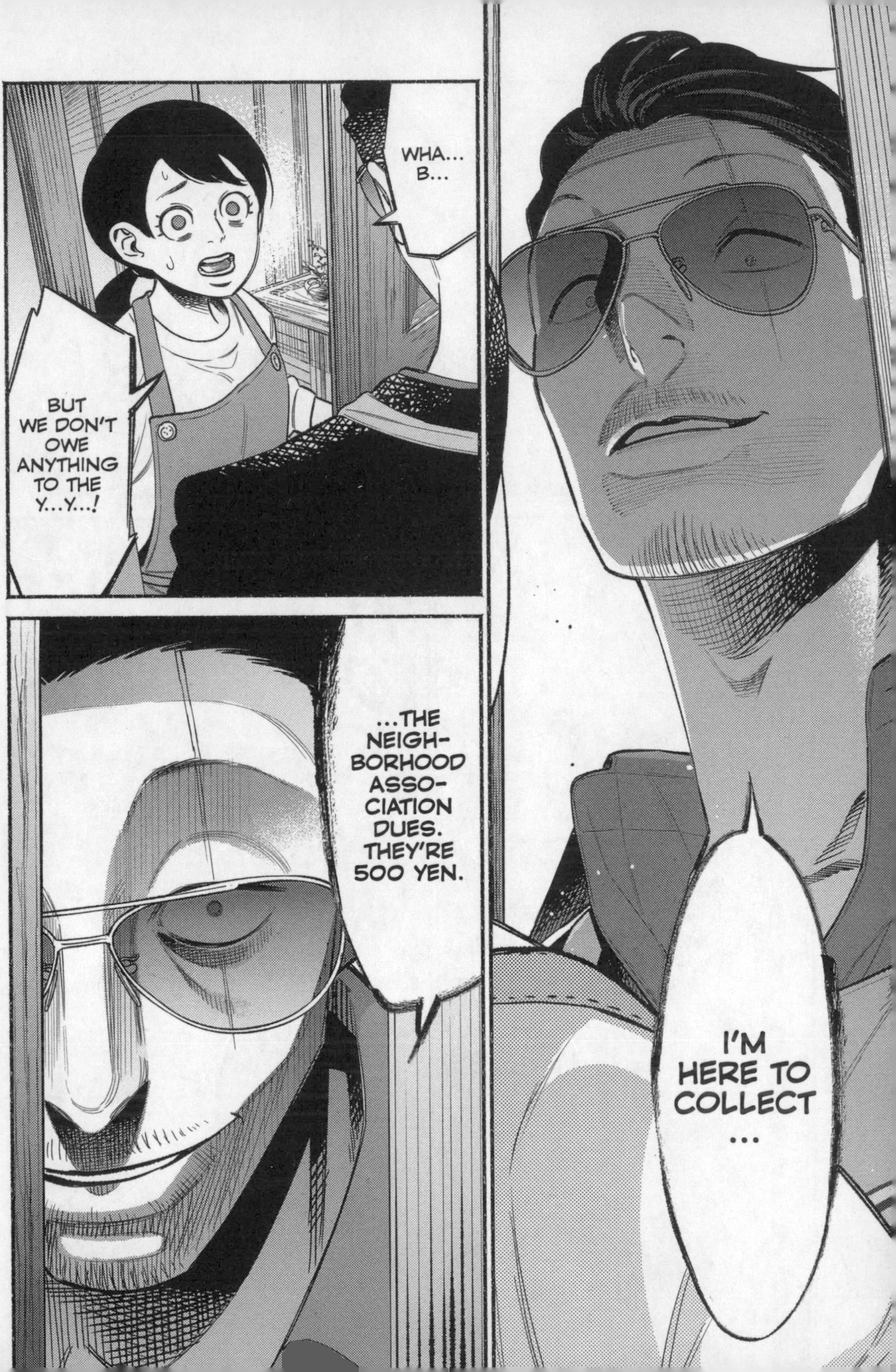
I'M HERE TO COLLECT ...
WHA... B...
BUT WE DON'T OWE ANYTHING TO THE Y...Y...!
...THE NEIGHBORHOOD ASSOCIATION DUES. THEY'RE 500 YEN.

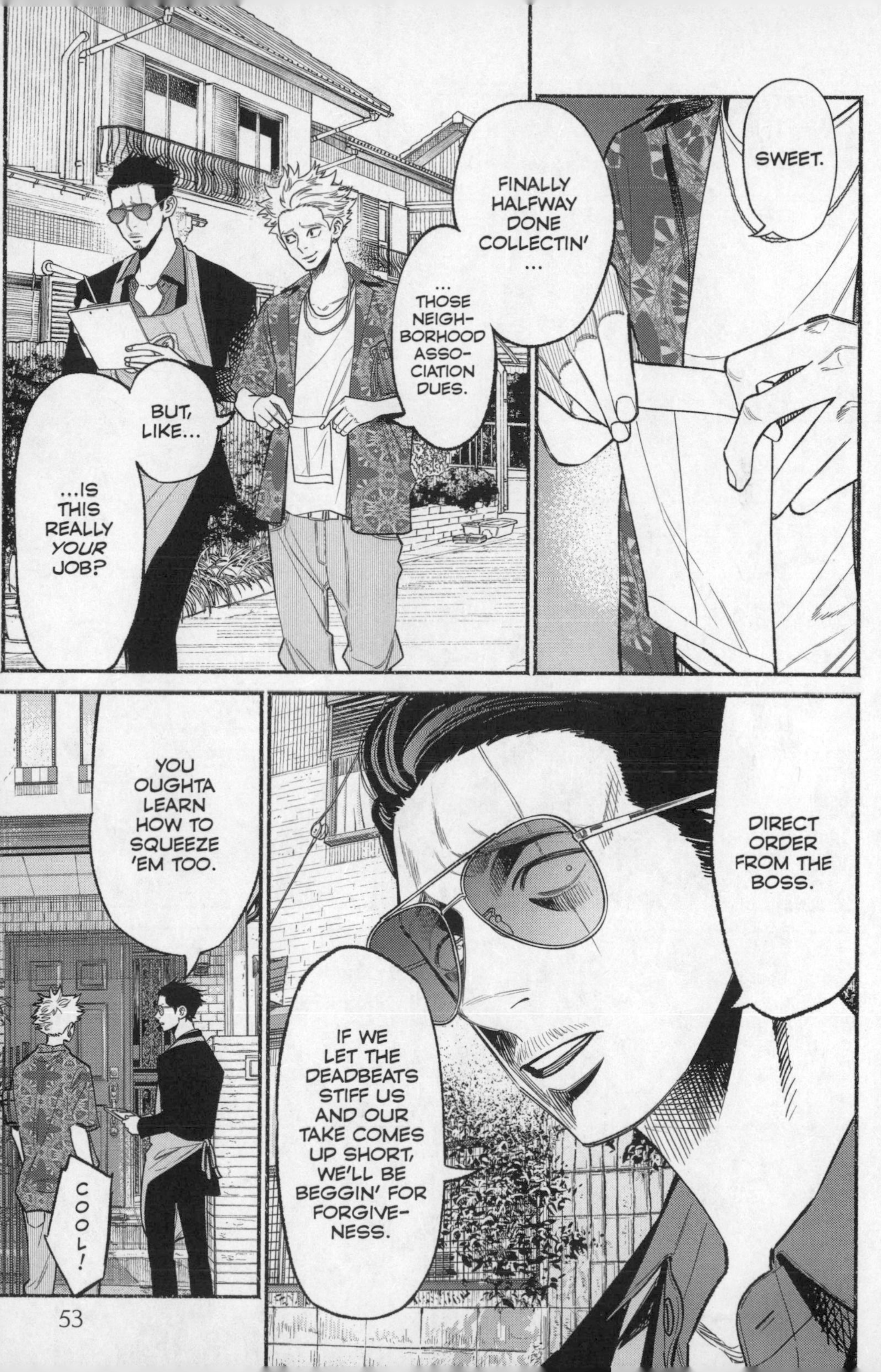
SWEET.
FINALLY HALFWAY DONE COLLECTIN' ...
... THOSE NEIGHBORHOOD ASSOCIATION DUES.
BUT, LIKE...
...IS THIS REALLY *YOUR* JOB?
DIRECT ORDER FROM THE BOSS.
IF WE LET THE DEADBEATS STIFF US AND OUR TAKE COMES UP SHORT, WE'LL BE BEGGIN' FOR FORGIVENESS.
YOU OUGHTA LEARN HOW TO SQUEEZE 'EM TOO.
COOL!

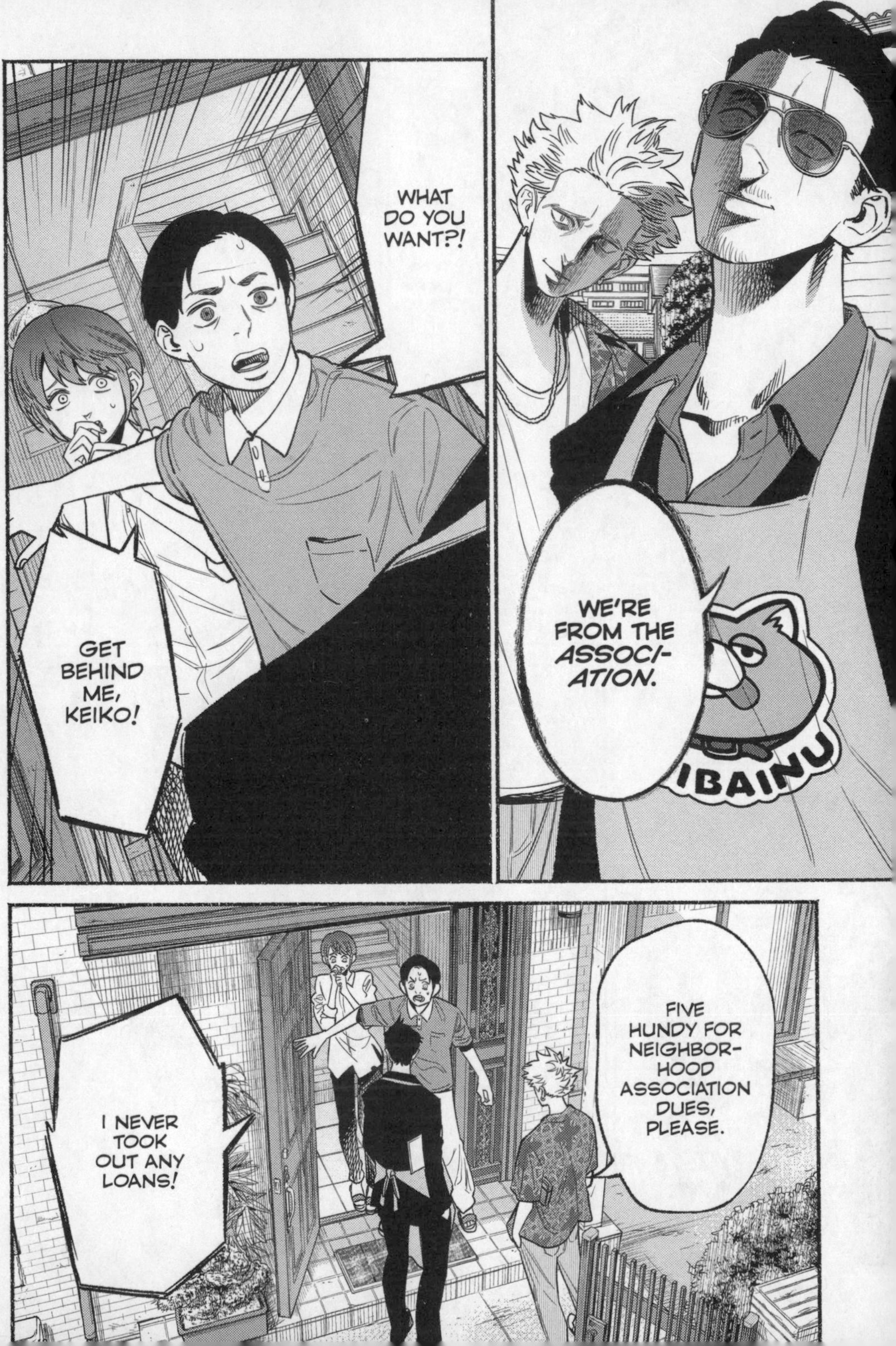
WE'RE FROM THE *ASSOCI-ATION*.
WHAT DO YOU WANT?!
GET BEHIND ME, KEIKO!
FIVE HUNDY FOR NEIGHBOR-HOOD ASSOCIATION DUES, PLEASE.
I NEVER TOOK OUT ANY LOANS!

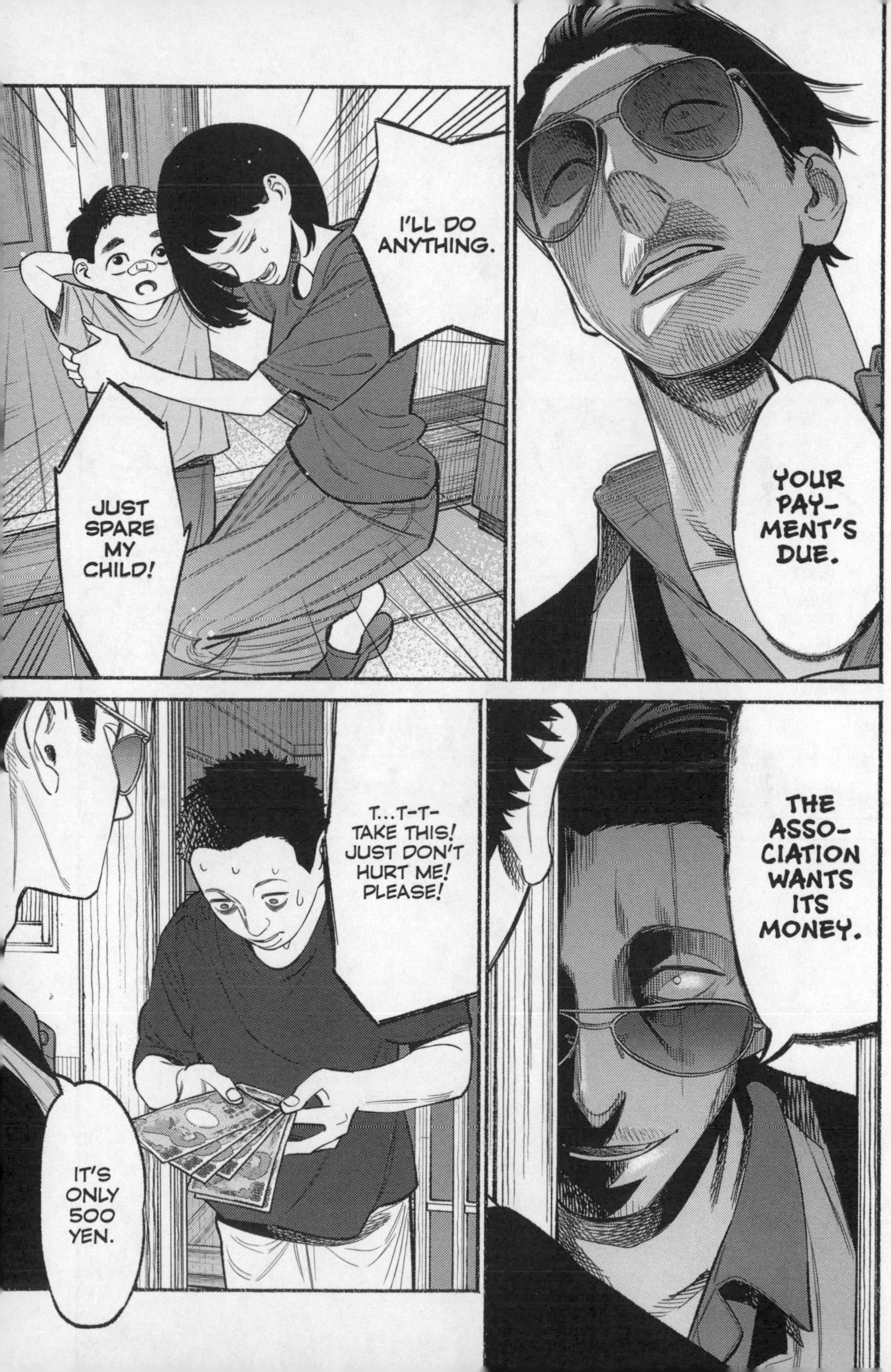
YOUR PAYMENT'S DUE.
I'LL DO ANYTHING.
JUST SPARE MY CHILD!
THE ASSOCIATION WANTS ITS MONEY.
T...T-T-TAKE THIS! JUST DON'T HURT ME! PLEASE!
IT'S ONLY 500 YEN.

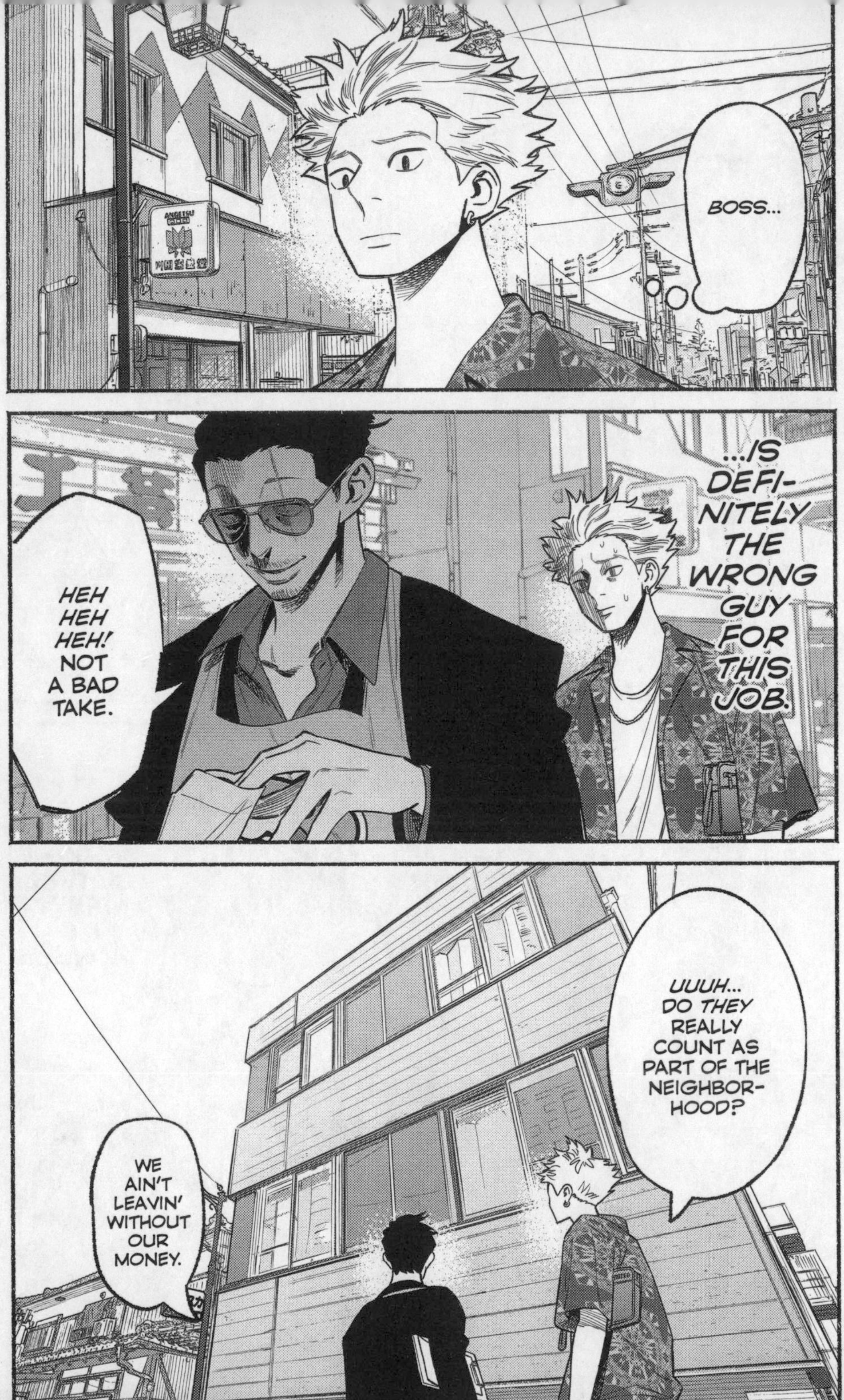
BOSS...
...IS DEFINITELY THE WRONG GUY FOR THIS JOB.
HEH HEH HEH! NOT A BAD TAKE.
UUUH... DO THEY REALLY COUNT AS PART OF THE NEIGHBORHOOD?
WE AIN'T LEAVIN' WITHOUT OUR MONEY.

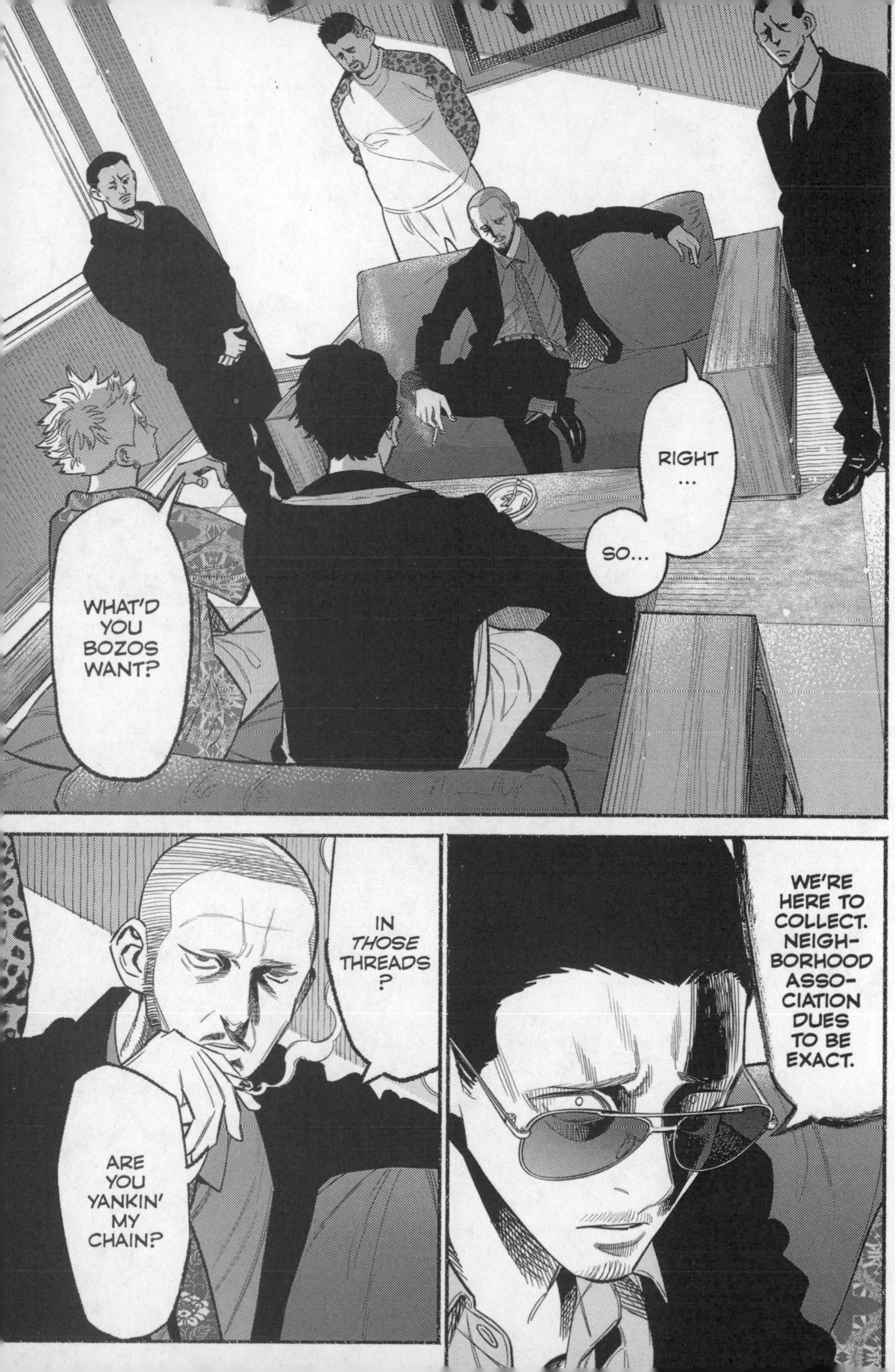
RIGHT...
SO...
WHAT'D YOU BOZOS WANT?
WE'RE HERE TO COLLECT. NEIGHBORHOOD ASSOCIATION DUES TO BE EXACT.
IN *THOSE* THREADS?
ARE YOU YANKIN' MY CHAIN?

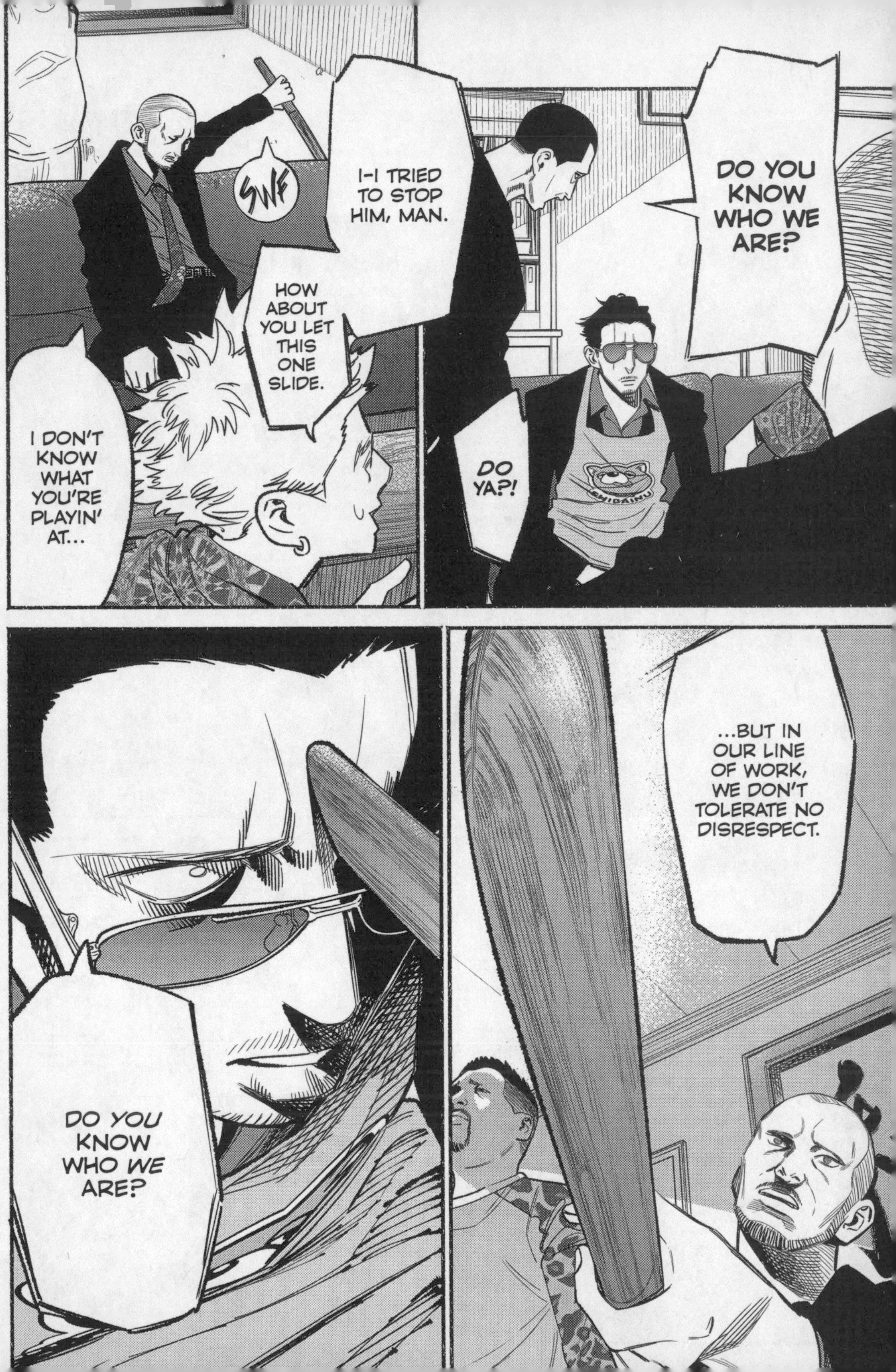
DO YOU KNOW WHO WE ARE?
DO YA?!
I-I TRIED TO STOP HIM, MAN.
SNF
HOW ABOUT YOU LET THIS ONE SLIDE.
I DON'T KNOW WHAT YOU'RE PLAYIN' AT...
...BUT IN OUR LINE OF WORK, WE DON'T TOLERATE NO DISRESPECT.
DO YOU KNOW WHO WE ARE?

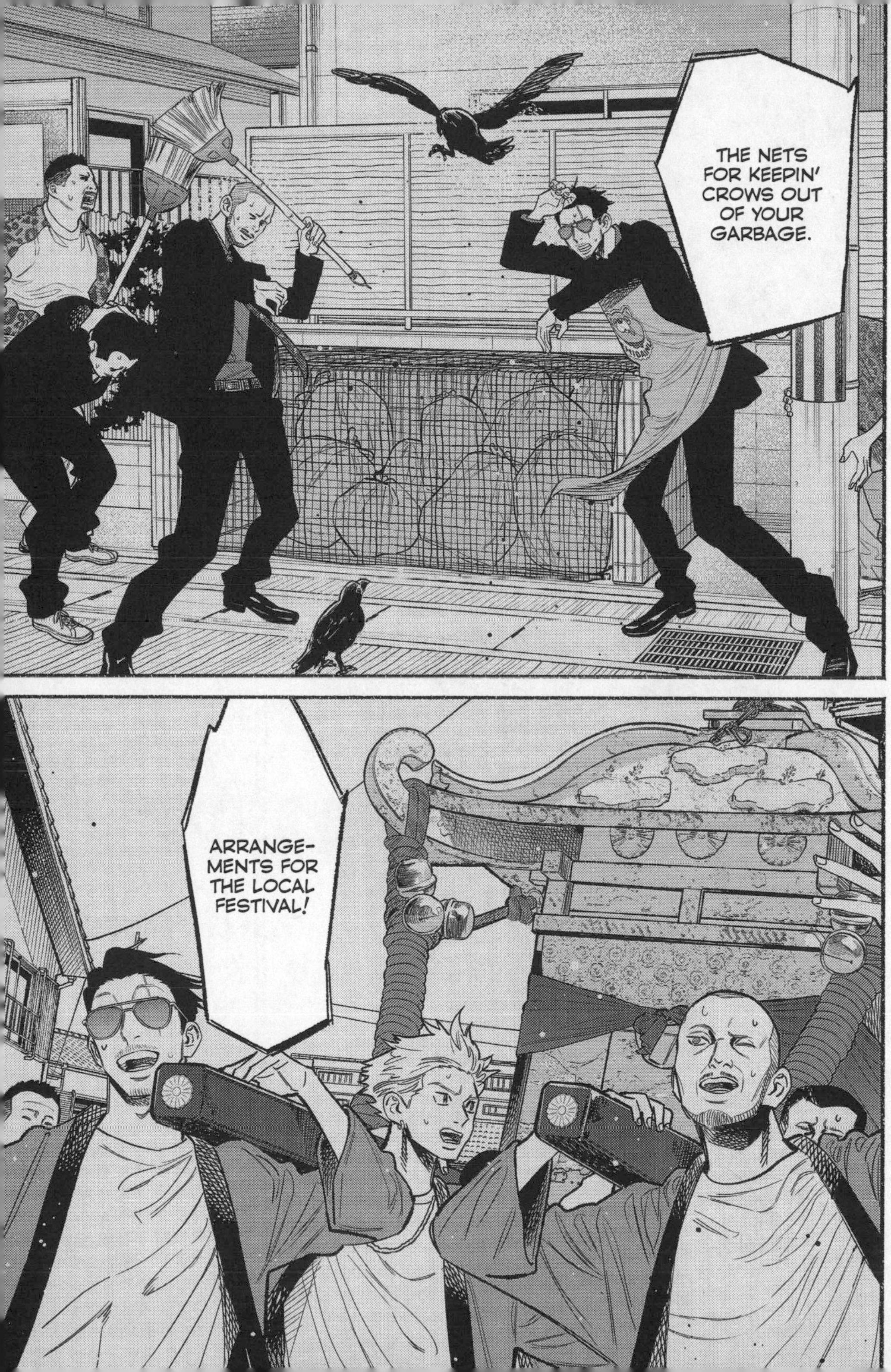
THE NETS FOR KEEPIN' CROWS OUT OF YOUR GARBAGE.
ARRANGE-MENTS FOR THE LOCAL FESTIVAL!

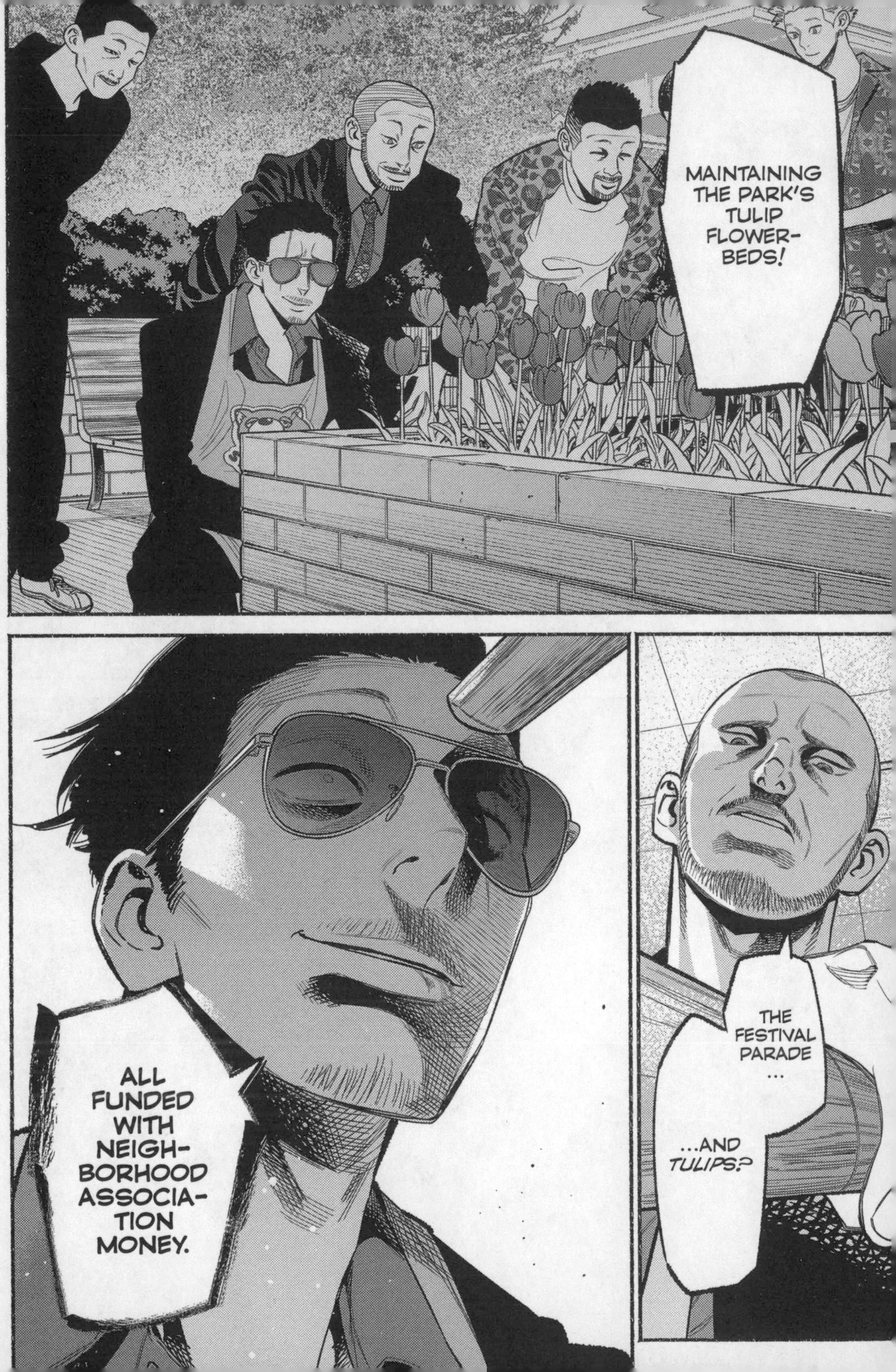
MAINTAINING THE PARK'S TULIP FLOWER-BEDS!
THE FESTIVAL PARADE ...
...AND *TULIPS?*
ALL FUNDED WITH NEIGHBORHOOD ASSOCIATION MONEY.

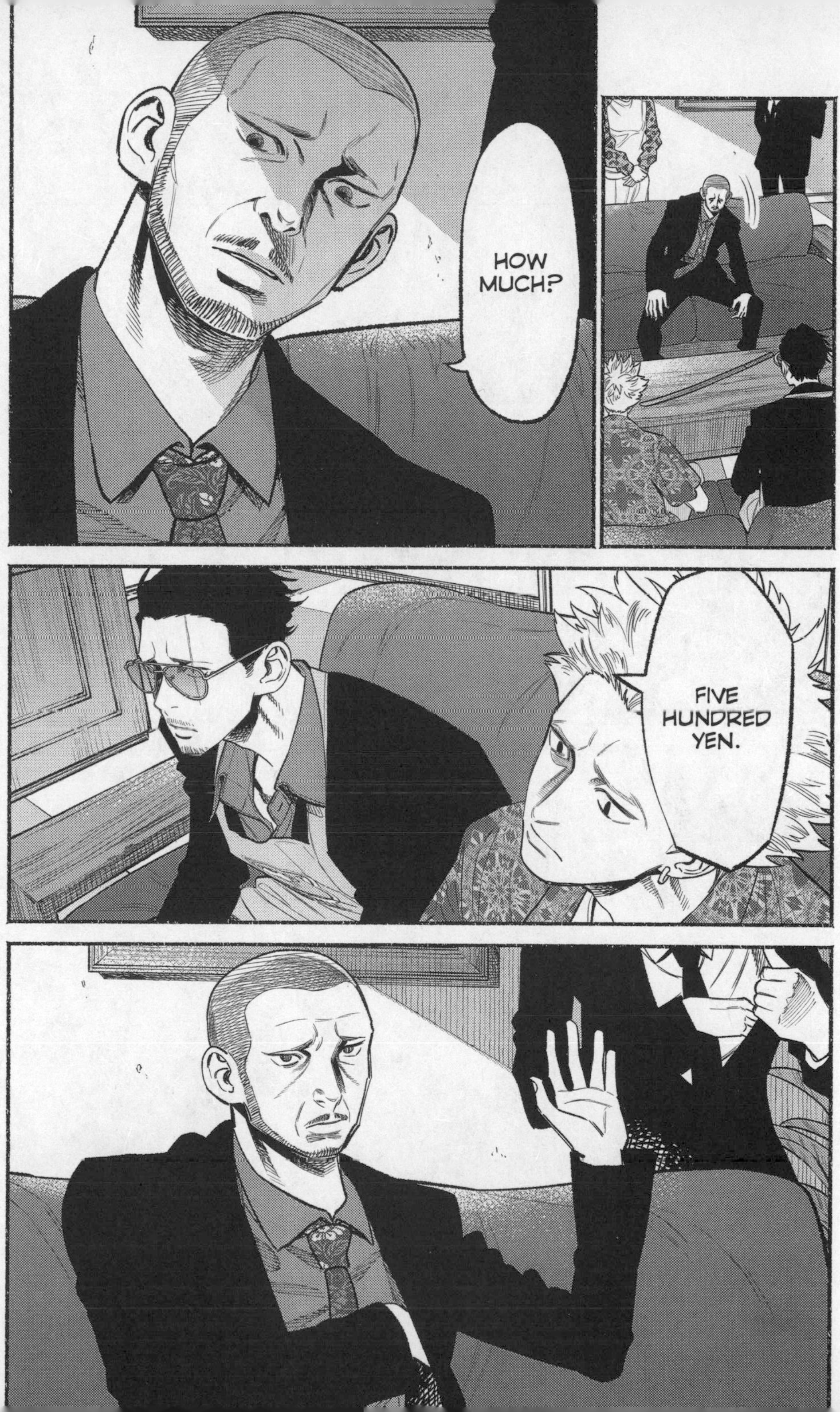
HOW MUCH?
FIVE HUNDRED YEN.

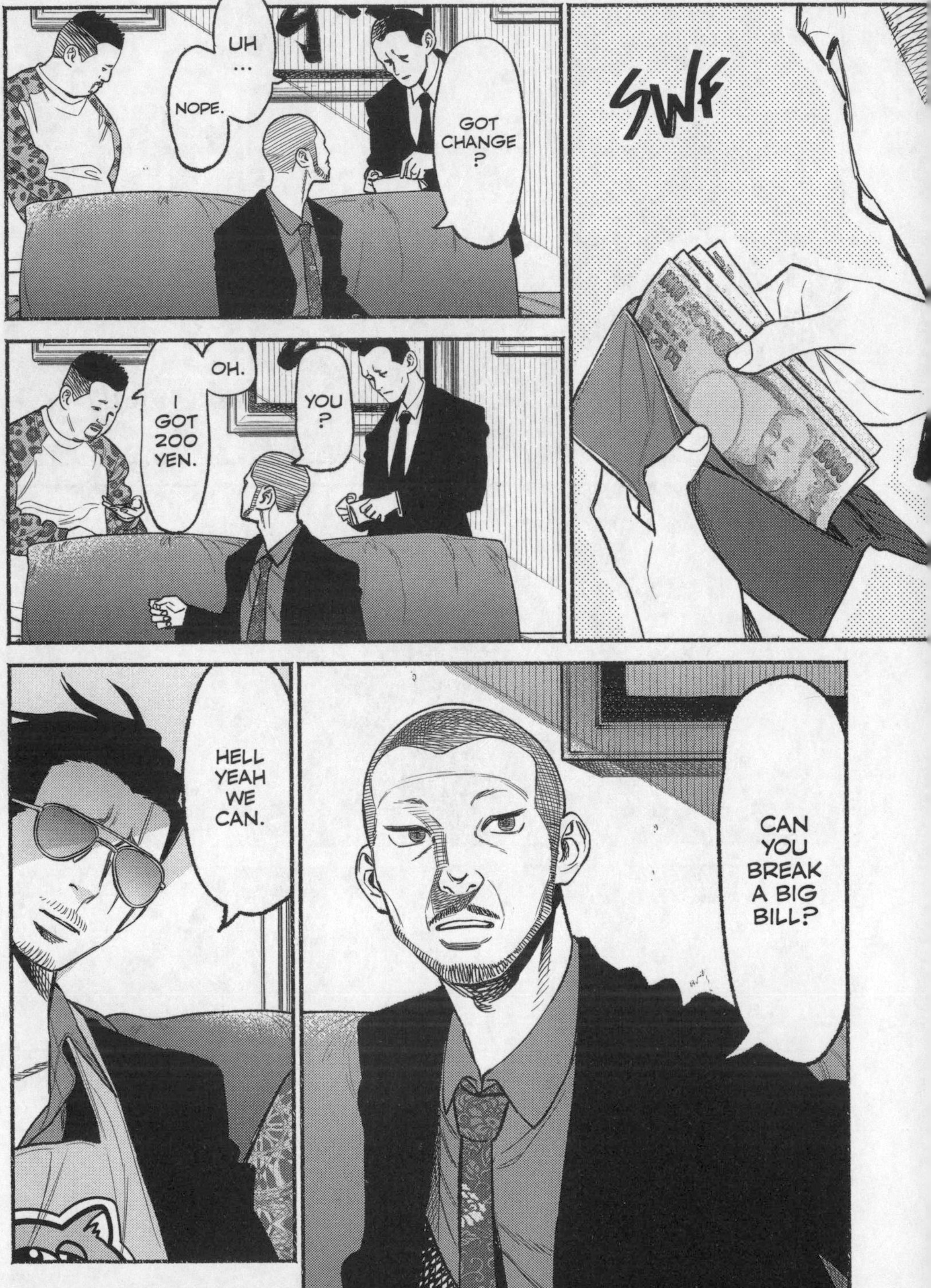
SWF
GOT CHANGE?
UH ... NOPE.
YOU?
OH. I GOT 200 YEN.
CAN YOU BREAK A BIG BILL?
HELL YEAH WE CAN.

IT'S ALL HERE.

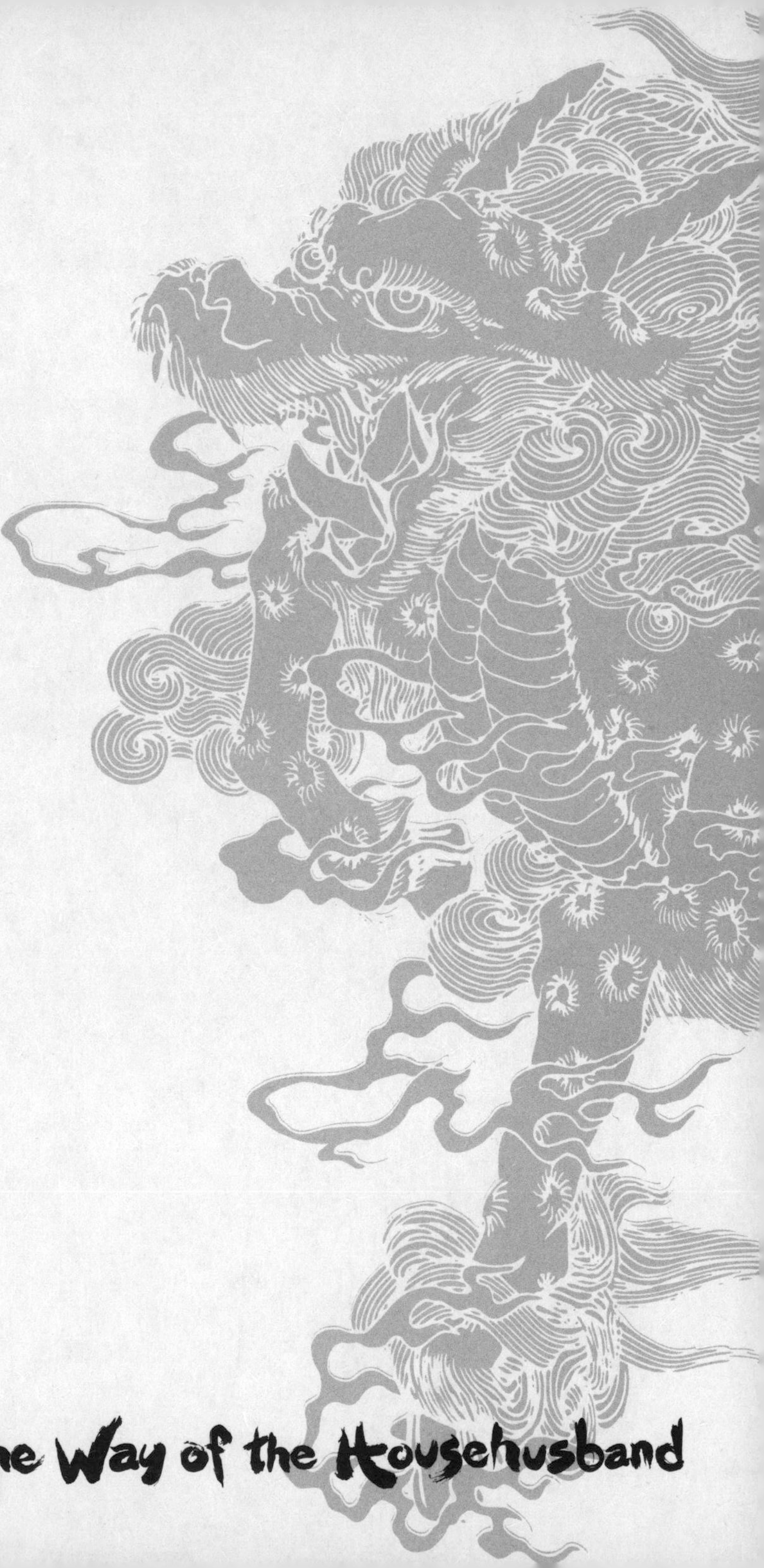

The Way of the Househusband

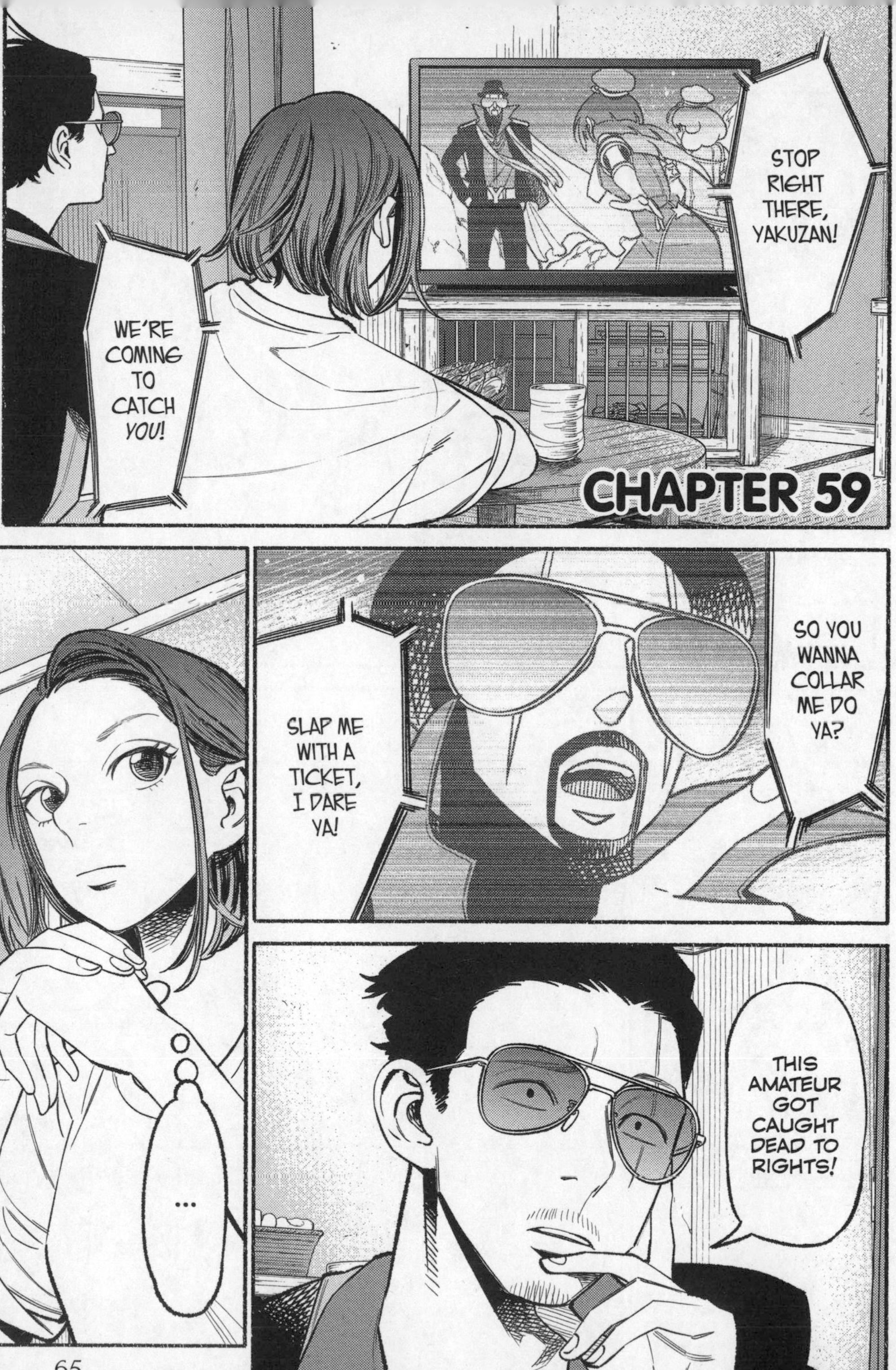
STOP RIGHT THERE, YAKUZAN!
WE'RE COMING TO CATCH *YOU*!
CHAPTER 59
SO YOU WANNA COLLAR ME DO YA?
SLAP ME WITH A TICKET, I DARE YA!
THIS AMATEUR GOT CAUGHT DEAD TO RIGHTS!
...

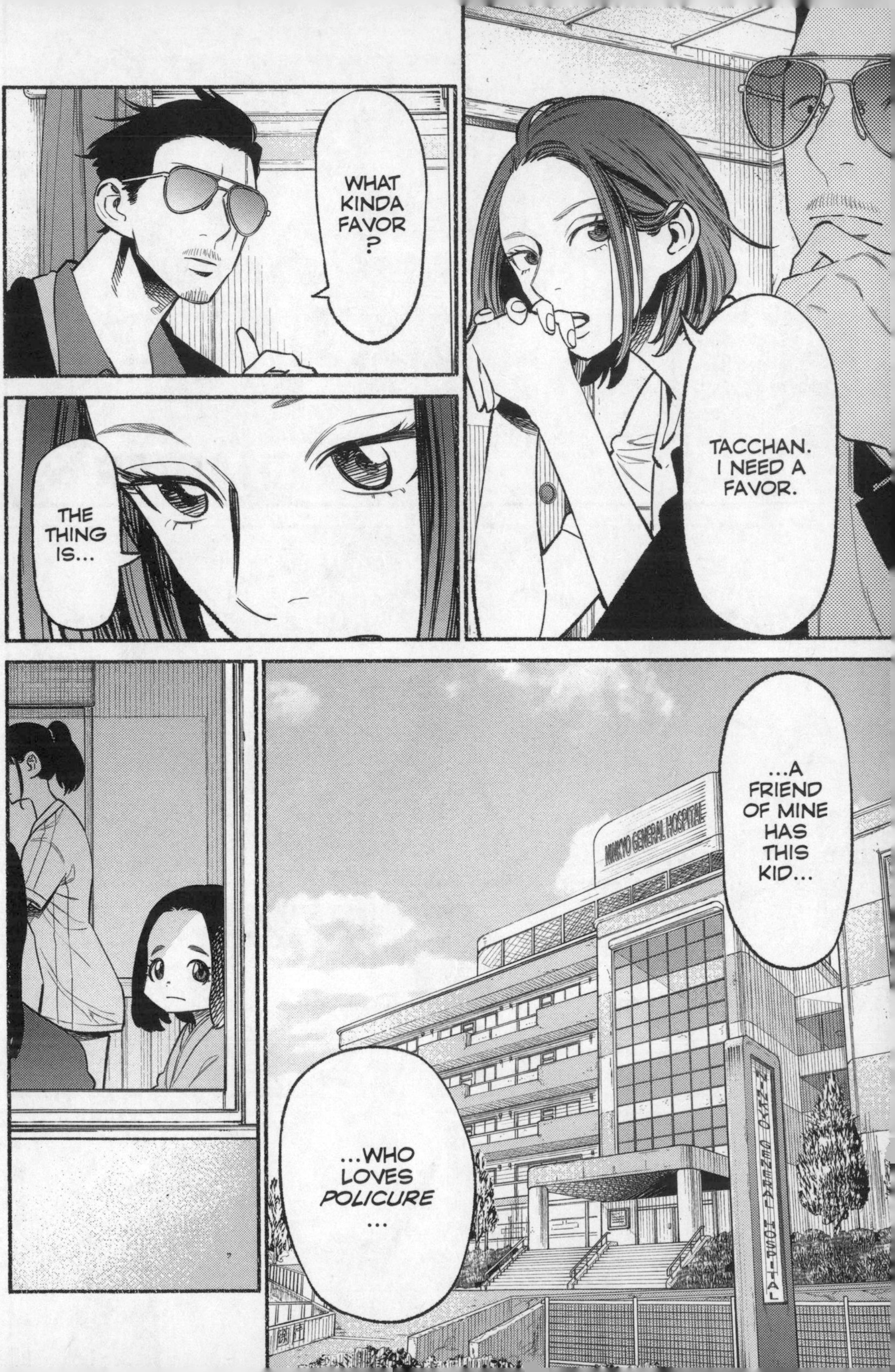
TACCHAN. I NEED A FAVOR.
WHAT KINDA FAVOR?
THE THING IS...
...A FRIEND OF MINE HAS THIS KID...
...WHO LOVES *POLICURE* ...

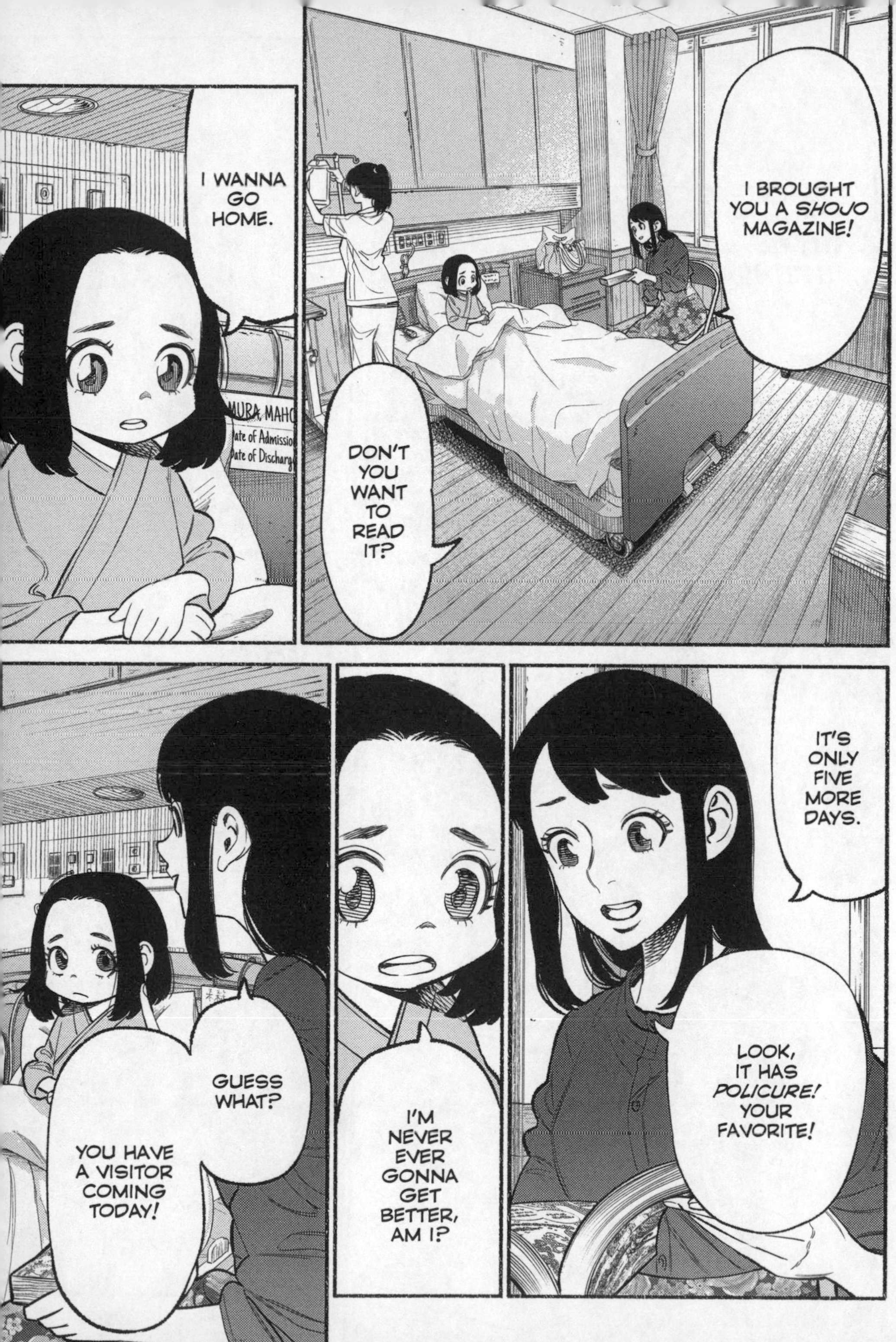
I BROUGHT YOU A *SHOJO* MAGAZINE!
DON'T YOU WANT TO READ IT?
I WANNA GO HOME.
MURA, MAHO
ate of Admissio
ate of Discharg
IT'S ONLY FIVE MORE DAYS.
LOOK, IT HAS *POLICURE!* YOUR FAVORITE!
I'M NEVER EVER GONNA GET BETTER, AM I?
GUESS WHAT?
YOU HAVE A VISITOR COMING TODAY!

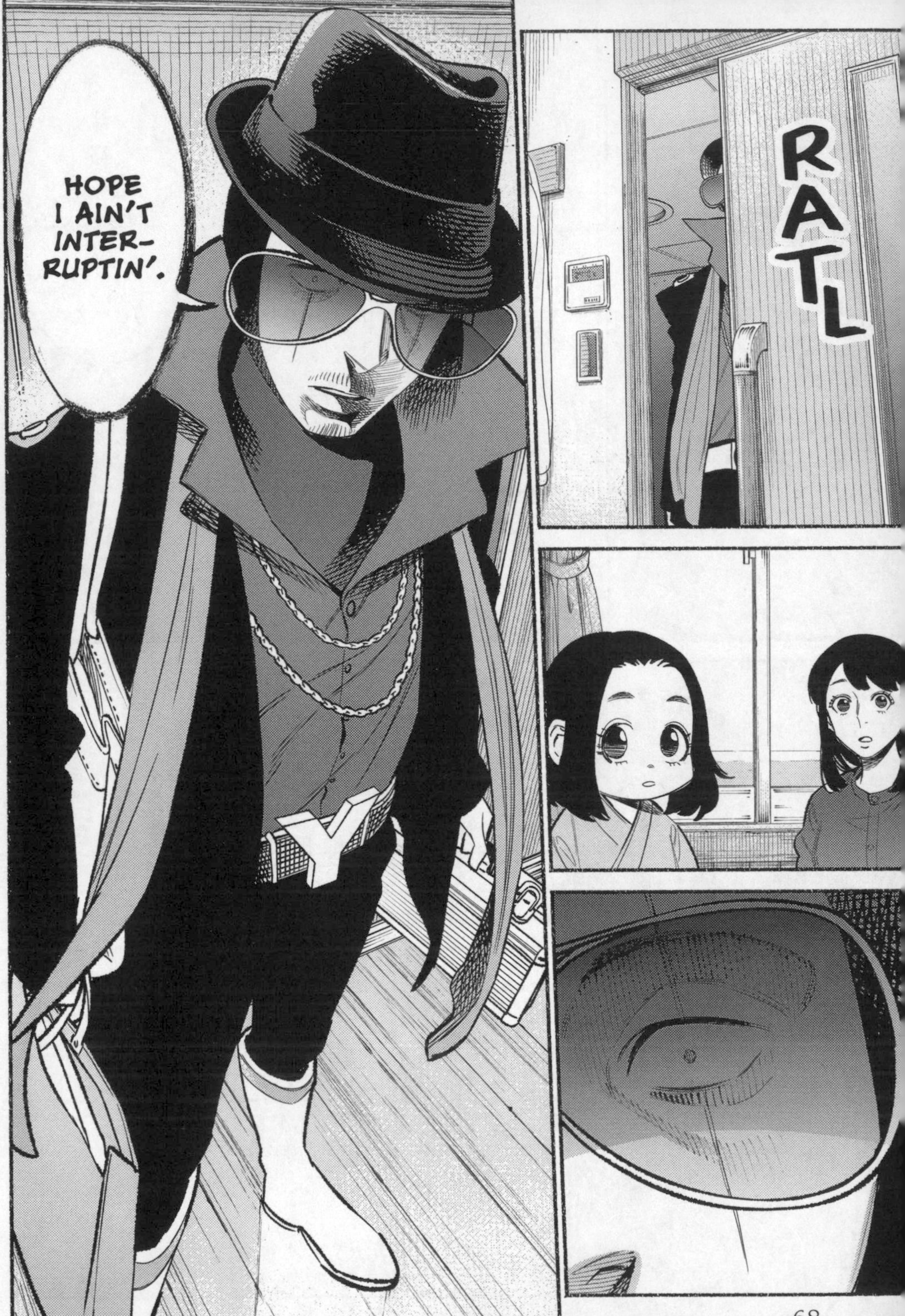
RATL
HOPE I AIN'T INTER- RUPTIN'.

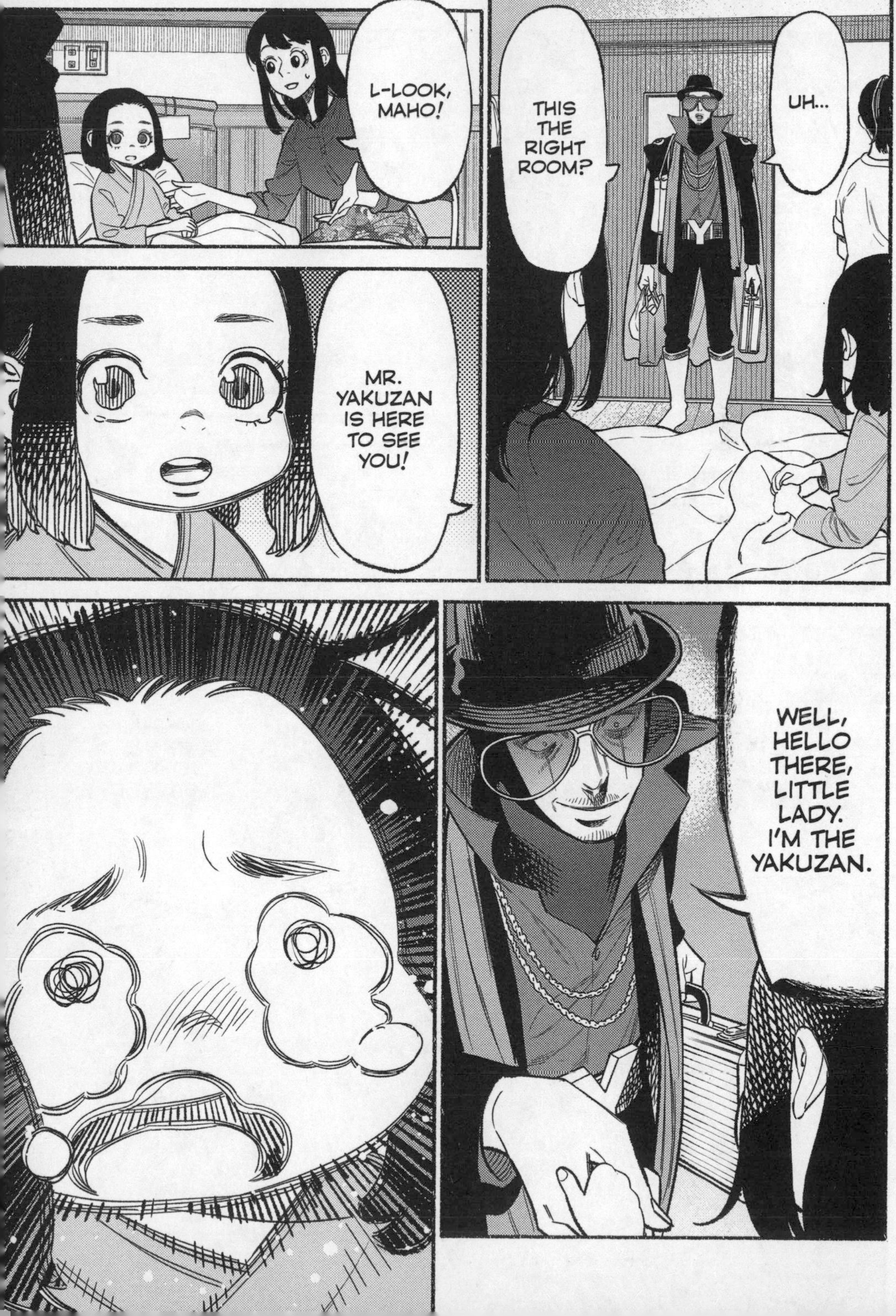
UH...
THIS THE RIGHT ROOM?
L-LOOK, MAHO!
MR. YAKUZAN IS HERE TO SEE YOU!
WELL, HELLO THERE, LITTLE LADY. I'M THE YAKUZAN.

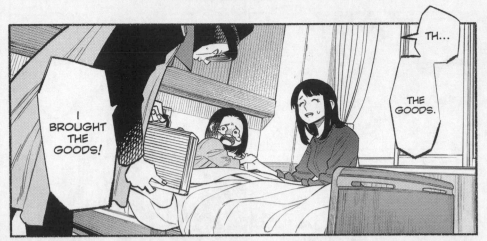

TH... THE GOODS.
I BROUGHT THE GOODS!
GCH
AK
TH-THAT'S A CHIVALRY CO. FRUIT BASKET!
THIS STUFF'S SO PRIMO THERE WAS A LINE FOR IT.
YOU SHOULDN'T HAVE! THANKS SO MUCH.

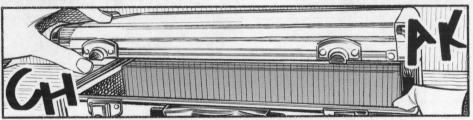

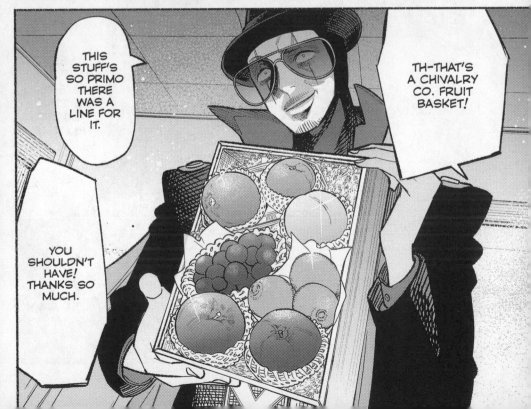

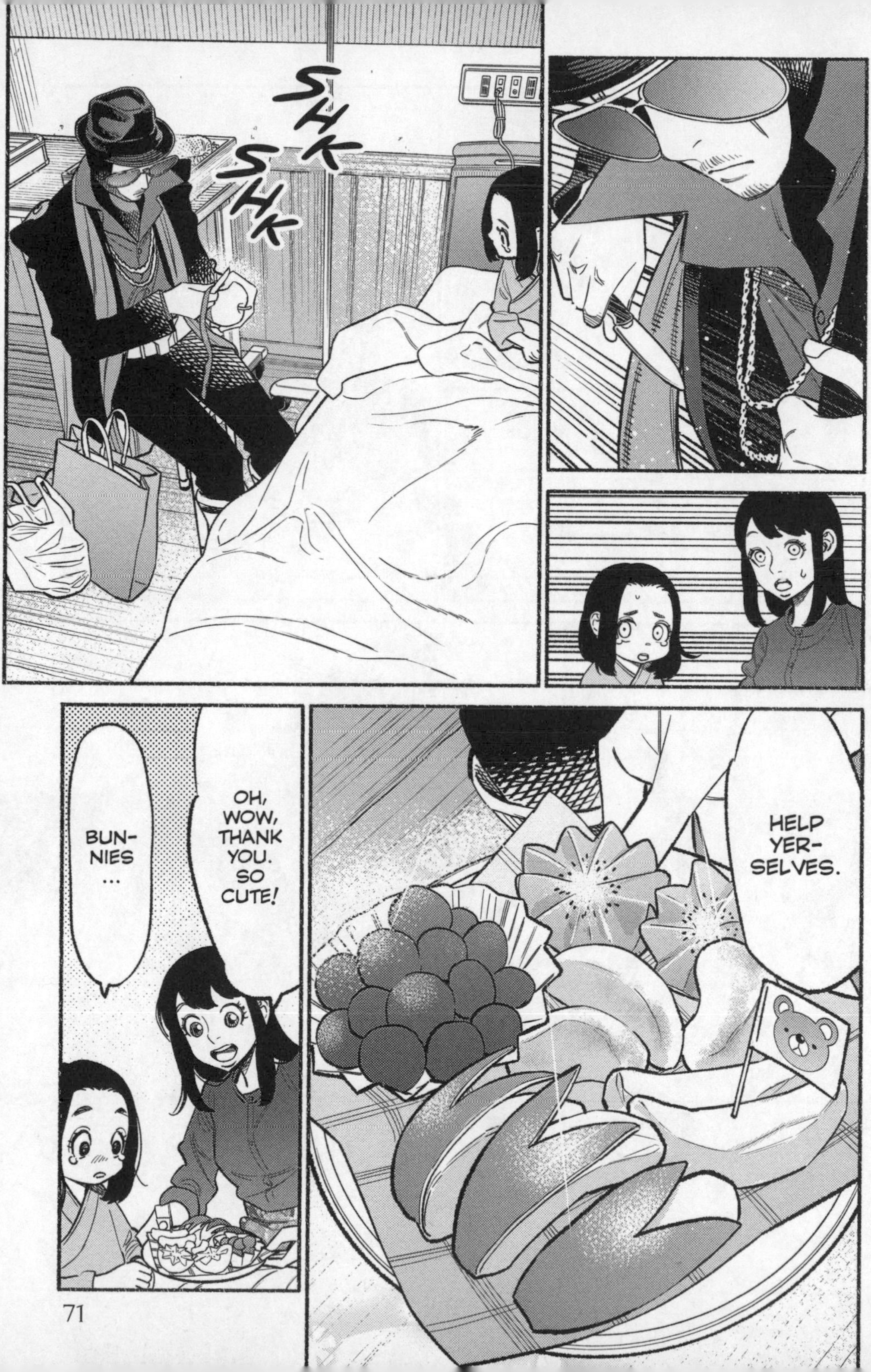
SHK SHK SHK
HELP YER-SELVES.
OH, WOW, THANK YOU. SO CUTE!
BUN-NIES ...

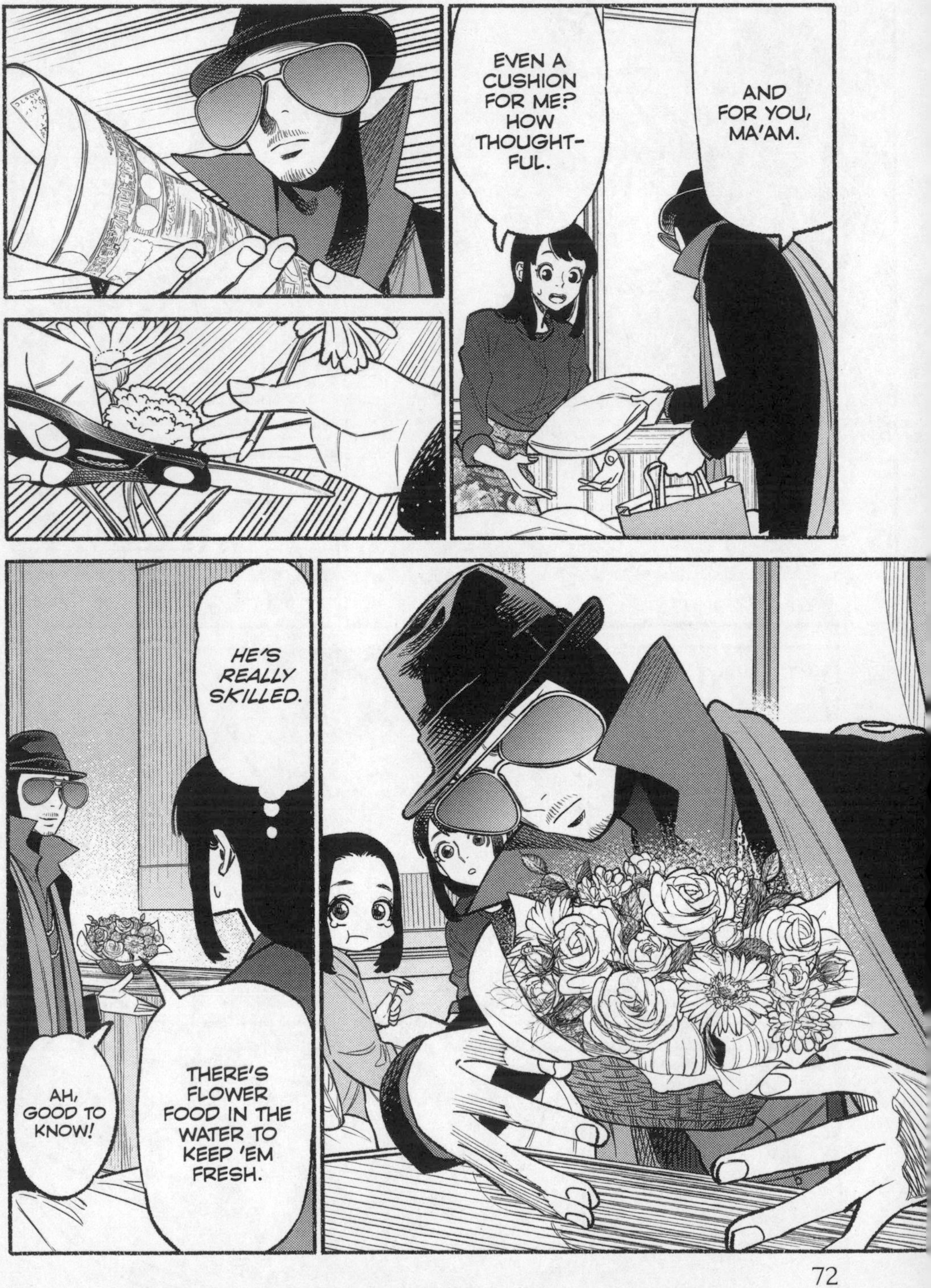
AND FOR YOU, MA'AM.
EVEN A CUSHION FOR ME? HOW THOUGHT-FUL.
HE'S REALLY SKILLED.
THERE'S FLOWER FOOD IN THE WATER TO KEEP 'EM FRESH.
AH, GOOD TO KNOW!

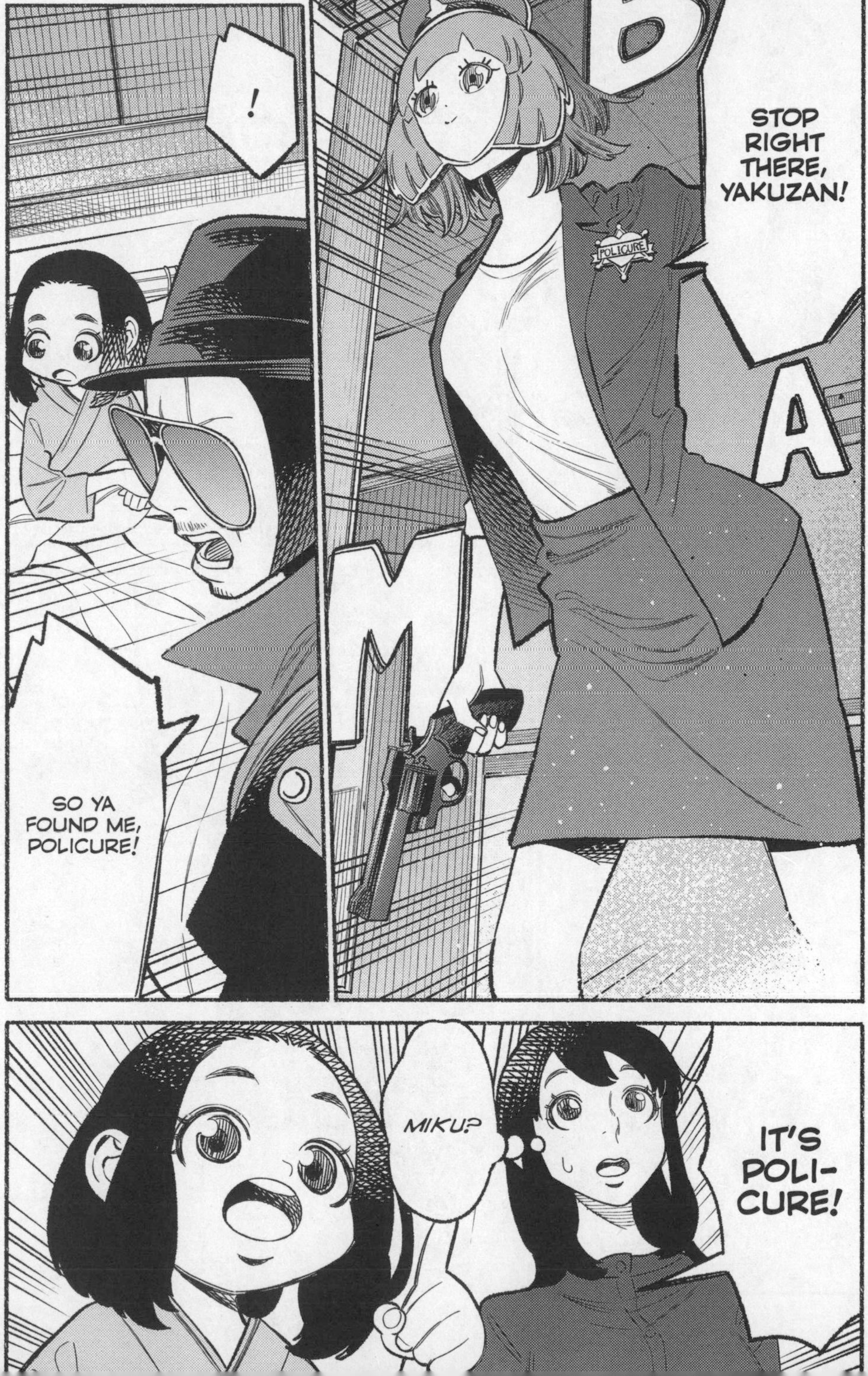
BAM
STOP RIGHT THERE, YAKUZAN!
!
SO YA FOUND ME, POLICURE!
IT'S POLI-CURE!
MIKU?

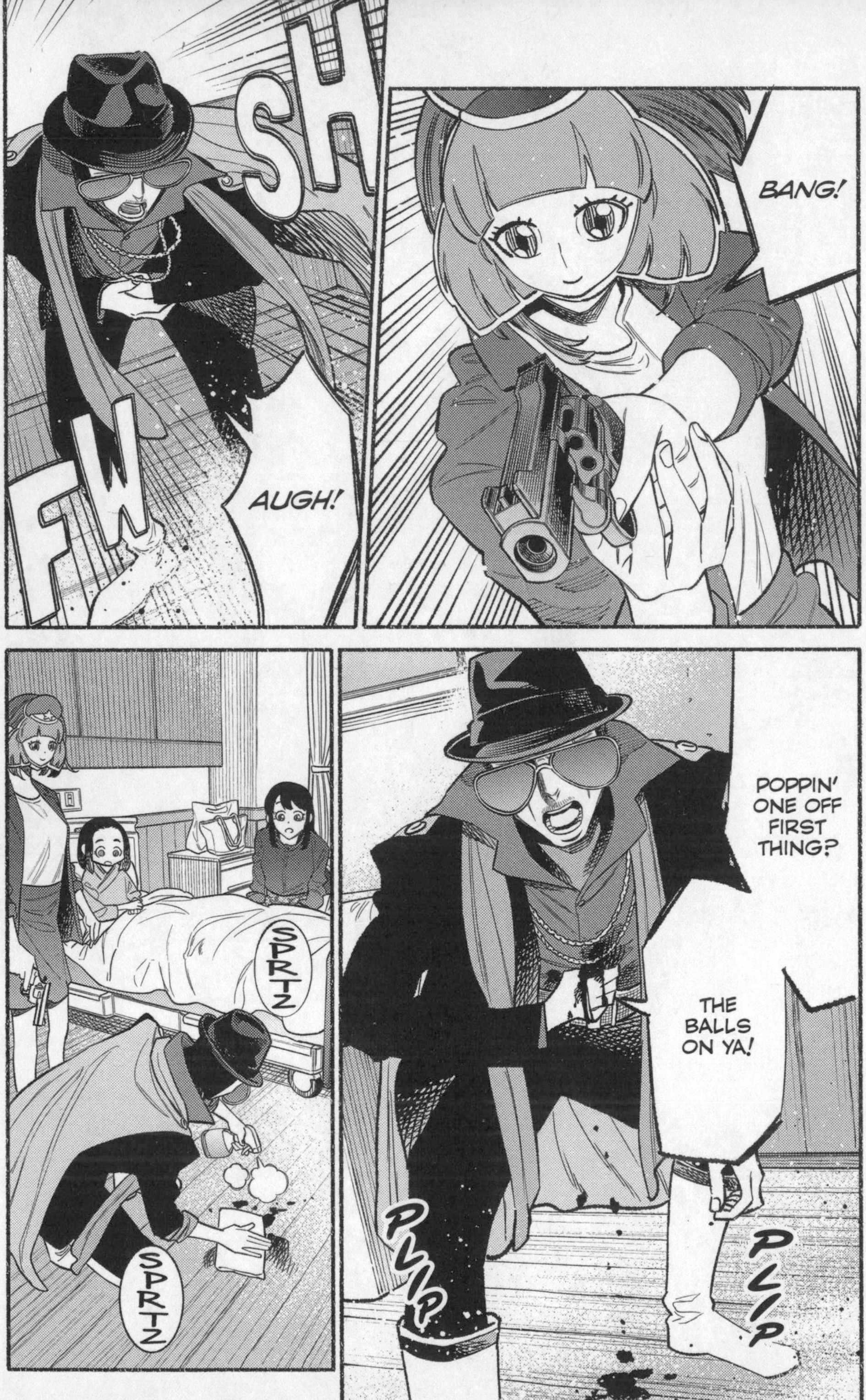
BANG!
SH
AUGH!
FW
POPPIN' ONE OFF FIRST THING?
THE BALLS ON YA!
PLIP
PLIP
SPRTZ
SPRTZ

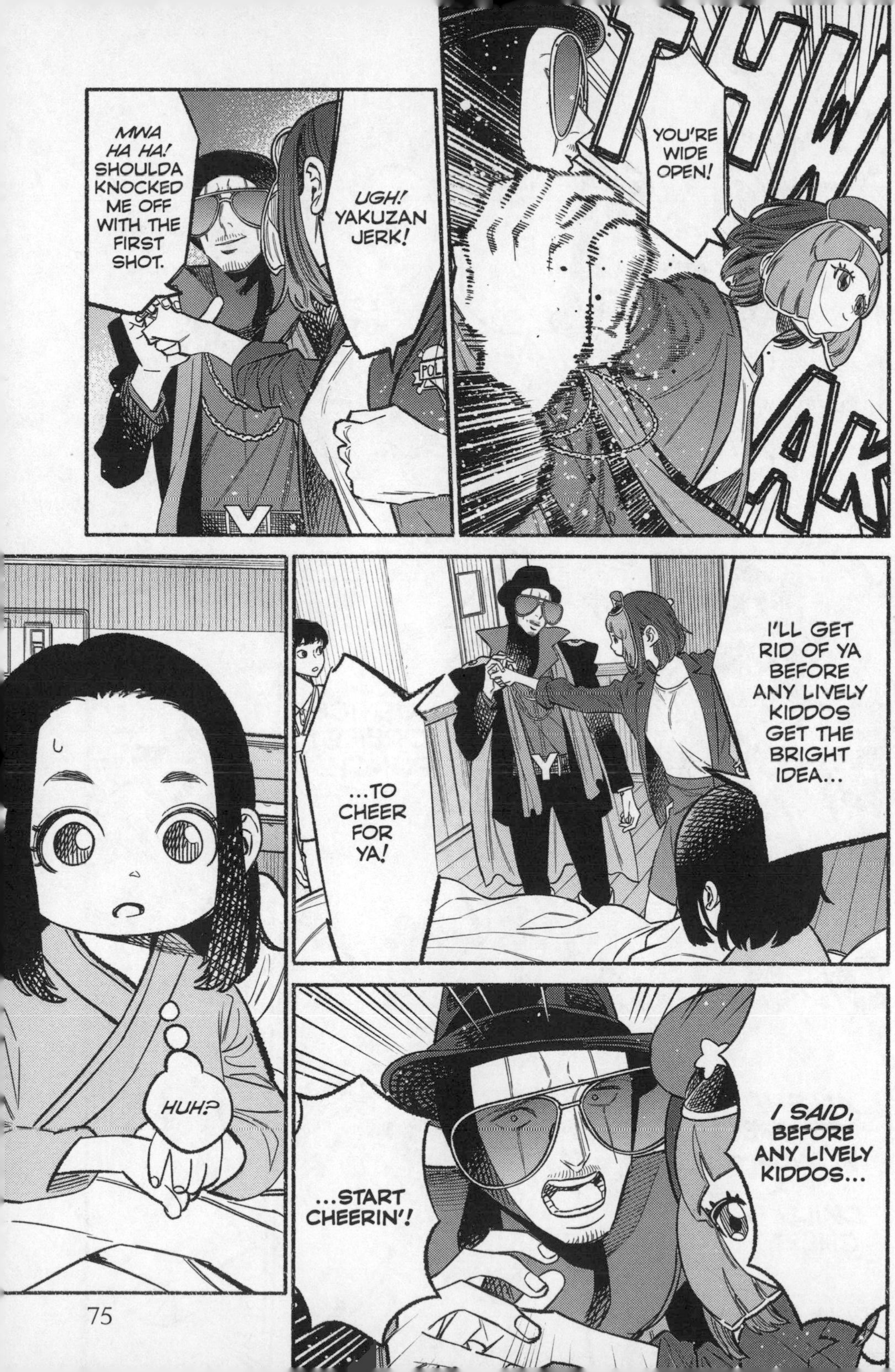
YOU'RE WIDE OPEN!
THWAK
UGH! YAKUZAN JERK!
MWA HA HA! SHOULDA KNOCKED ME OFF WITH THE FIRST SHOT.
I'LL GET RID OF YA BEFORE ANY LIVELY KIDDOS GET THE BRIGHT IDEA...
...TO CHEER FOR YA!
I SAID, BEFORE ANY LIVELY KIDDOS...
...START CHEERIN'!
HUH?

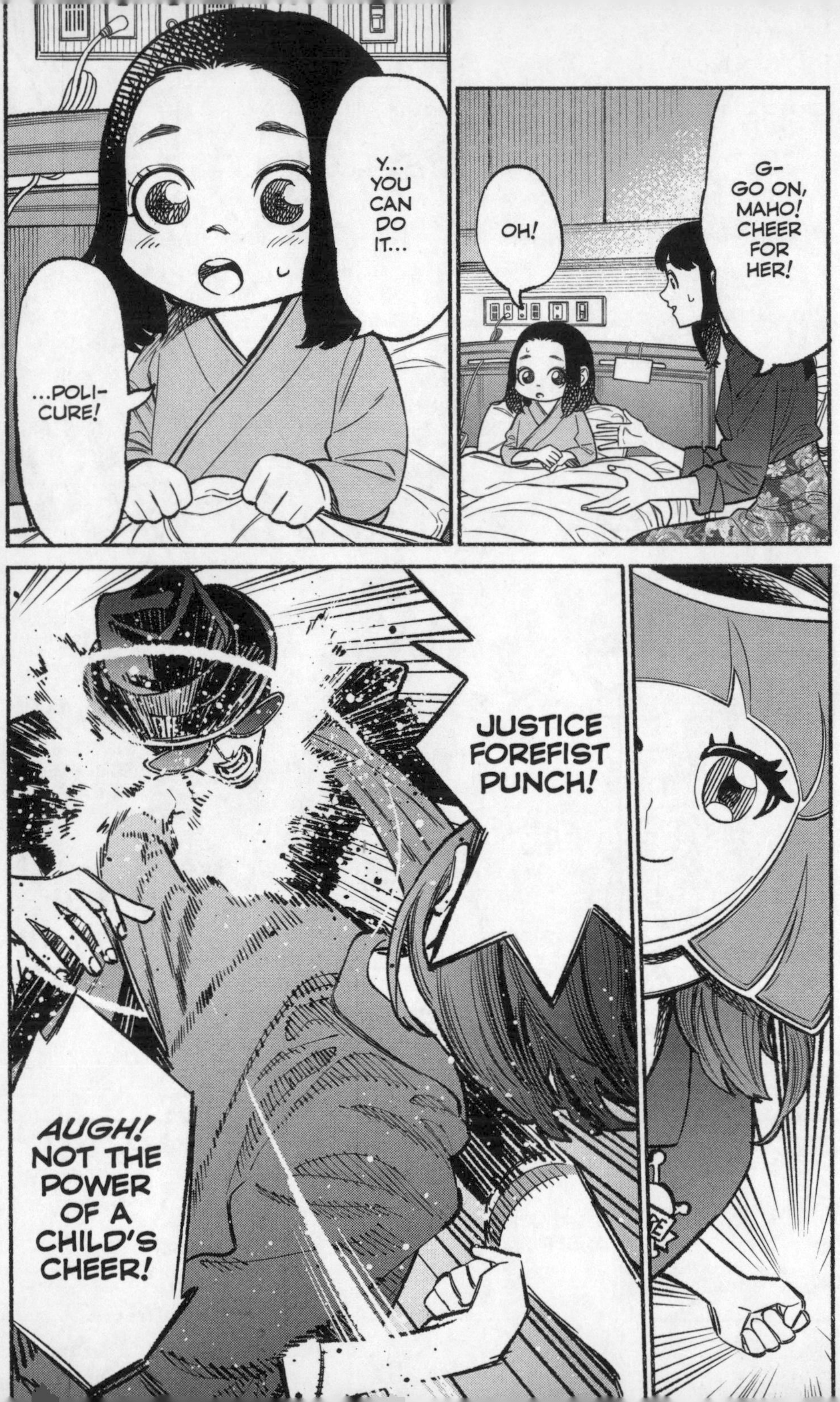
G-GO ON, MAHO! CHEER FOR HER!
OH!
Y... YOU CAN DO IT...
...POLI-CURE!
JUSTICE FOREFIST PUNCH!
AUGH! NOT THE POWER OF A CHILD'S CHEER!

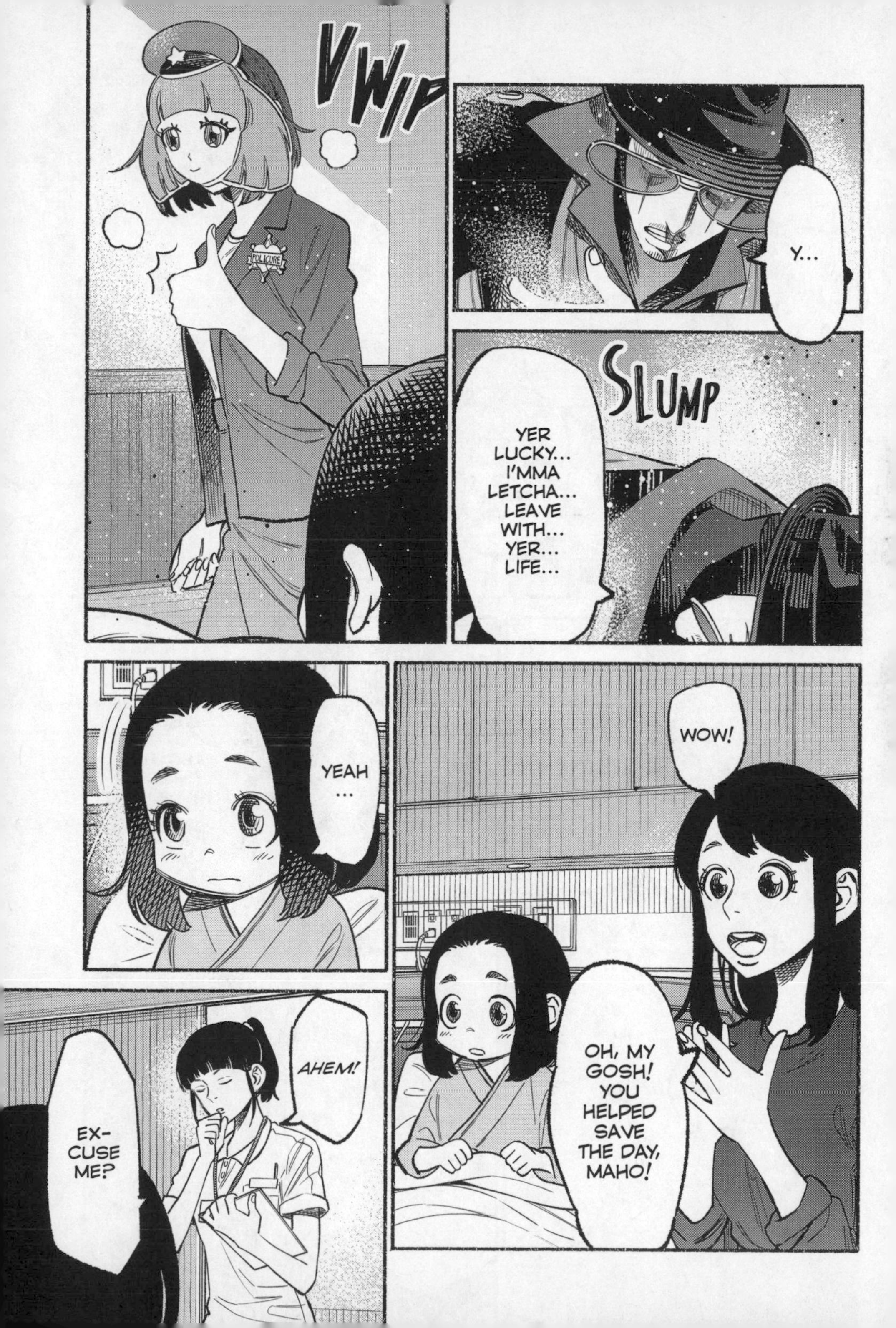
Y...
SLUMP
YER LUCKY... I'MMA LETCHA... LEAVE WITH... YER... LIFE...
VWIP
WOW!
OH, MY GOSH! YOU HELPED SAVE THE DAY, MAHO!
YEAH ...
AHEM!
EX-CUSE ME?

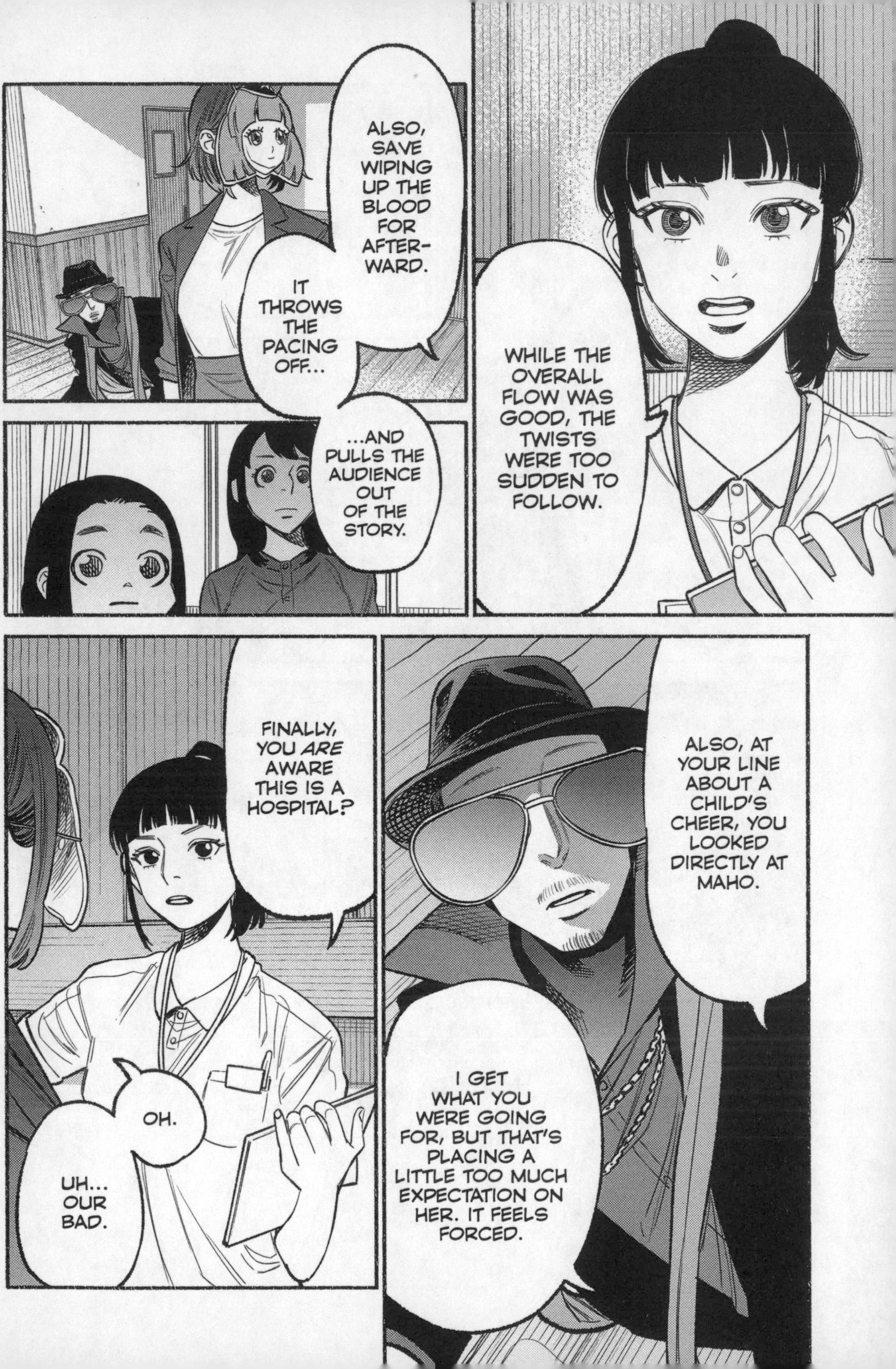
WHILE THE OVERALL FLOW WAS GOOD, THE TWISTS WERE TOO SUDDEN TO FOLLOW.
ALSO, SAVE WIPING UP THE BLOOD FOR AFTER-WARD.
IT THROWS THE PACING OFF...
...AND PULLS THE AUDIENCE OUT OF THE STORY.
ALSO, AT YOUR LINE ABOUT A CHILD'S CHEER, YOU LOOKED DIRECTLY AT MAHO.
I GET WHAT YOU WERE GOING FOR, BUT THAT'S PLACING A LITTLE TOO MUCH EXPECTATION ON HER. IT FEELS FORCED.
FINALLY, YOU *ARE* AWARE THIS IS A HOSPITAL?
OH.
UH... OUR BAD.

FOR
SHAME...

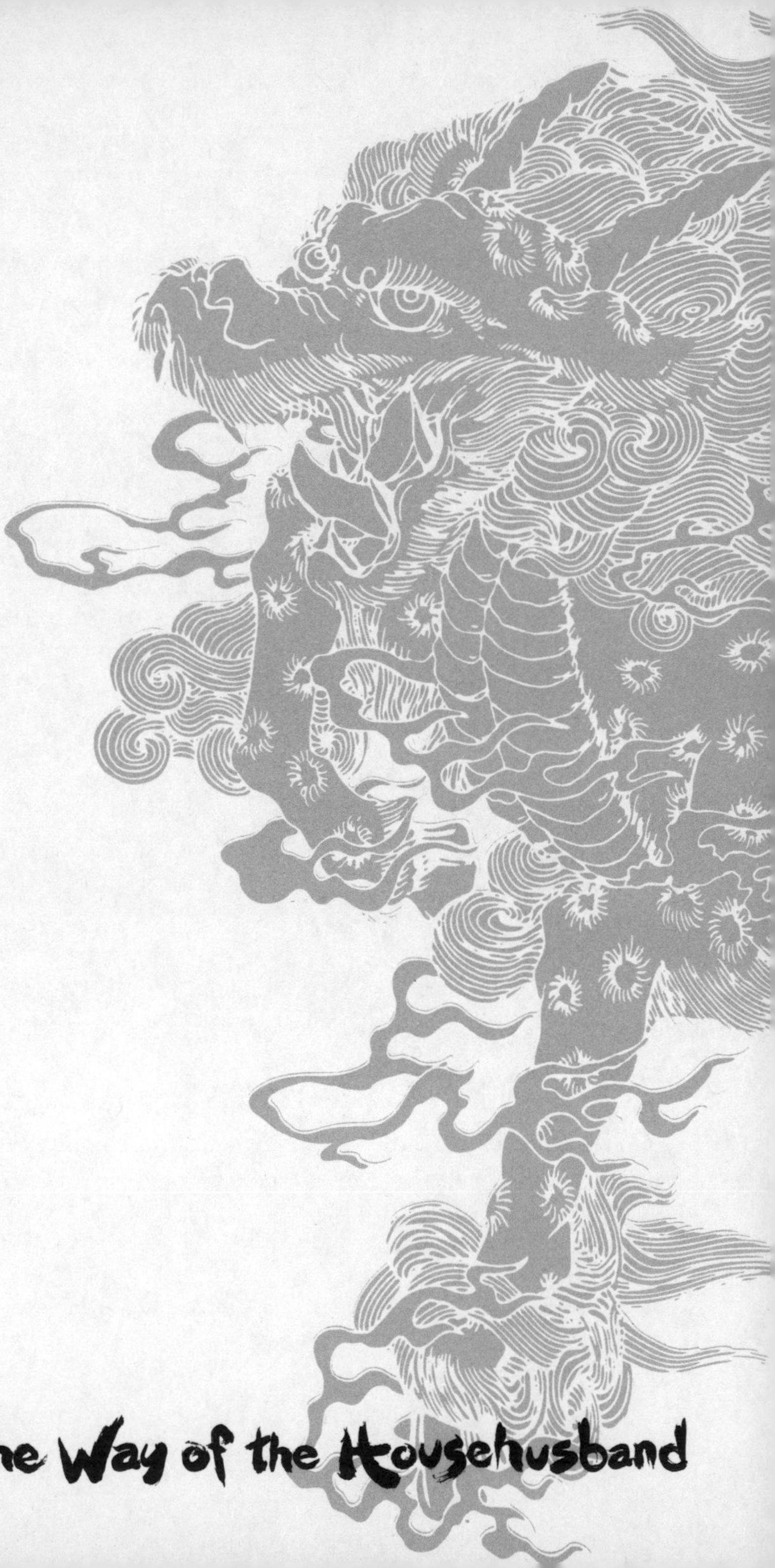

The Way of the Househusband

CHAPTER 60

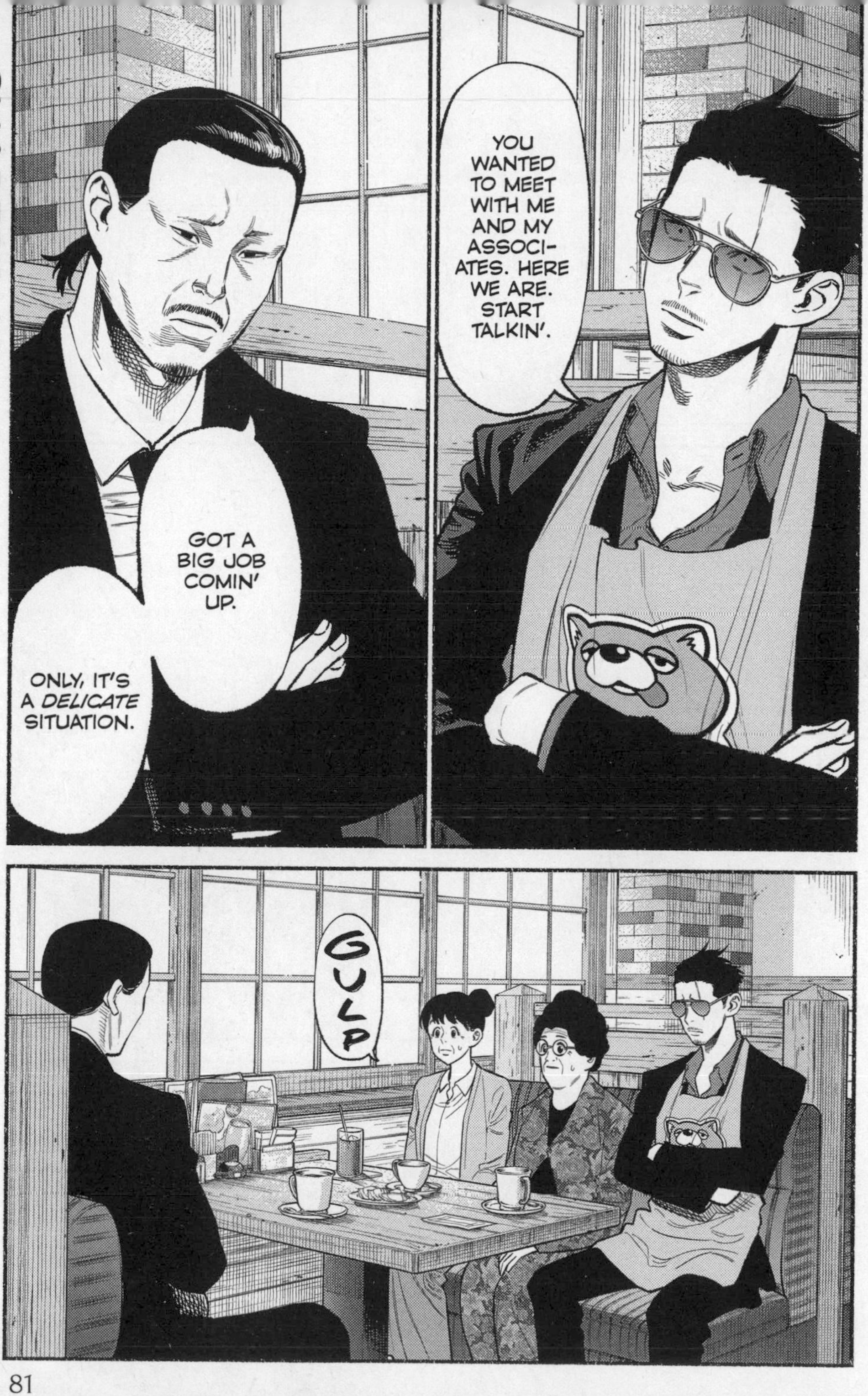
YOU WANTED TO MEET WITH ME AND MY ASSOCI-ATES. HERE WE ARE. START TALKIN'.
GOT A BIG JOB COMIN' UP.
ONLY, IT'S A *DELICATE* SITUATION.
GULP

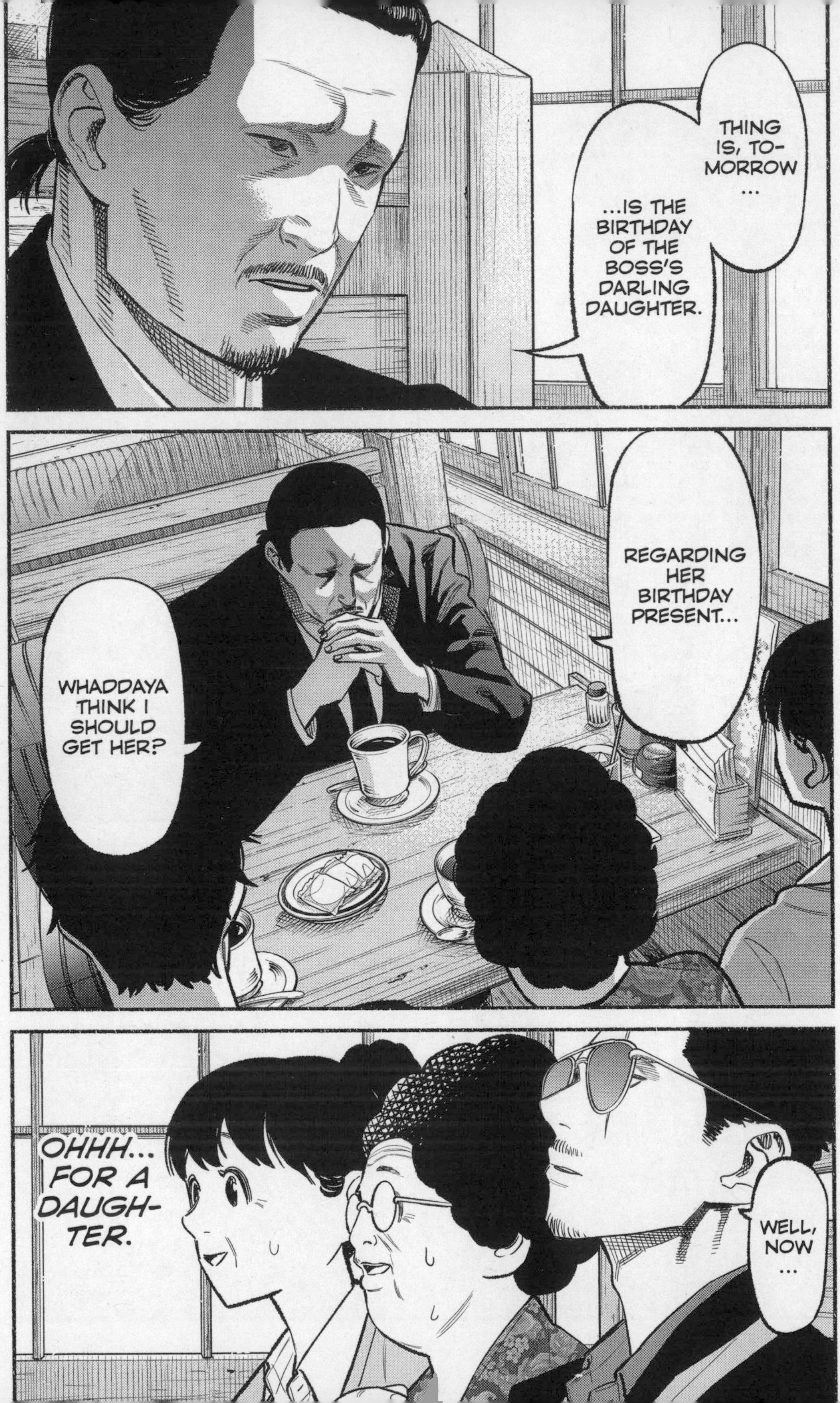
THING IS, TO-MORROW ...
...IS THE BIRTHDAY OF THE BOSS'S DARLING DAUGHTER.
REGARDING HER BIRTHDAY PRESENT...
WHADDAYA THINK I SHOULD GET HER?
WELL, NOW ...
OHHH... FOR A DAUGH-TER.

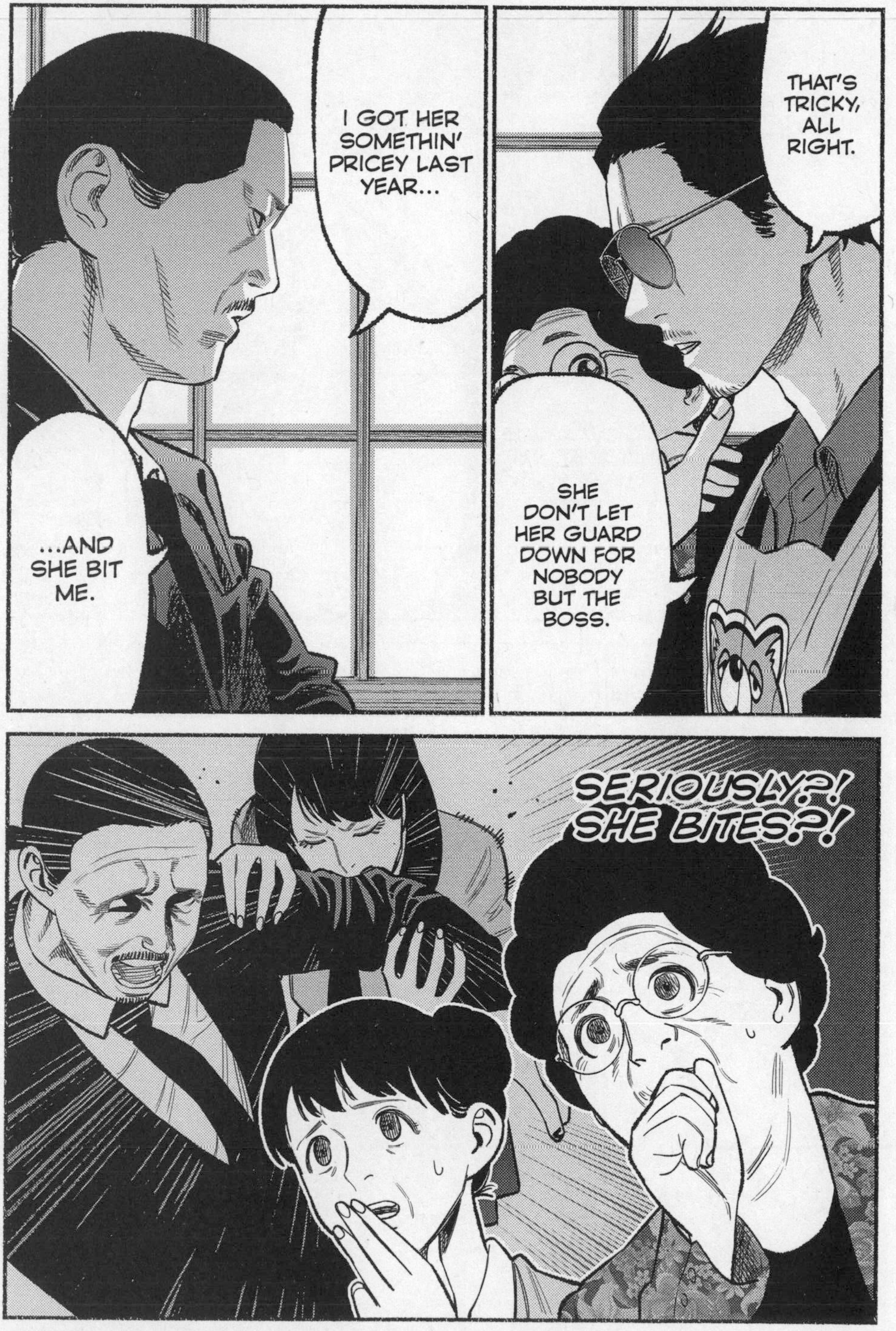
THAT'S TRICKY, ALL RIGHT.
SHE DON'T LET HER GUARD DOWN FOR NOBODY BUT THE BOSS.
I GOT HER SOMETHIN' PRICEY LAST YEAR...
...AND SHE BIT ME.
SERIOUSLY?! SHE BITES?!

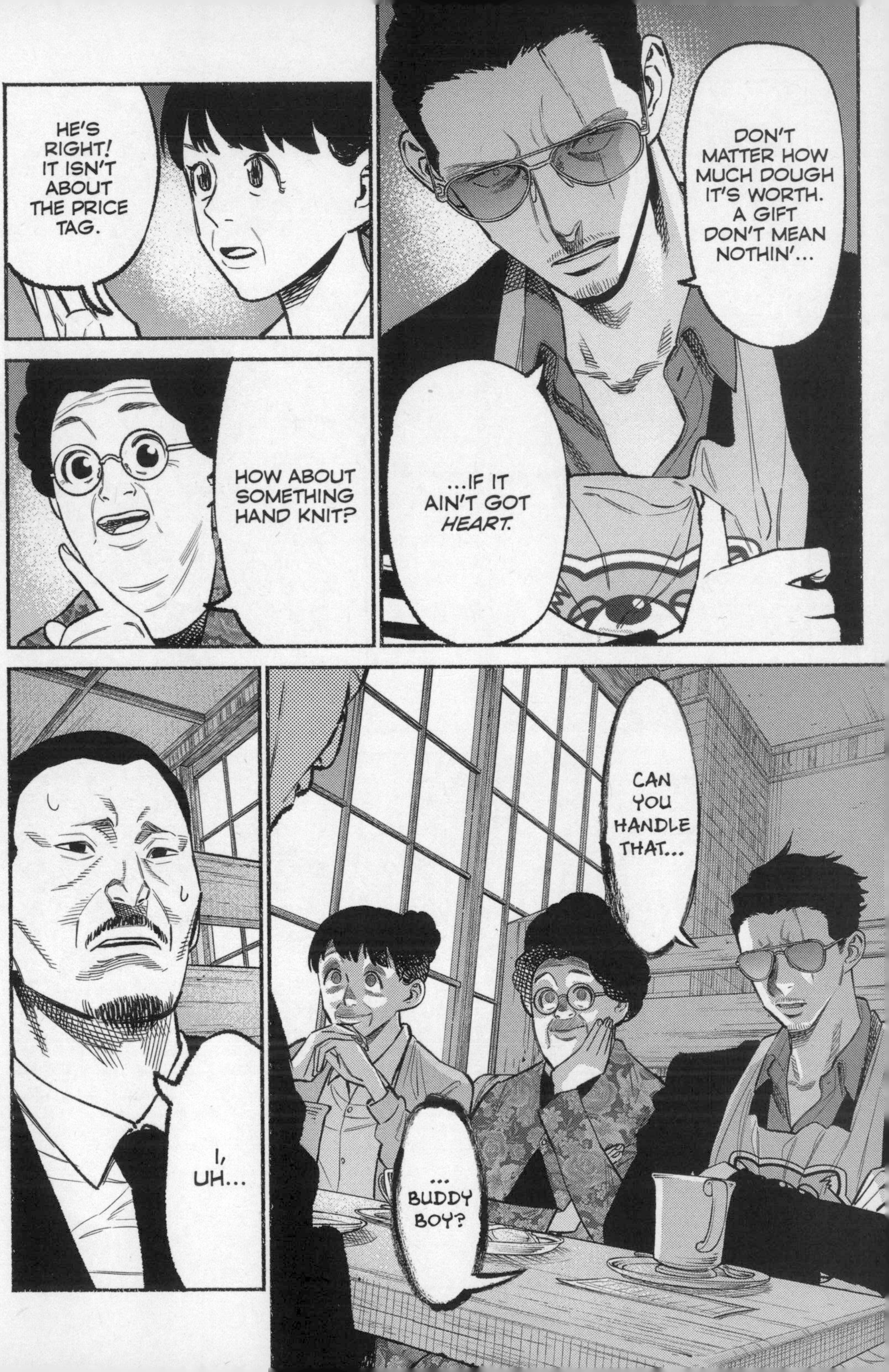
DON'T MATTER HOW MUCH DOUGH IT'S WORTH. A GIFT DON'T MEAN NOTHIN'...
...IF IT AIN'T GOT *HEART.*
HE'S RIGHT! IT ISN'T ABOUT THE PRICE TAG.
HOW ABOUT SOMETHING HAND KNIT?
CAN YOU HANDLE THAT...
...BUDDY BOY?
I, UH...

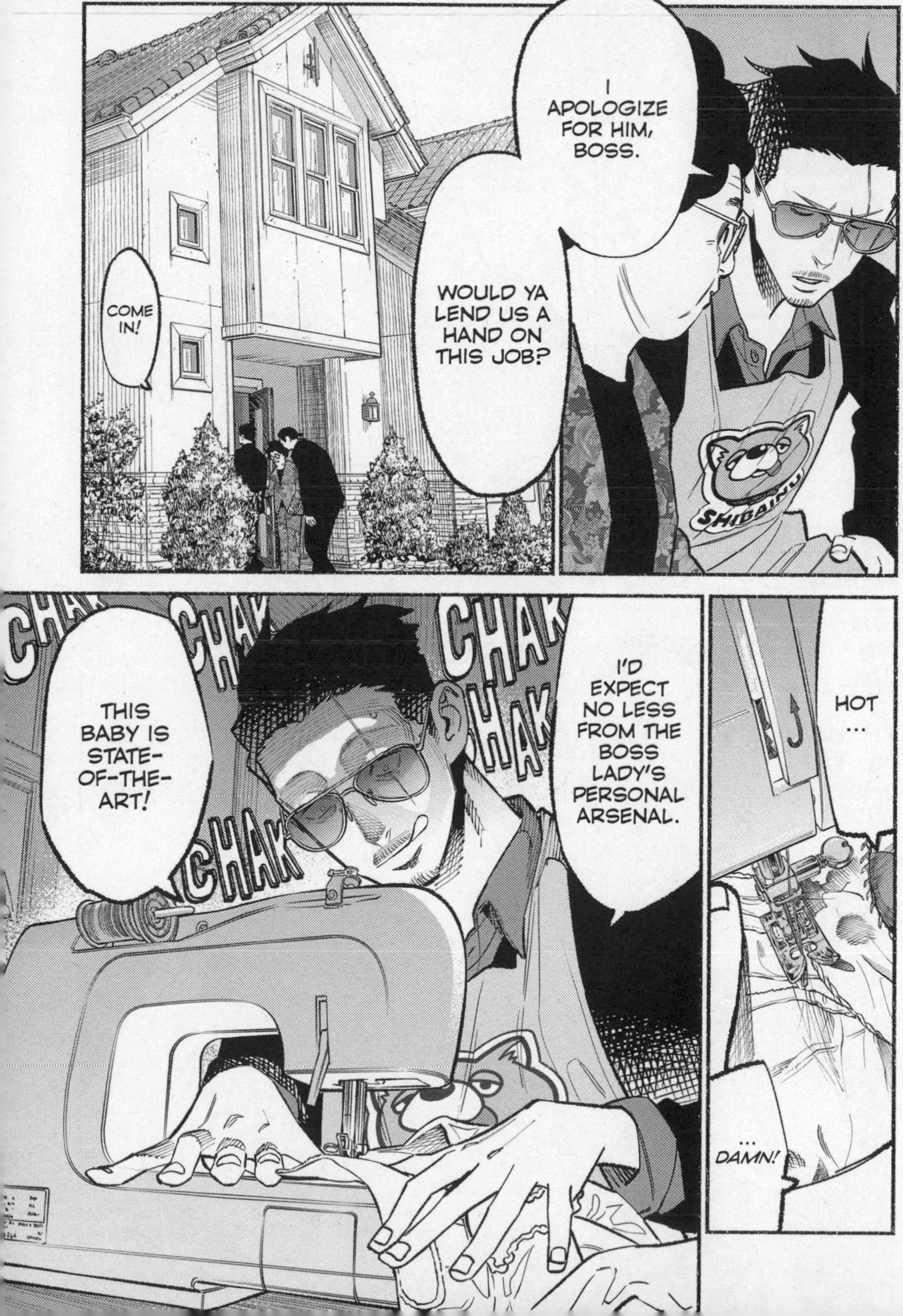
I APOLOGIZE FOR HIM, BOSS.
WOULD YA LEND US A HAND ON THIS JOB?
COME IN!
HOT ...
... DAMN!
CHAK
CHAK
CHAK
CHAK
CHAK
I'D EXPECT NO LESS FROM THE BOSS LADY'S PERSONAL ARSENAL.
THIS BABY IS STATE-OF-THE-ART!

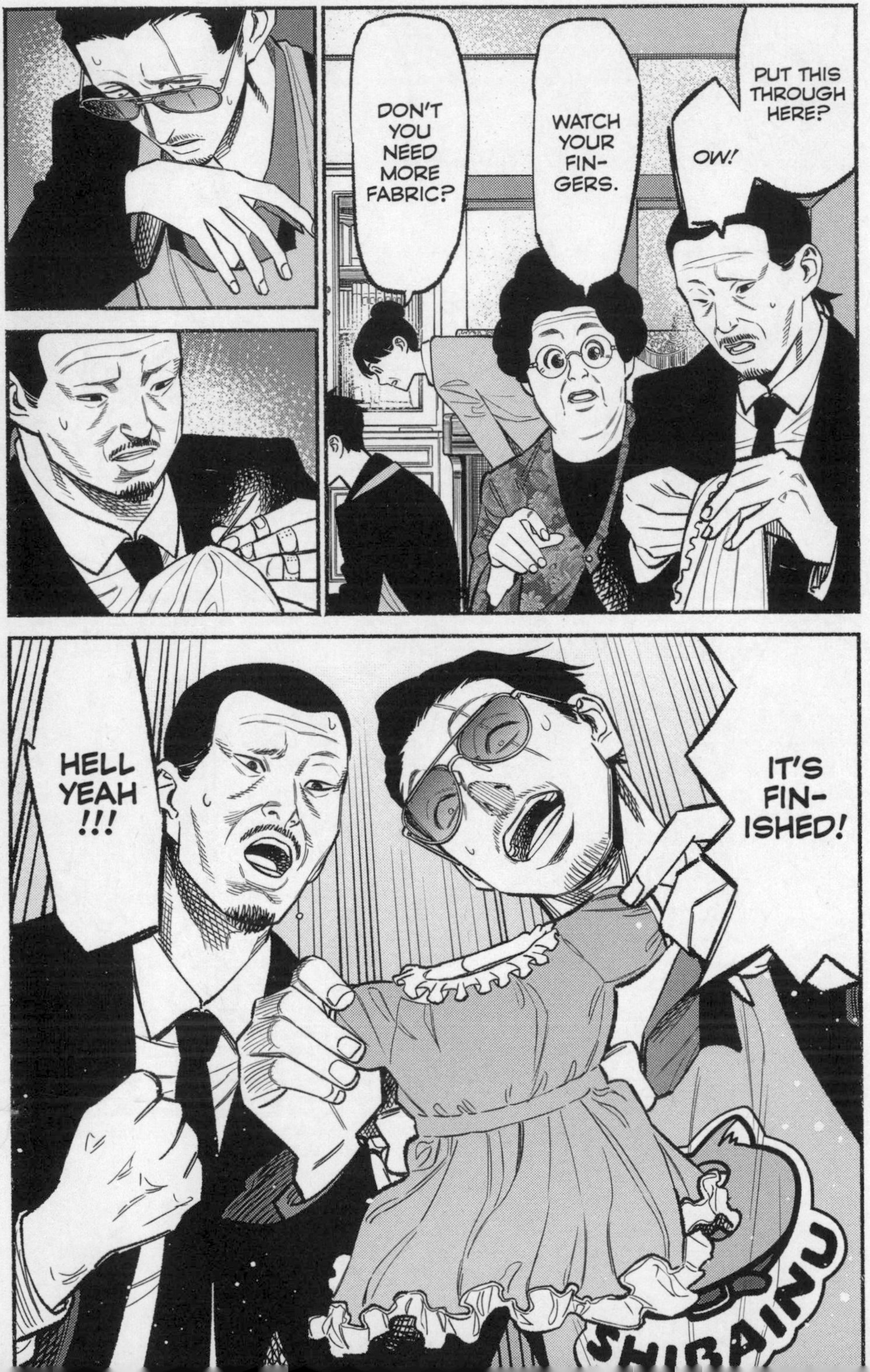
PUT THIS THROUGH HERE?
OW!
WATCH YOUR FIN-GERS.
DON'T YOU NEED MORE FABRIC?
IT'S FIN-ISHED!
HELL YEAH!!!
SHIBAINU

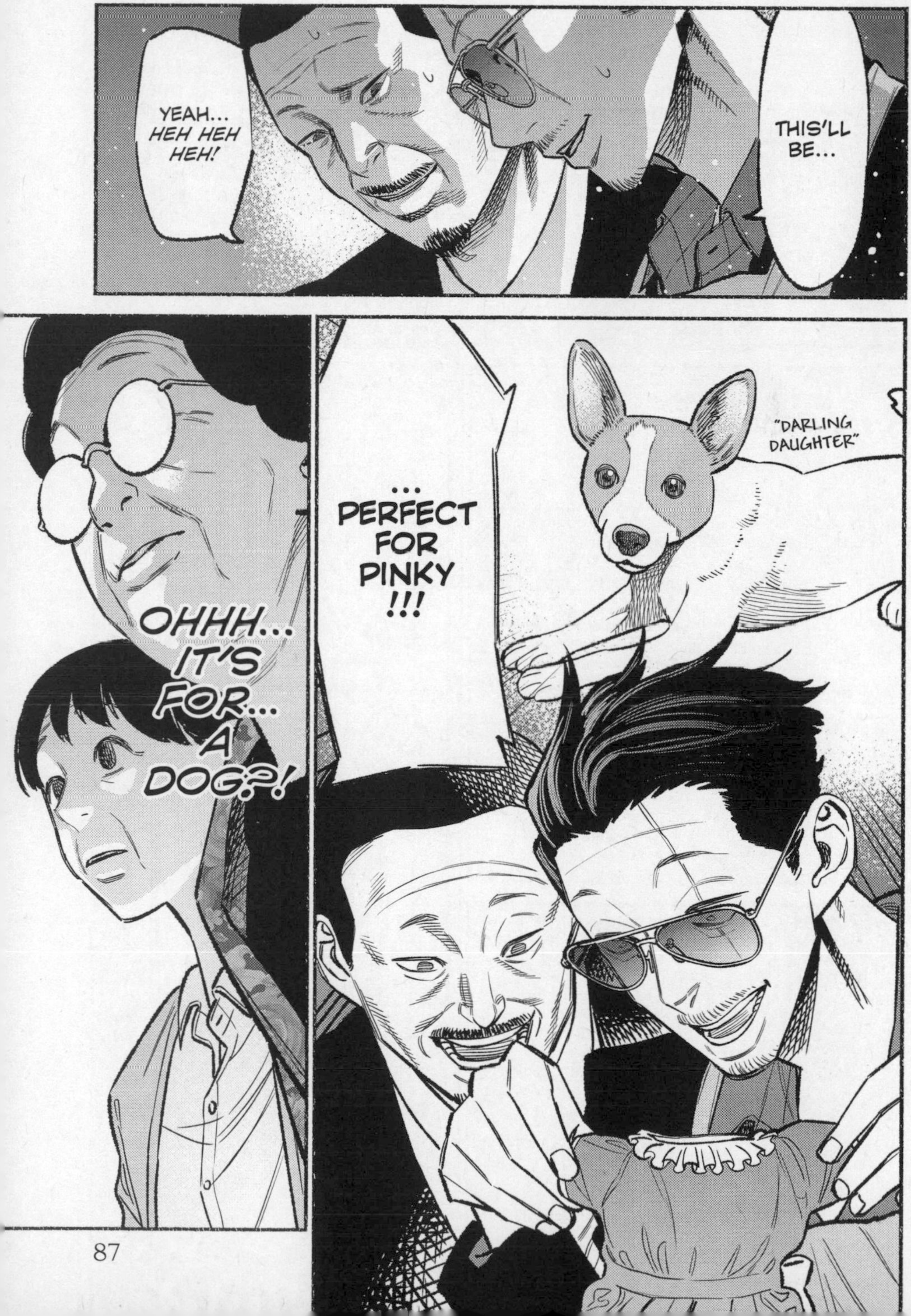
THIS'LL BE...
YEAH... HEH HEH HEH!
"DARLING DAUGHTER"
... PERFECT FOR PINKY !!!
OHHH... IT'S FOR... A DOG?!

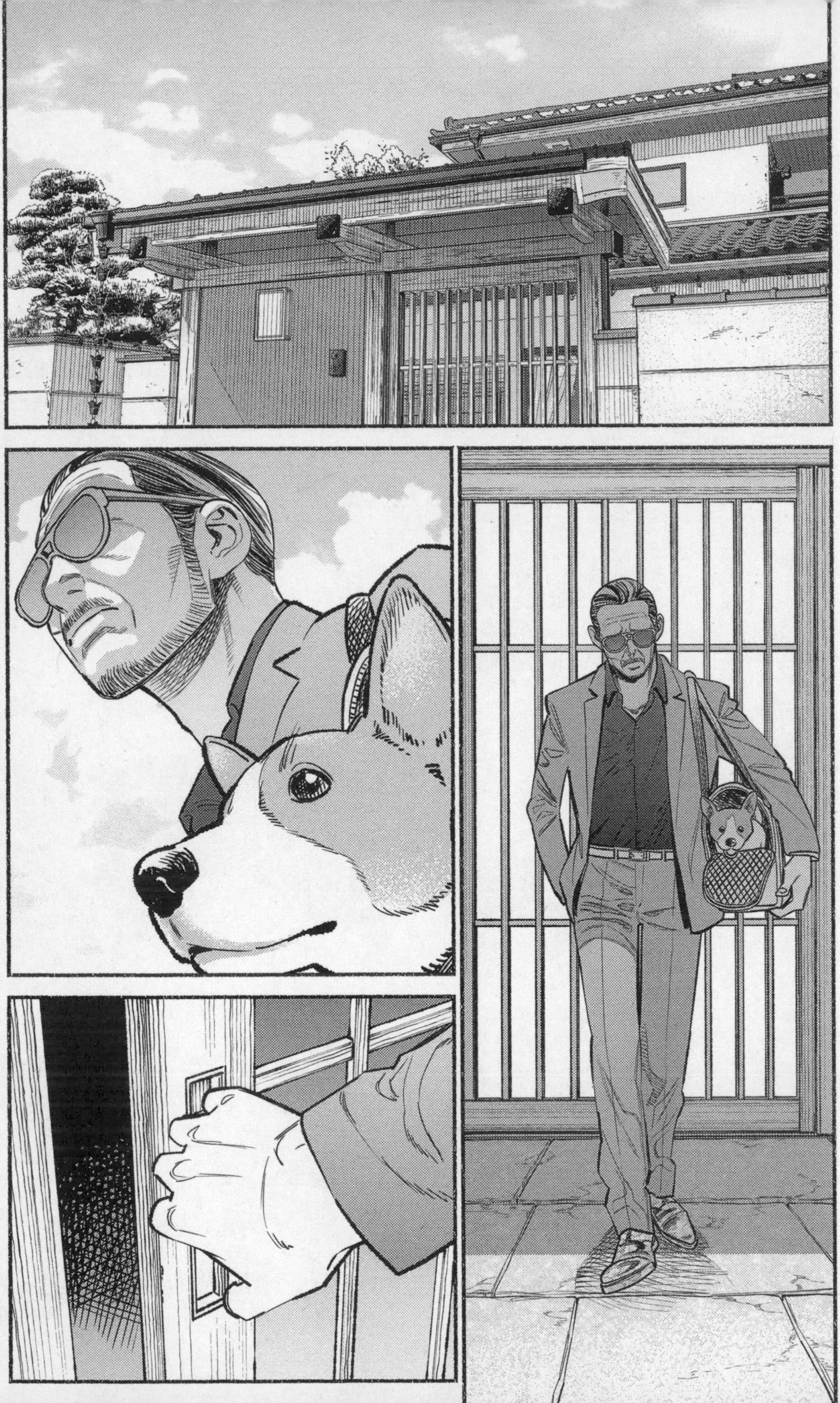

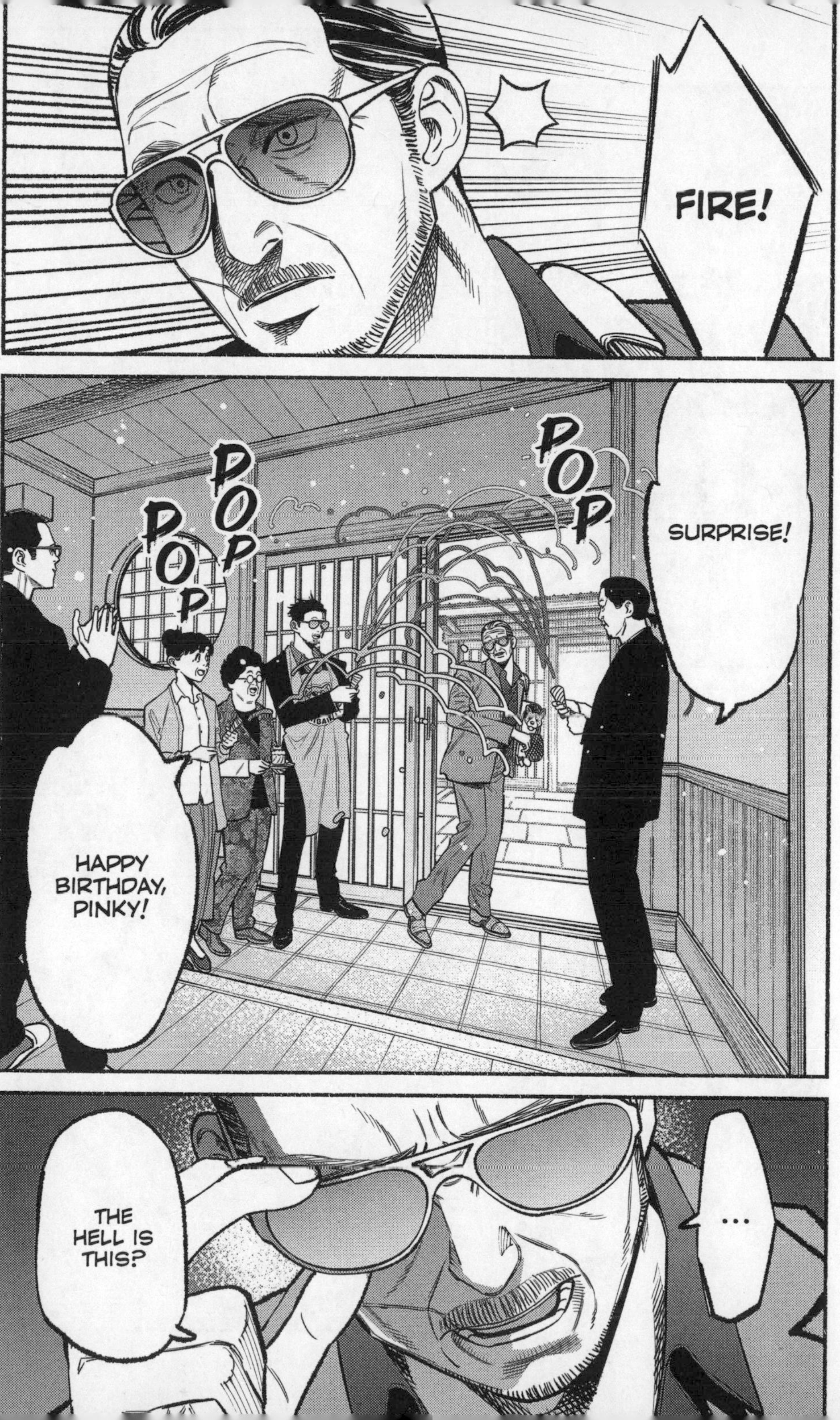
FIRE!
SURPRISE!
POP
POP
POP
HAPPY BIRTHDAY, PINKY!
...
THE HELL IS THIS?

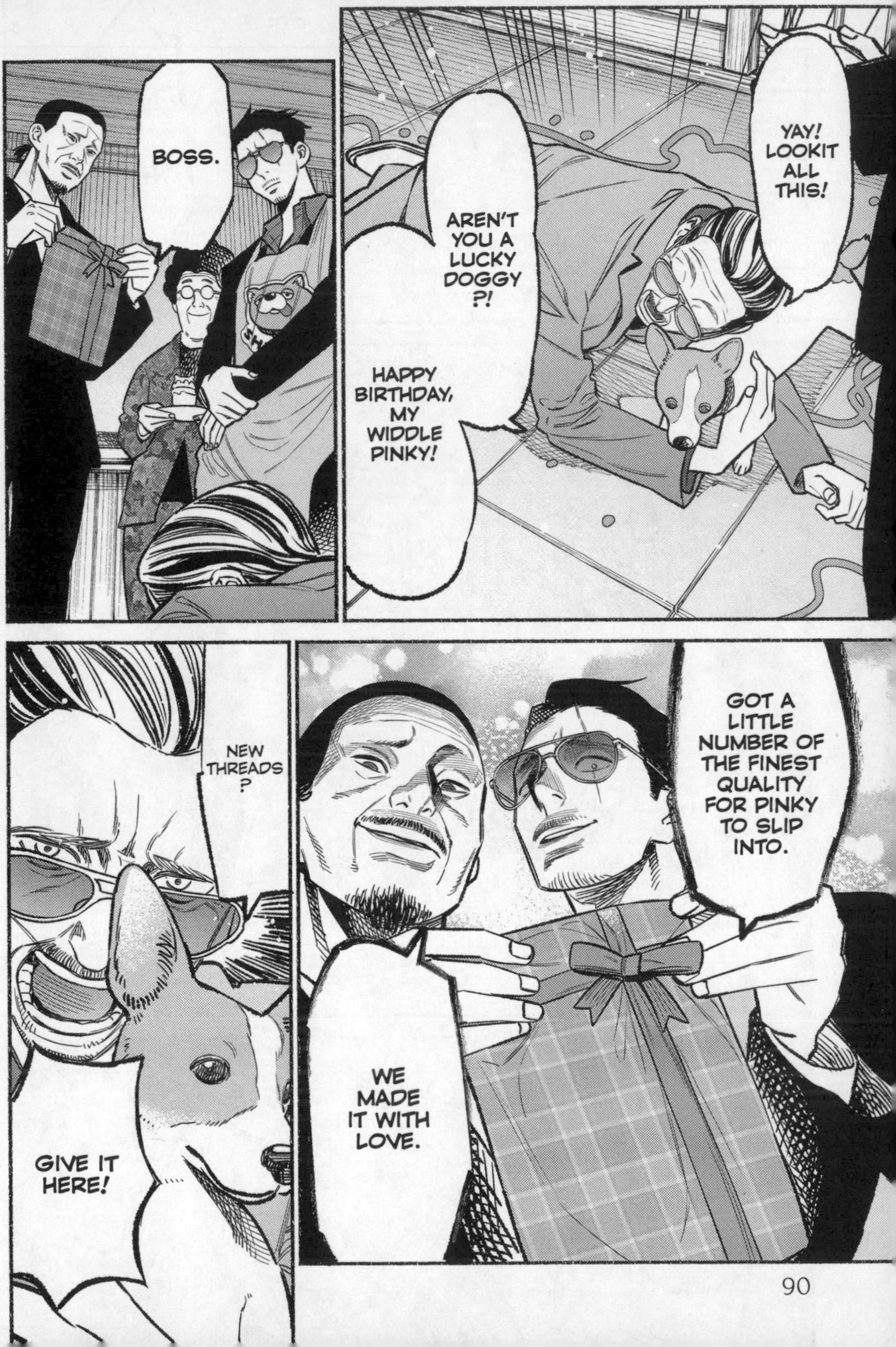
YAY! LOOKIT ALL THIS!
AREN'T YOU A LUCKY DOGGY ?!
HAPPY BIRTHDAY, MY WIDDLE PINKY!
BOSS.
GOT A LITTLE NUMBER OF THE FINEST QUALITY FOR PINKY TO SLIP INTO.
WE MADE IT WITH LOVE.
NEW THREADS ?
GIVE IT HERE!

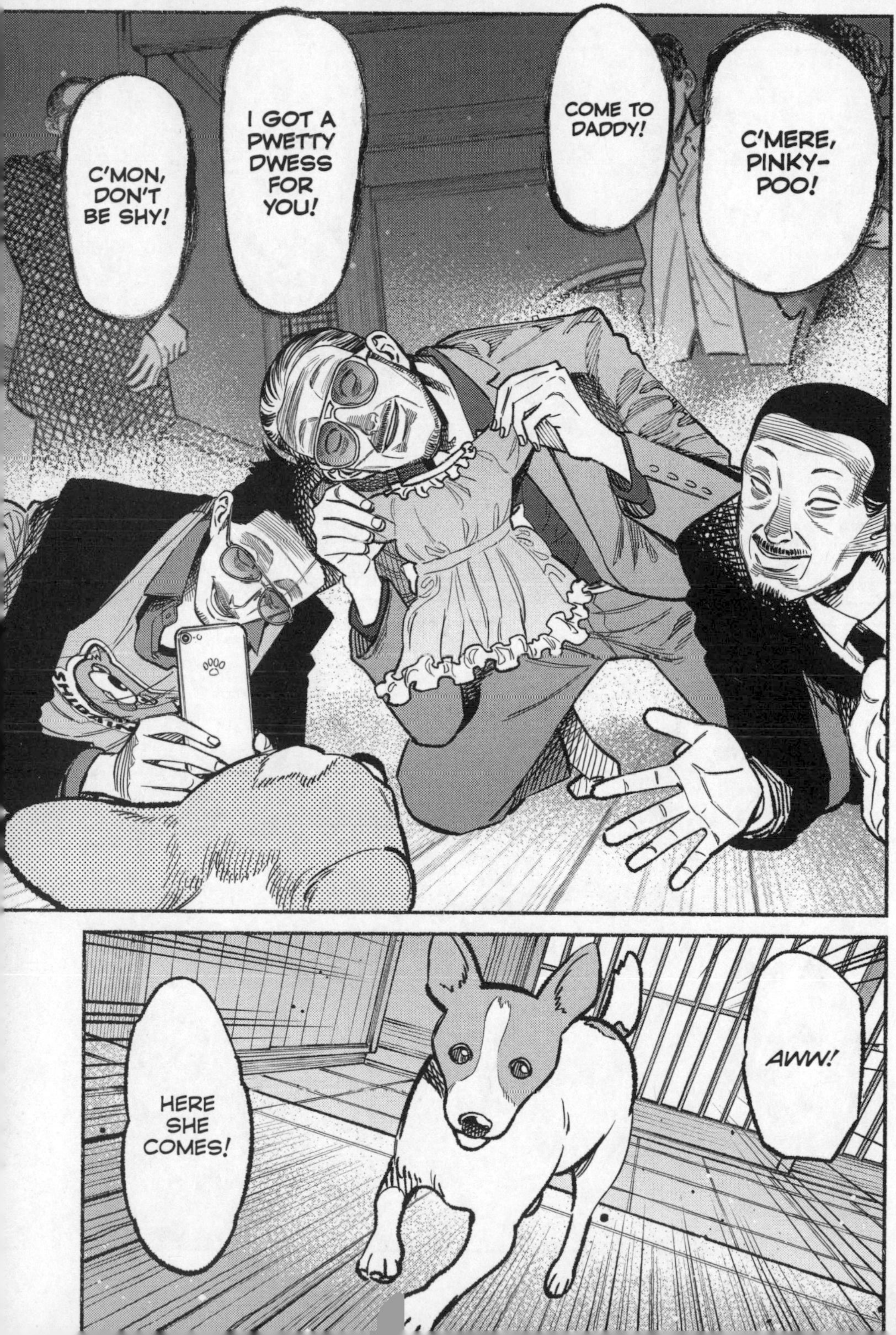
C'MERE, PINKY-POO!
COME TO DADDY!
I GOT A PWETTY DWESS FOR YOU!
C'MON, DON'T BE SHY!
AWW!
HERE SHE COMES!

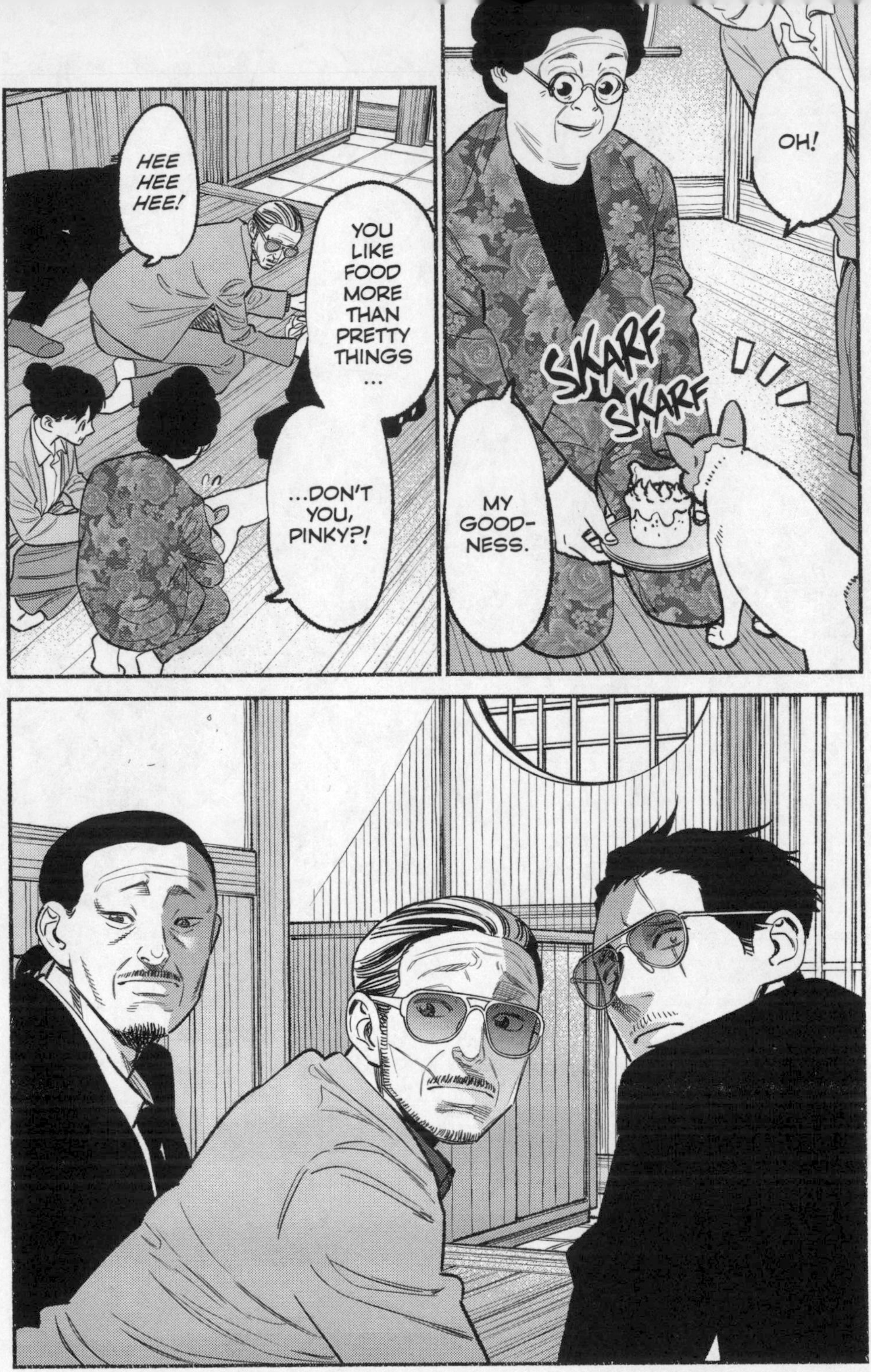
OH!
SKARF SKARF
MY GOODNESS.
YOU LIKE FOOD MORE THAN PRETTY THINGS...
...DON'T YOU, PINKY?!
HEE HEE HEE!

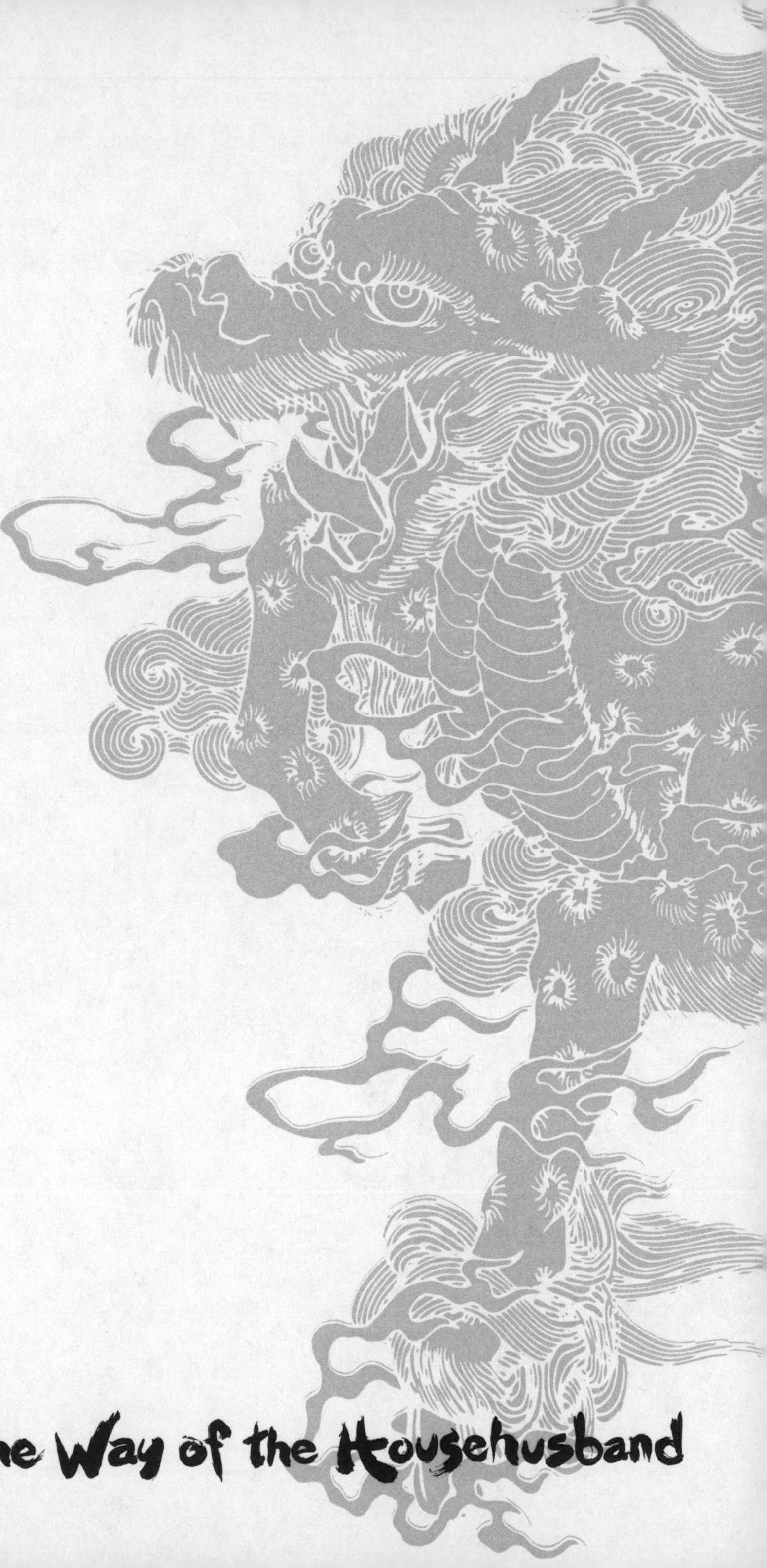

The Way of the Househusband

CHAPTER 61

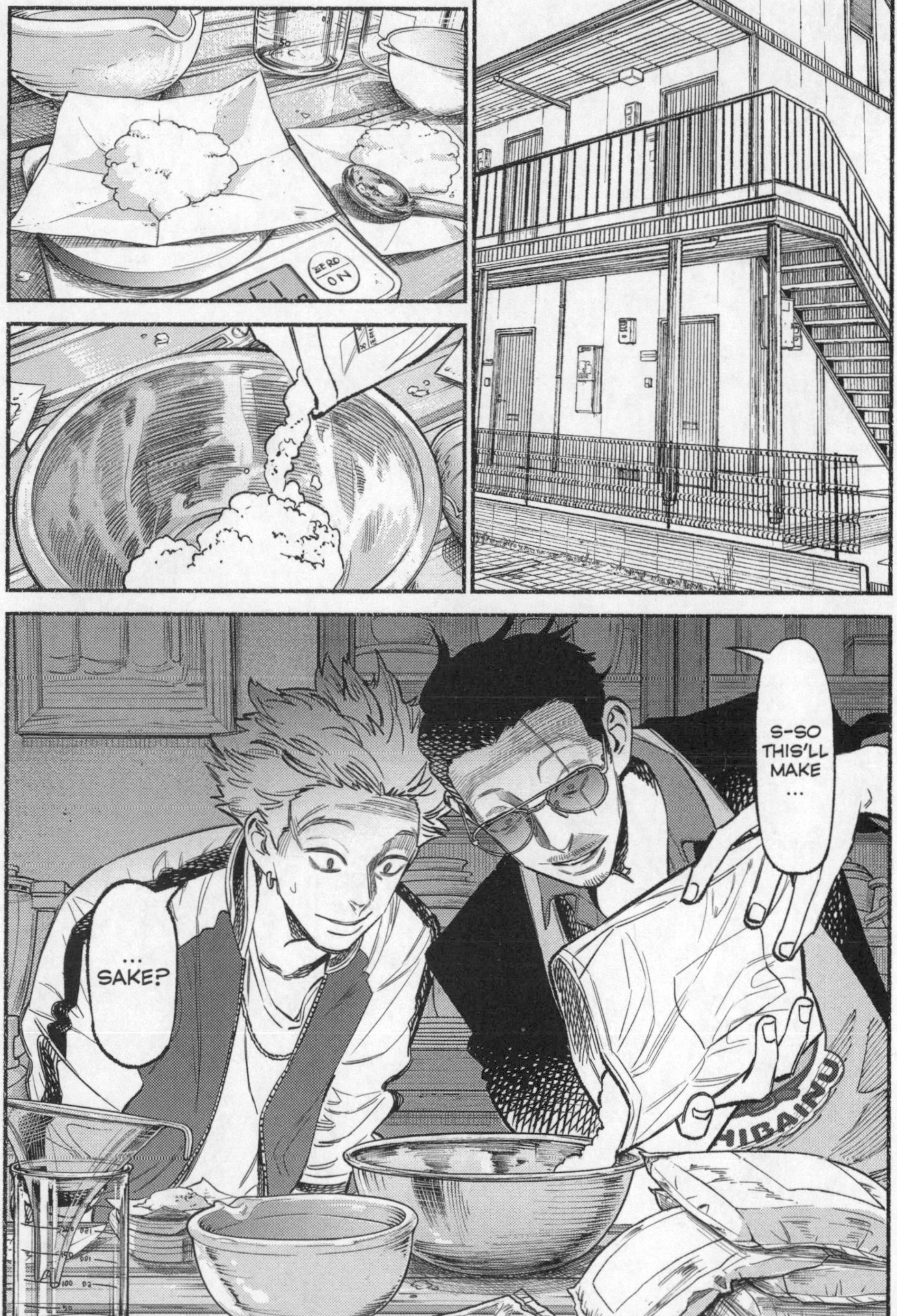
S-SO THIS'LL MAKE ...
... SAKE?

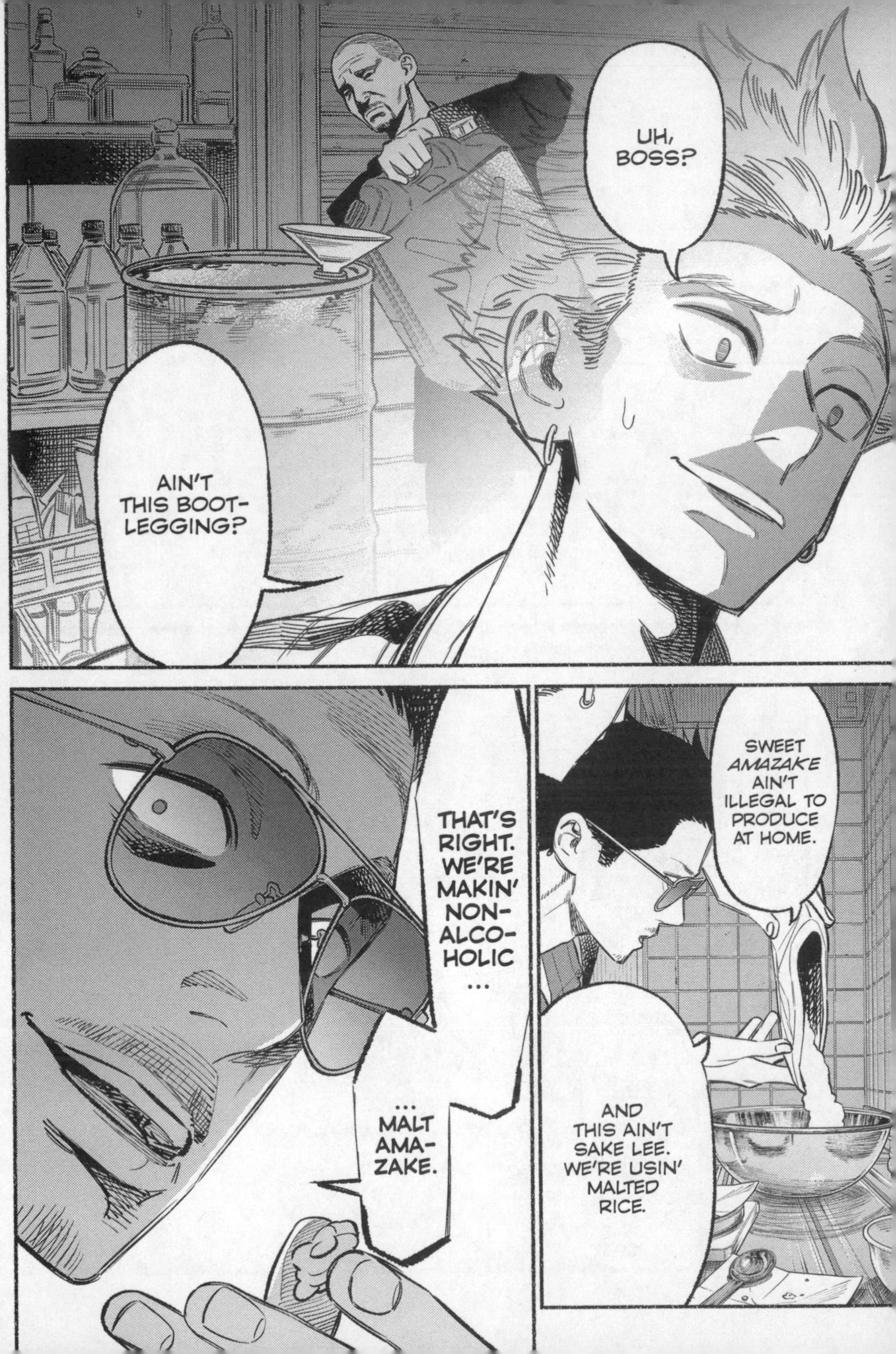
UH, BOSS?
AIN'T THIS BOOT-LEGGING?
SWEET *AMAZAKE* AIN'T ILLEGAL TO PRODUCE AT HOME.
AND THIS AIN'T SAKE LEE. WE'RE USIN' MALTED RICE.
THAT'S RIGHT. WE'RE MAKIN' NON-ALCOHOLIC ...
... MALT AMA-ZAKE.

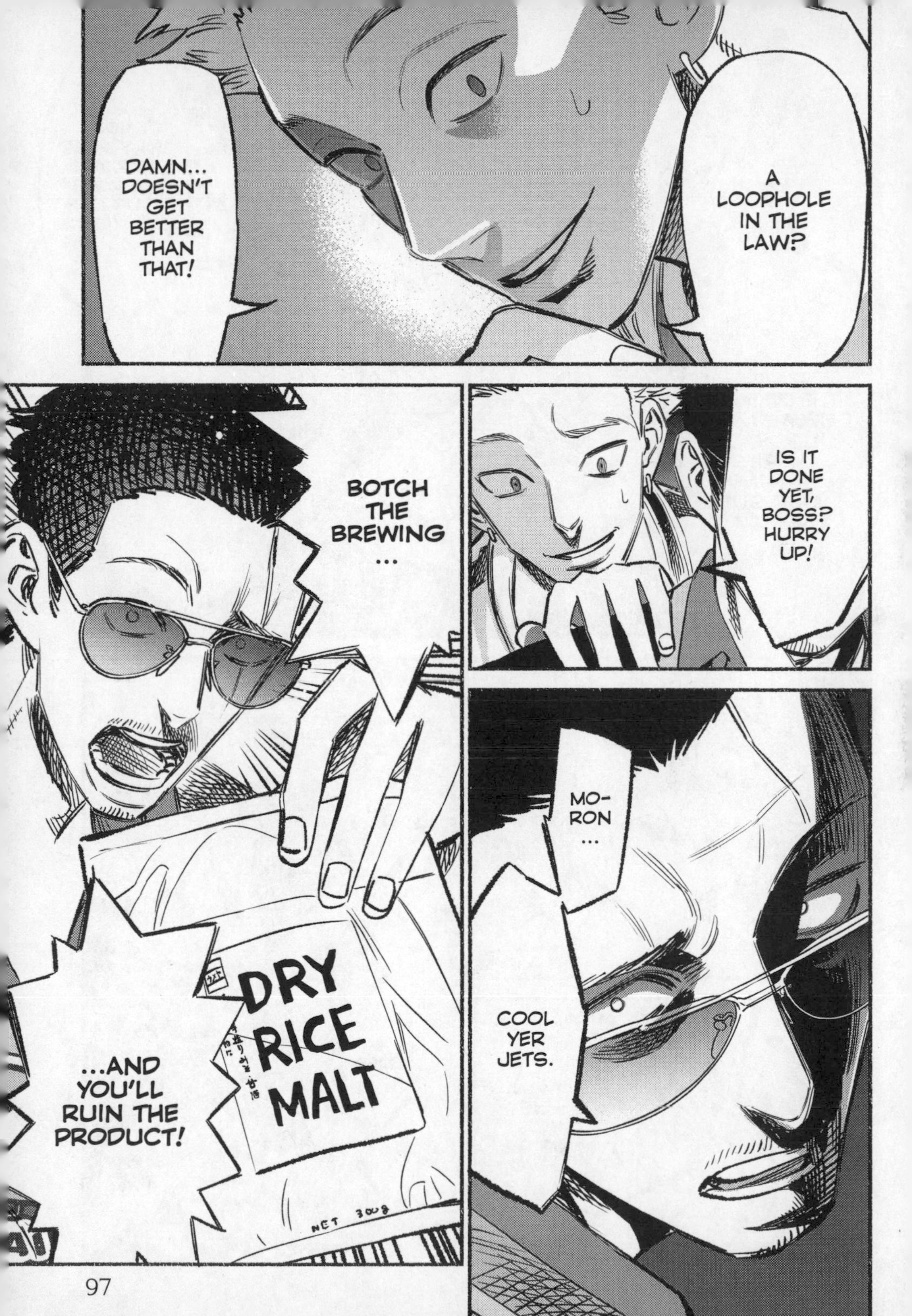
A LOOPHOLE IN THE LAW?
DAMN... DOESN'T GET BETTER THAN THAT!
IS IT DONE YET, BOSS? HURRY UP!
MO-RON ...
COOL YER JETS.
BOTCH THE BREWING ...
DRY RICE MALT
...AND YOU'LL RUIN THE PRODUCT!

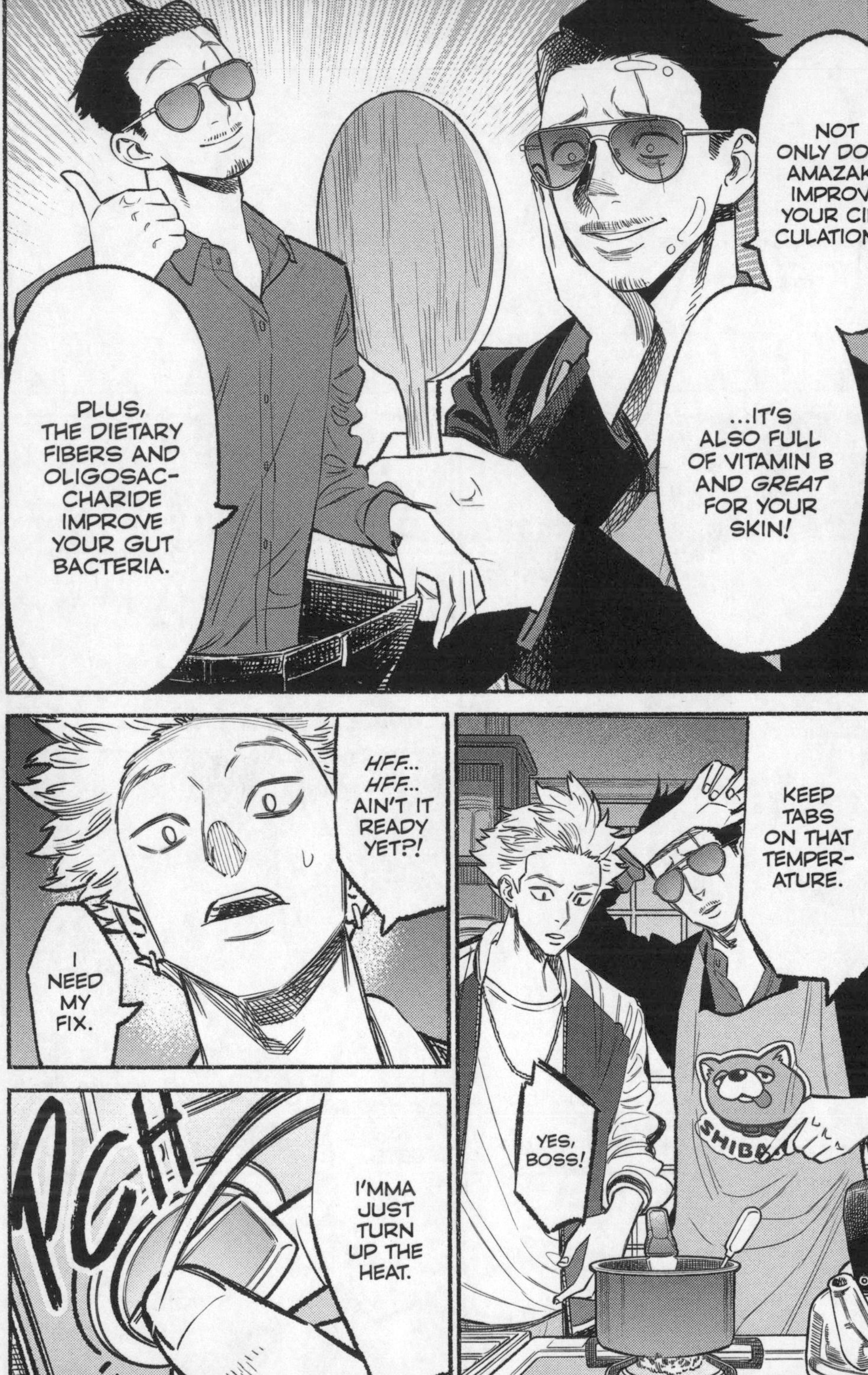
NOT ONLY DOES AMAZAKE IMPROVE YOUR CIRCULATION...
...IT'S ALSO FULL OF VITAMIN B AND *GREAT* FOR YOUR SKIN!
PLUS, THE DIETARY FIBERS AND OLIGOSACCHARIDE IMPROVE YOUR GUT BACTERIA.
KEEP TABS ON THAT TEMPERATURE.
YES, BOSS!
SHIBA
HFF.. HFF.. AIN'T IT READY YET?!
I NEED MY FIX.
I'MMA JUST TURN UP THE HEAT.
PCH
HIGH

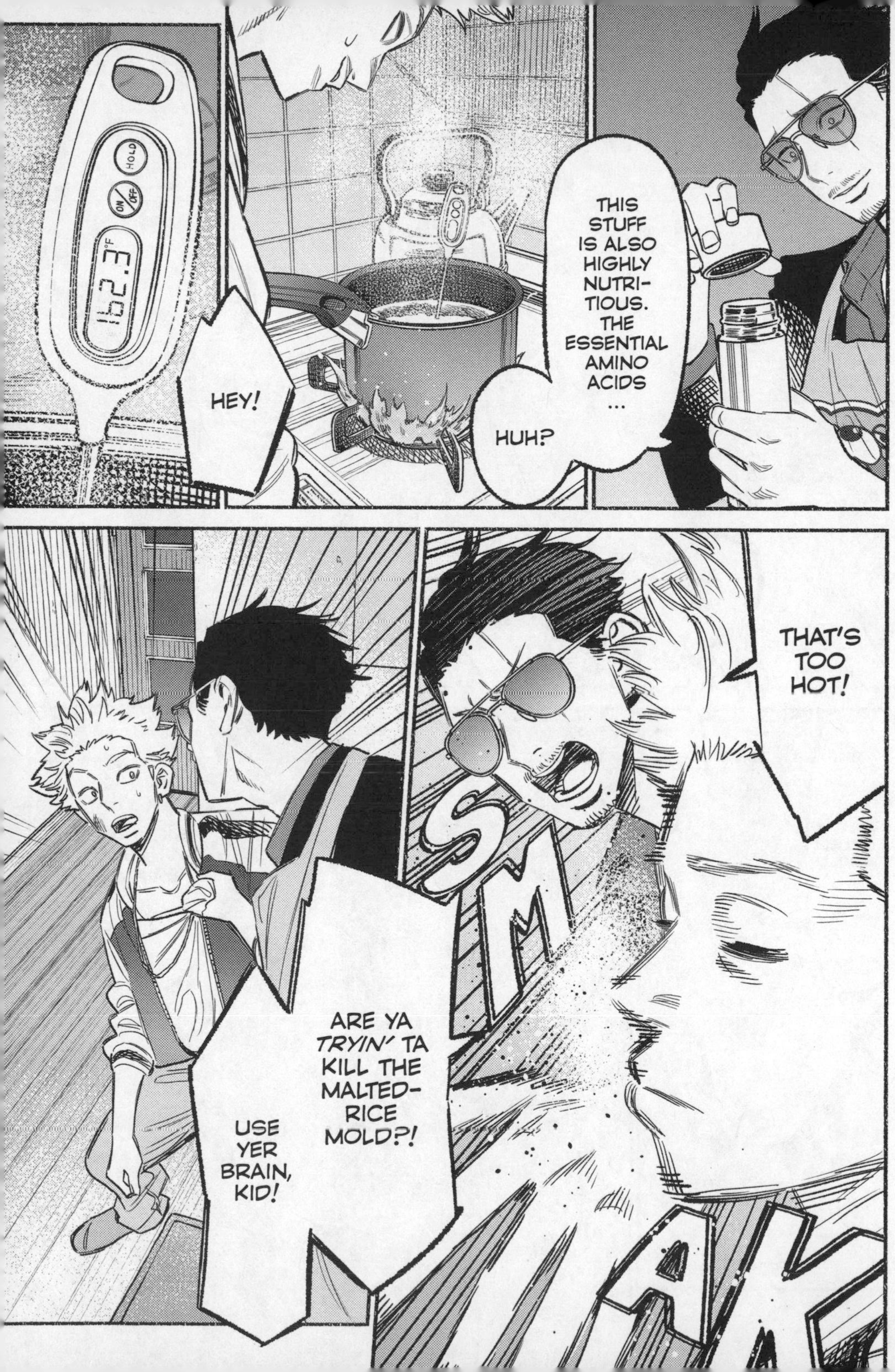
THIS STUFF IS ALSO HIGHLY NUTRITIOUS. THE ESSENTIAL AMINO ACIDS ...
HUH?
HEY!
HOLD
ON/OFF
162.3 °F
THAT'S TOO HOT!
ARE YA *TRYIN'* TA KILL THE MALTED-RICE MOLD?!
USE YER BRAIN, KID!

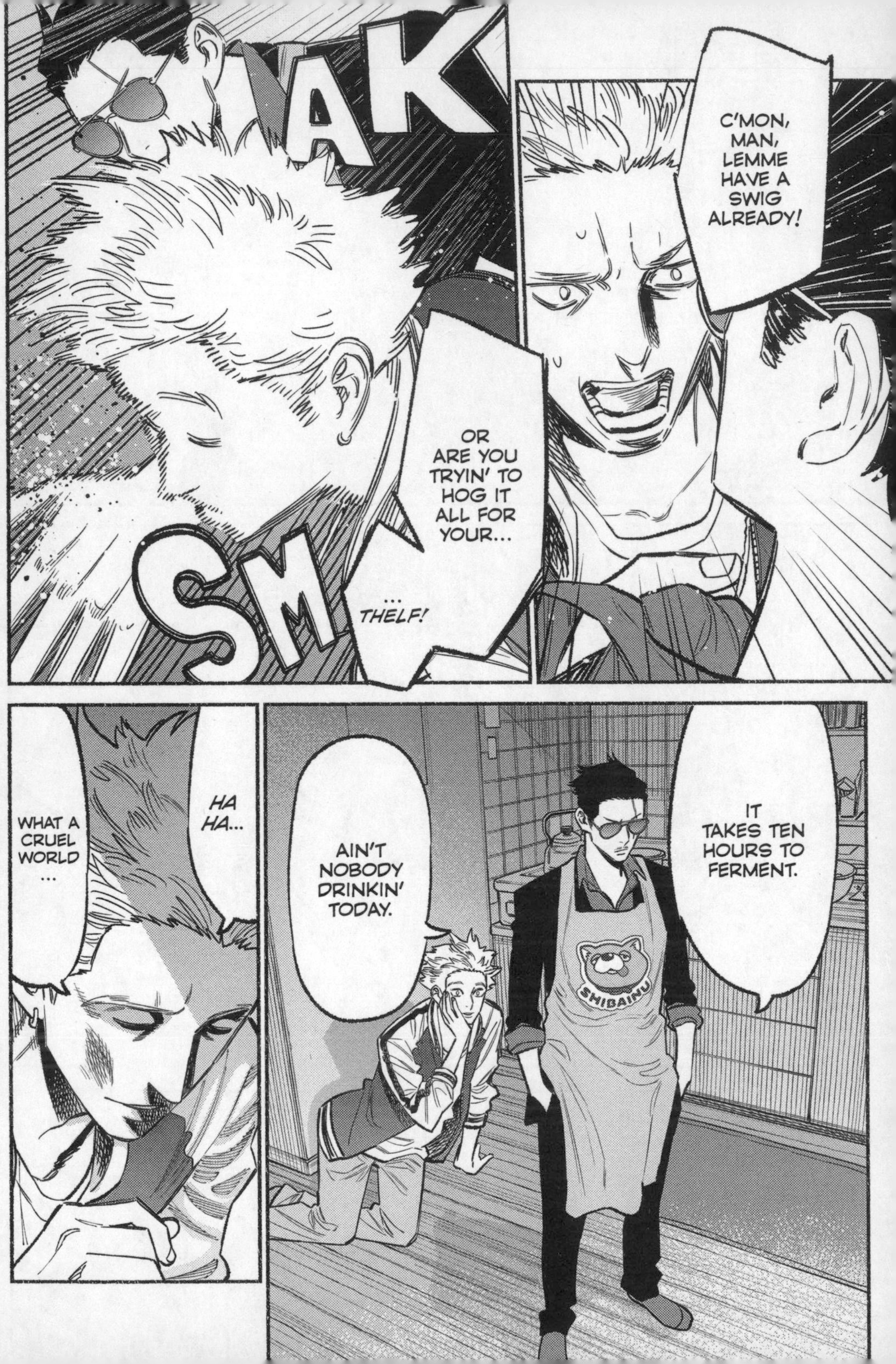
C'MON, MAN, LEMME HAVE A SWIG ALREADY!
OR ARE YOU TRYIN' TO HOG IT ALL FOR YOUR...
AK
SM
... THELF!
IT TAKES TEN HOURS TO FERMENT.
AIN'T NOBODY DRINKIN' TODAY.
SHIBAINU
HA HA...
WHAT A CRUEL WORLD ...

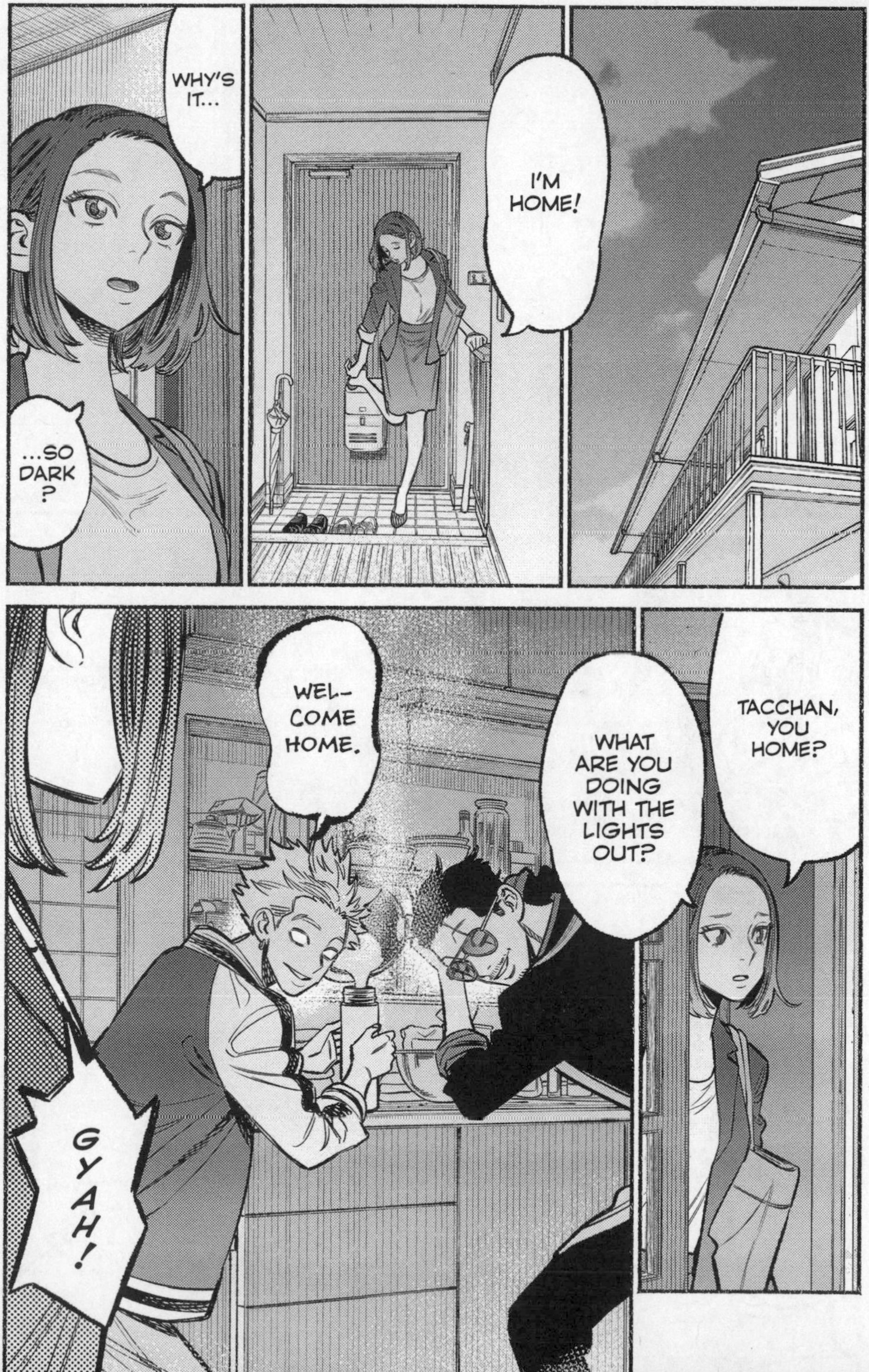
I'M HOME!
WHY'S IT...
...SO DARK?
TACCHAN, YOU HOME?
WHAT ARE YOU DOING WITH THE LIGHTS OUT?
WEL-COME HOME.
GYAH!

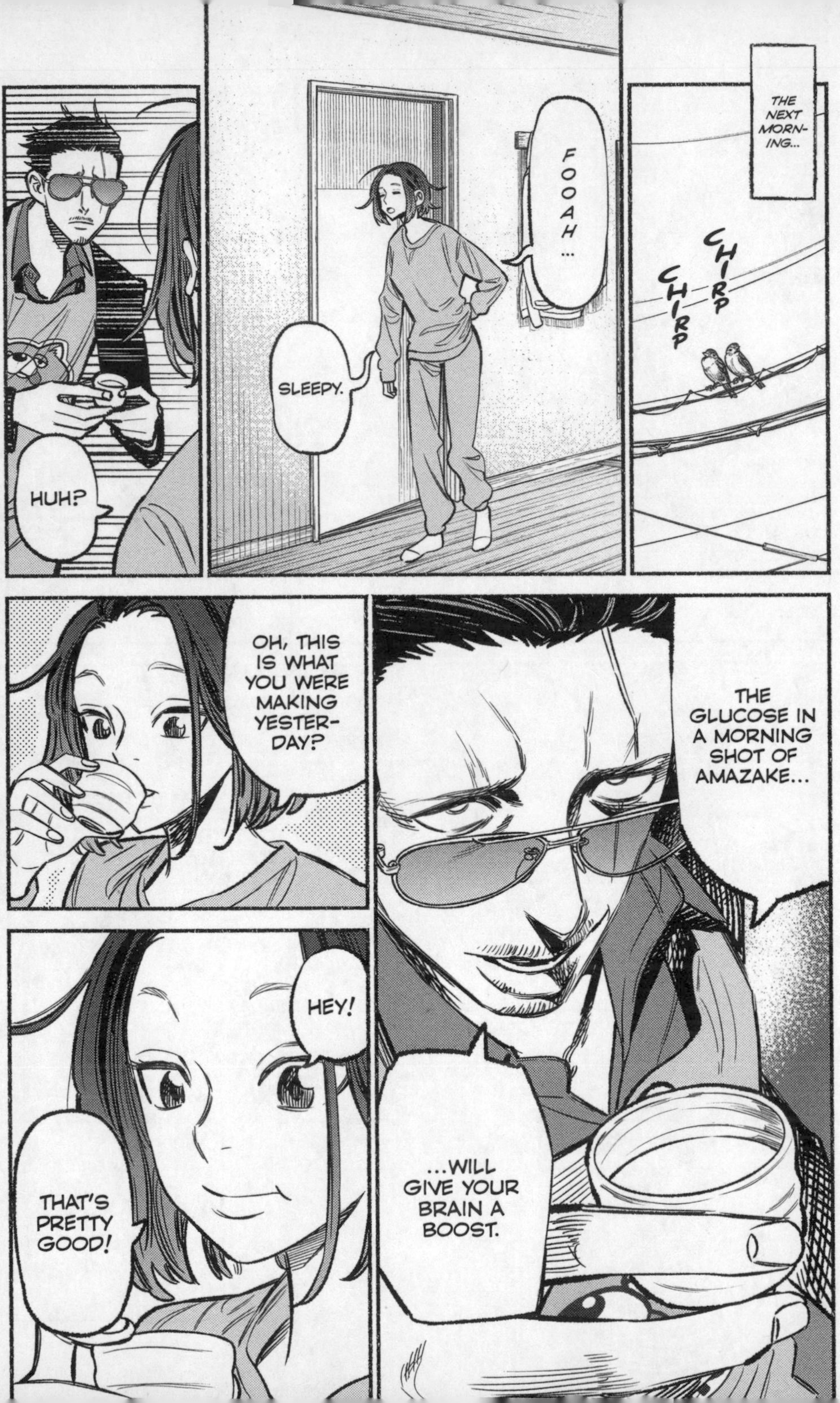
THE NEXT MORNING...
CHIRP
CHIRP
FOOAAH...
SLEEPY.
HUH?
THE GLUCOSE IN A MORNING SHOT OF AMAZAKE...
...WILL GIVE YOUR BRAIN A BOOST.
OH, THIS IS WHAT YOU WERE MAKING YESTERDAY?
HEY!
THAT'S PRETTY GOOD!

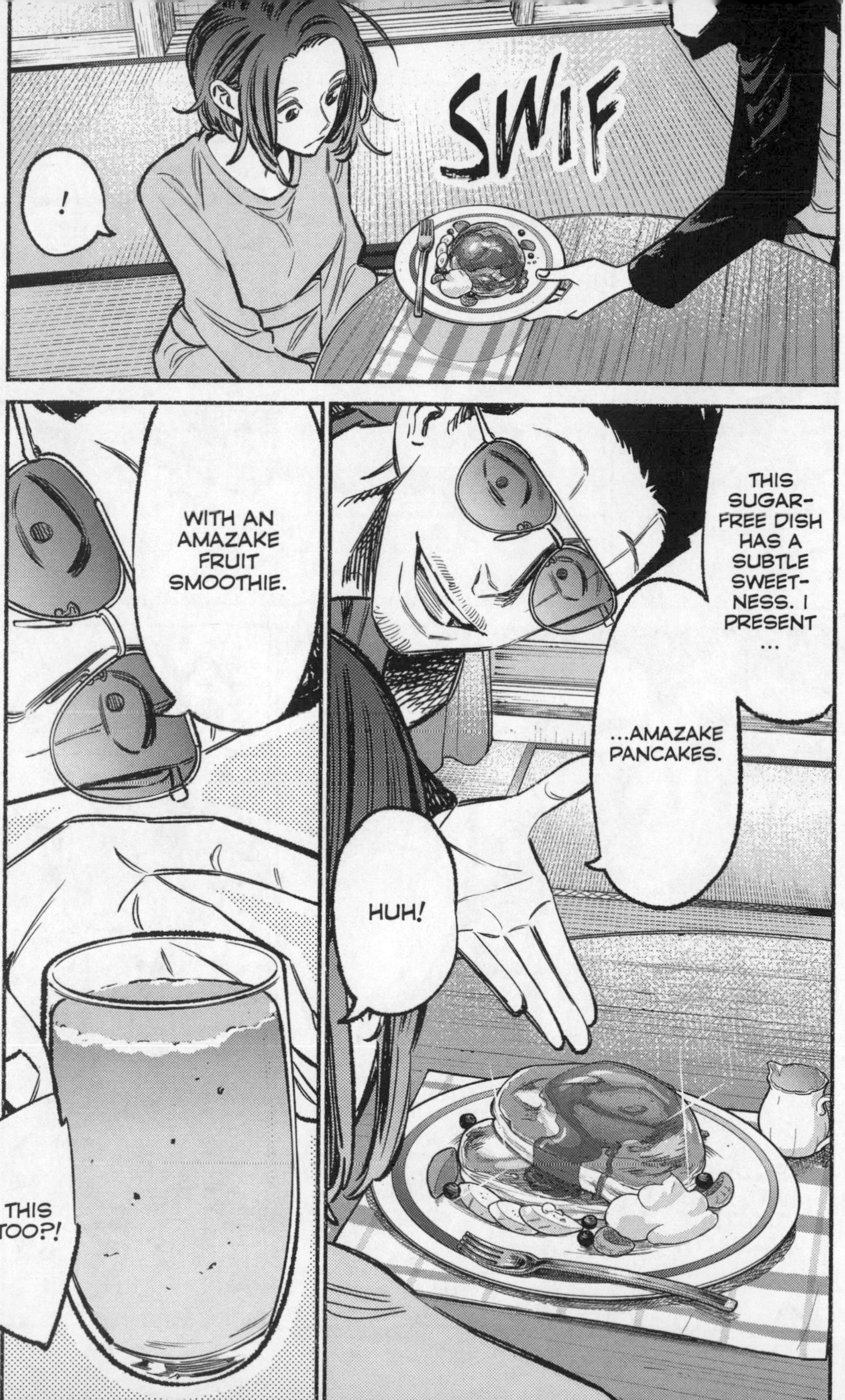
SWIF
!
THIS SUGAR-FREE DISH HAS A SUBTLE SWEETNESS. I PRESENT ...
...AMAZAKE PANCAKES.
HUH!
WITH AN AMAZAKE FRUIT SMOOTHIE.
THIS TOO?!

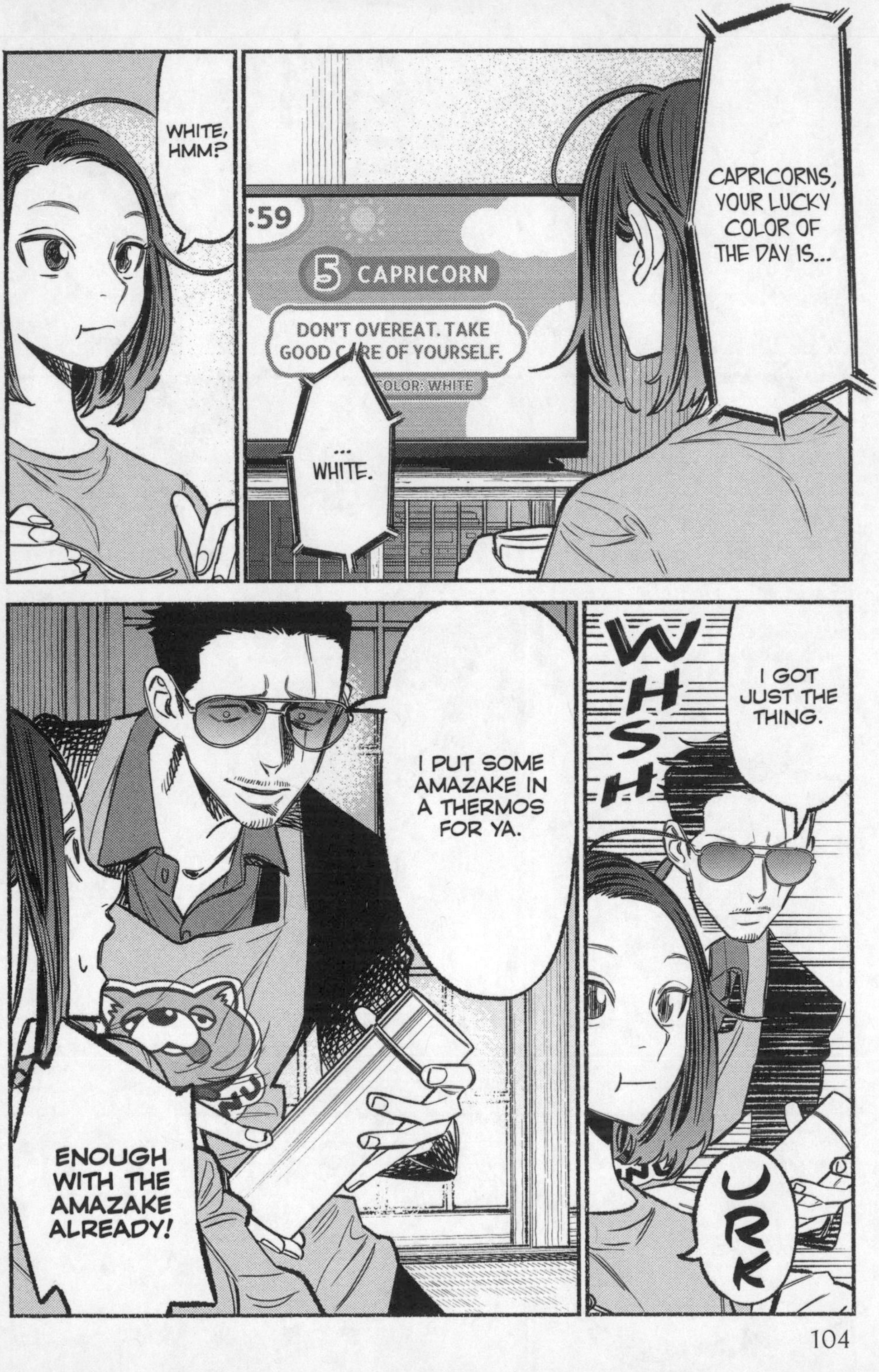
CAPRICORNS, YOUR LUCKY COLOR OF THE DAY IS...
:59
5 CAPRICORN
DON'T OVEREAT. TAKE GOOD CARE OF YOURSELF.
COLOR: WHITE
... WHITE.
WHITE, HMM?
WHSH
I GOT JUST THE THING.
URK
I PUT SOME AMAZAKE IN A THERMOS FOR YA.
ENOUGH WITH THE AMAZAKE ALREADY!

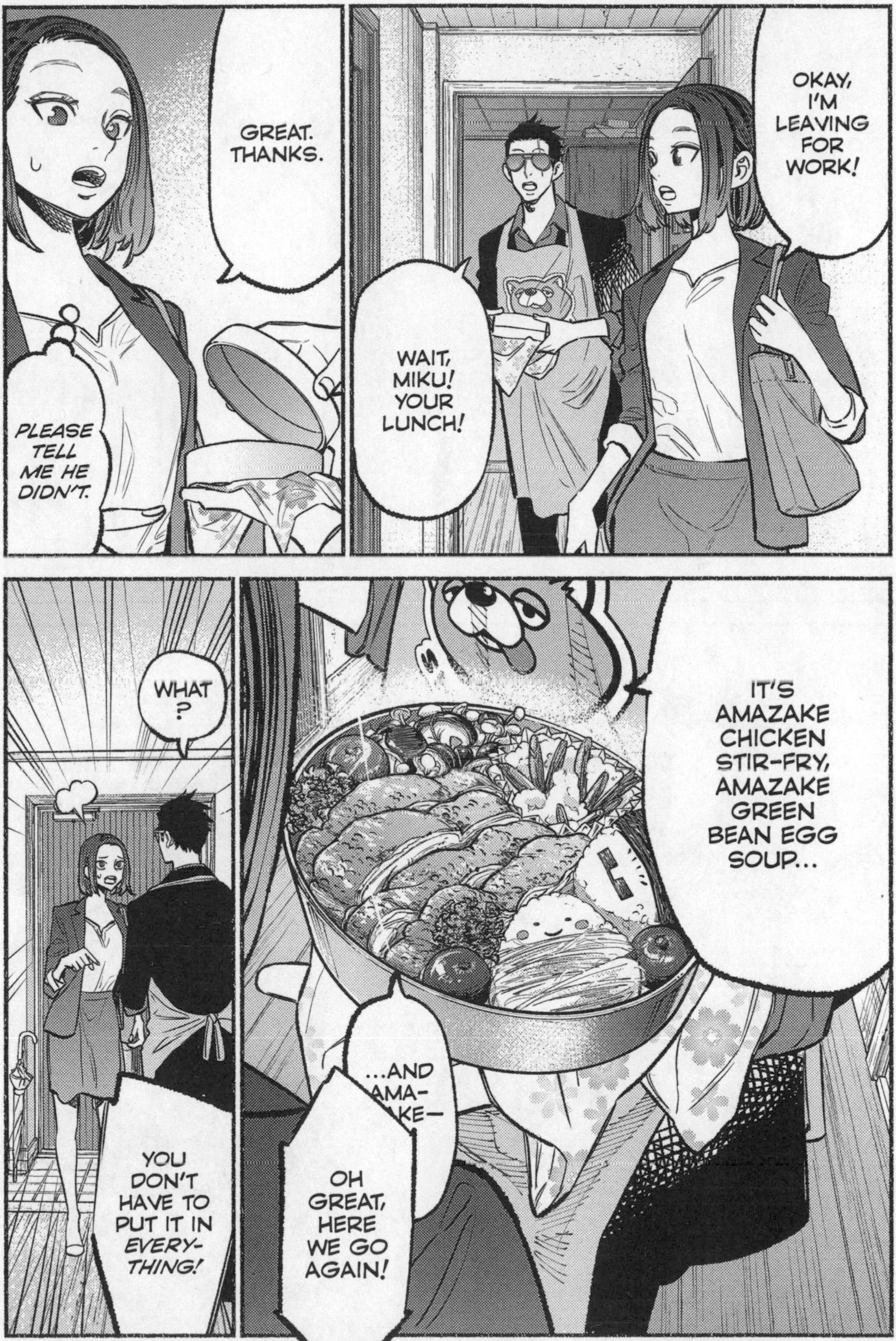
OKAY, I'M LEAVING FOR WORK!
WAIT, MIKU! YOUR LUNCH!
GREAT. THANKS.
PLEASE TELL ME HE DIDN'T.
IT'S AMAZAKE CHICKEN STIR-FRY, AMAZAKE GREEN BEAN EGG SOUP...
...AND AMA- KE—
OH GREAT, HERE WE GO AGAIN!
WHAT?
YOU DON'T HAVE TO PUT IT IN *EVERY-THING!*

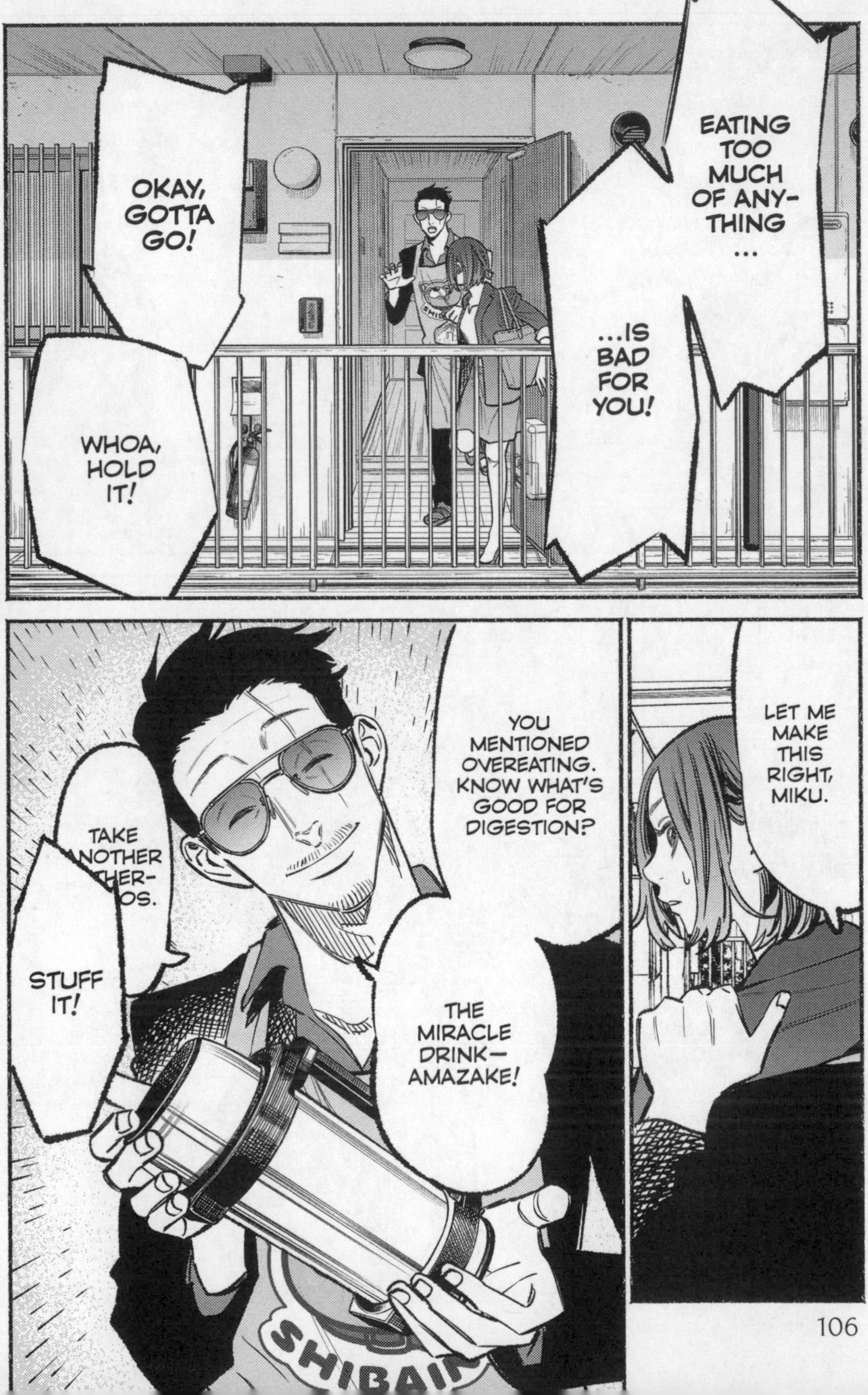
EATING TOO MUCH OF ANY-THING...
...IS BAD FOR YOU!
OKAY, GOTTA GO!
WHOA, HOLD IT!
LET ME MAKE THIS RIGHT, MIKU.
YOU MENTIONED OVEREATING. KNOW WHAT'S GOOD FOR DIGESTION?
THE MIRACLE DRINK—AMAZAKE!
TAKE ANOTHER THER- OS.
STUFF IT!
SHIBAI

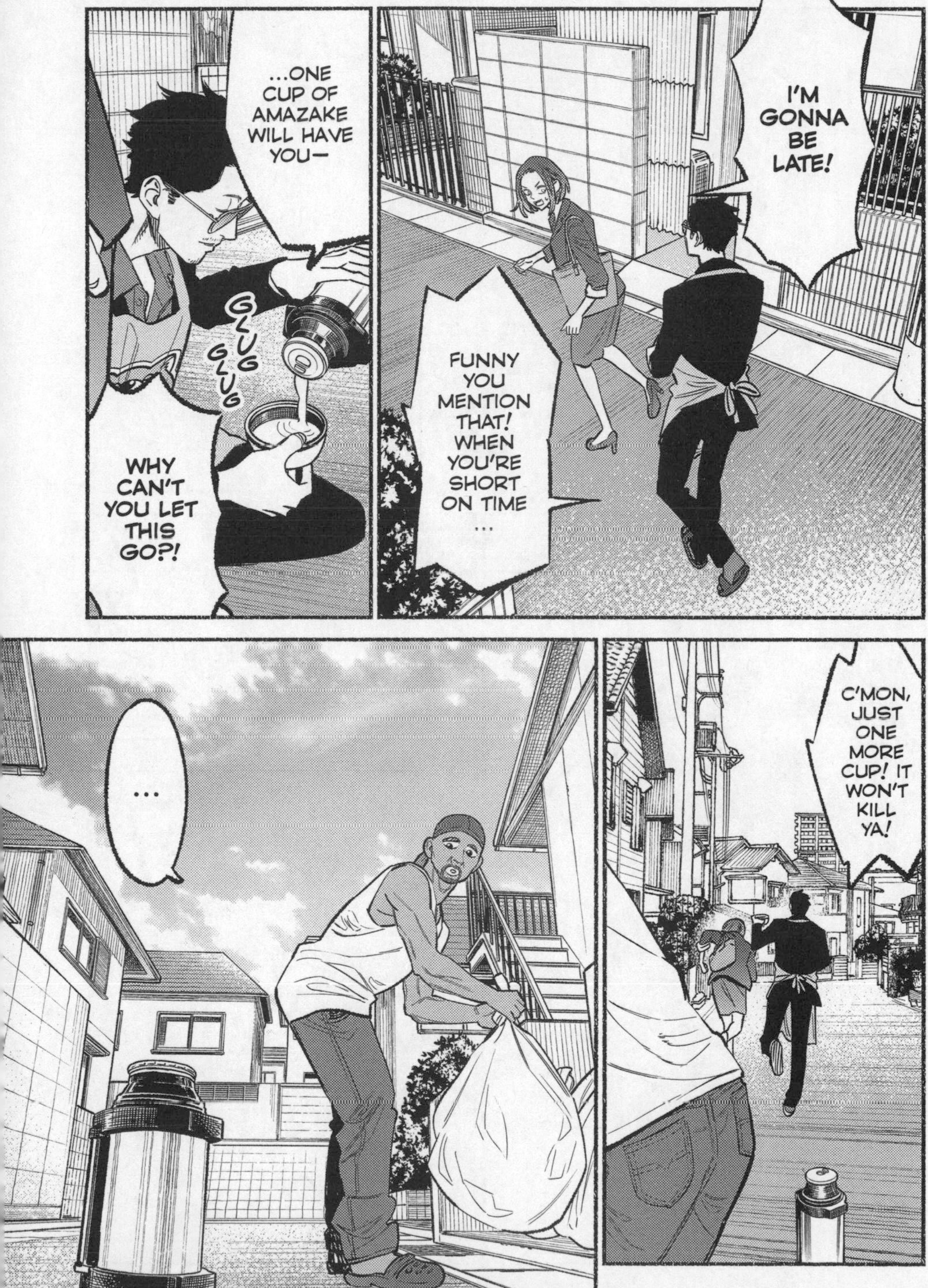
I'M GONNA BE LATE!
FUNNY YOU MENTION THAT! WHEN YOU'RE SHORT ON TIME ...
...ONE CUP OF AMAZAKE WILL HAVE YOU—
GLUG GLUG
WHY CAN'T YOU LET THIS GO?!
C'MON, JUST ONE MORE CUP! IT WON'T KILL YA!
...

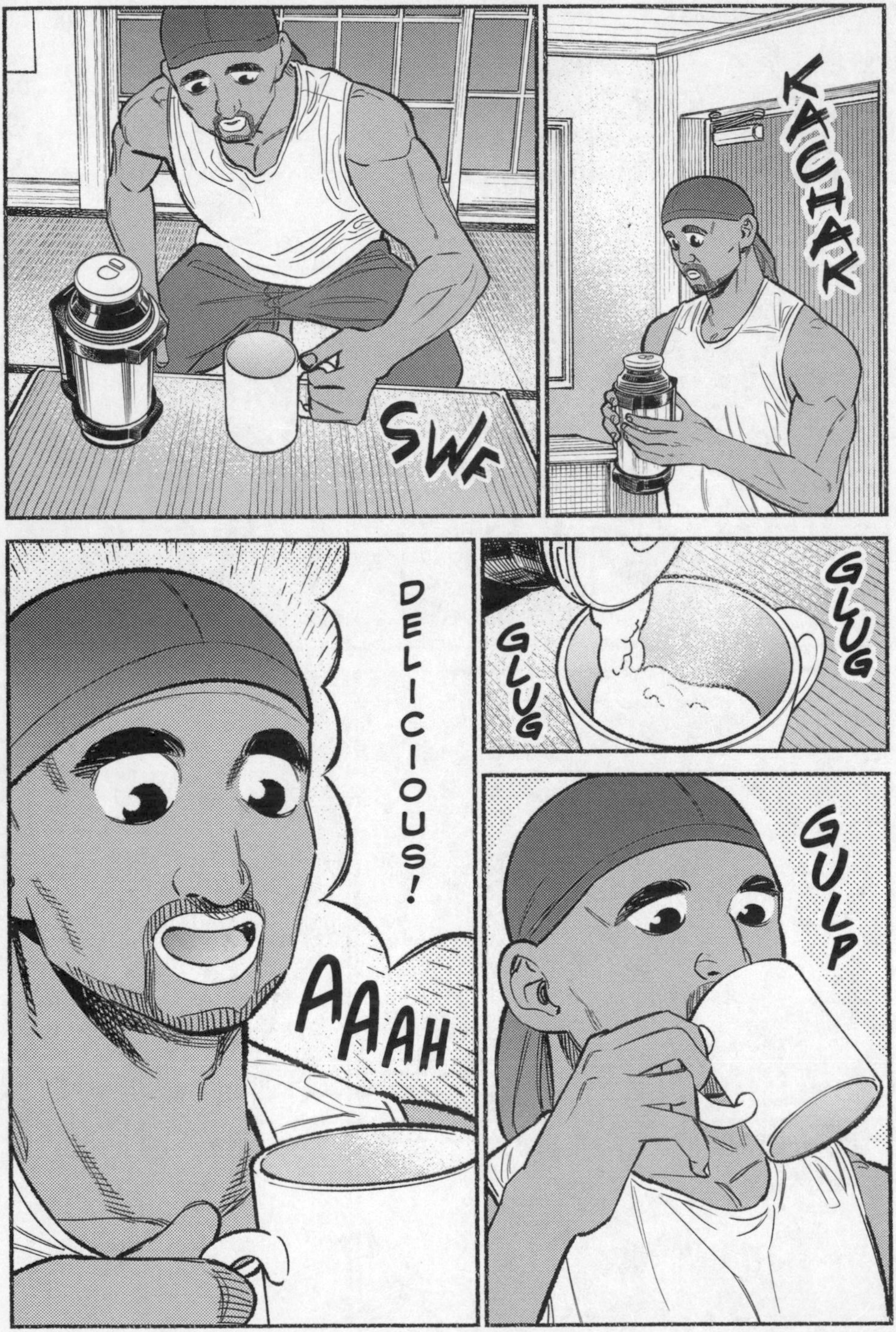
KACHAK
SWF
GLUG
GLUG
GULP
DELICIOUS!
AAAH

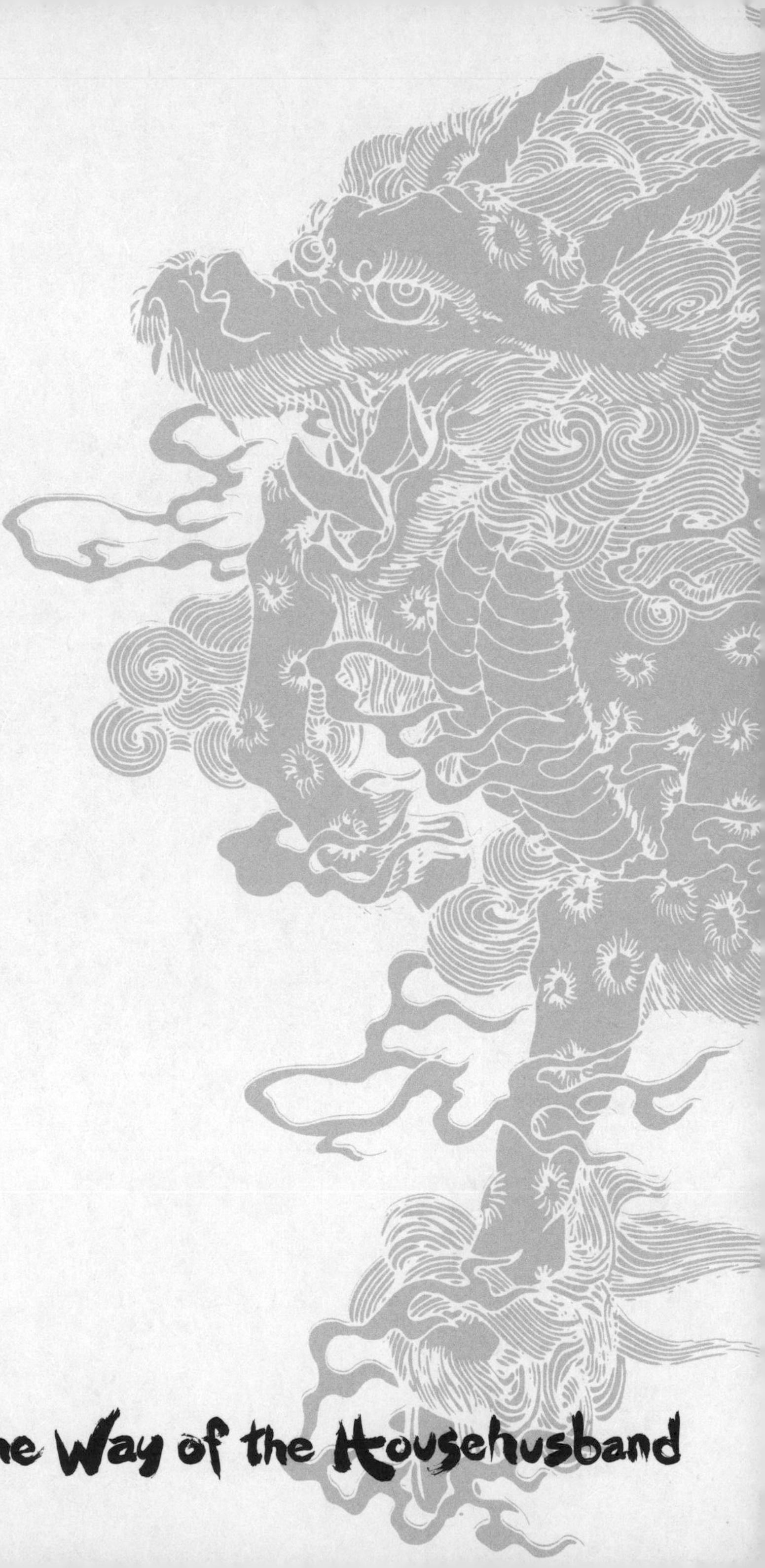

The Way of the Househusband

CHAPTER 62

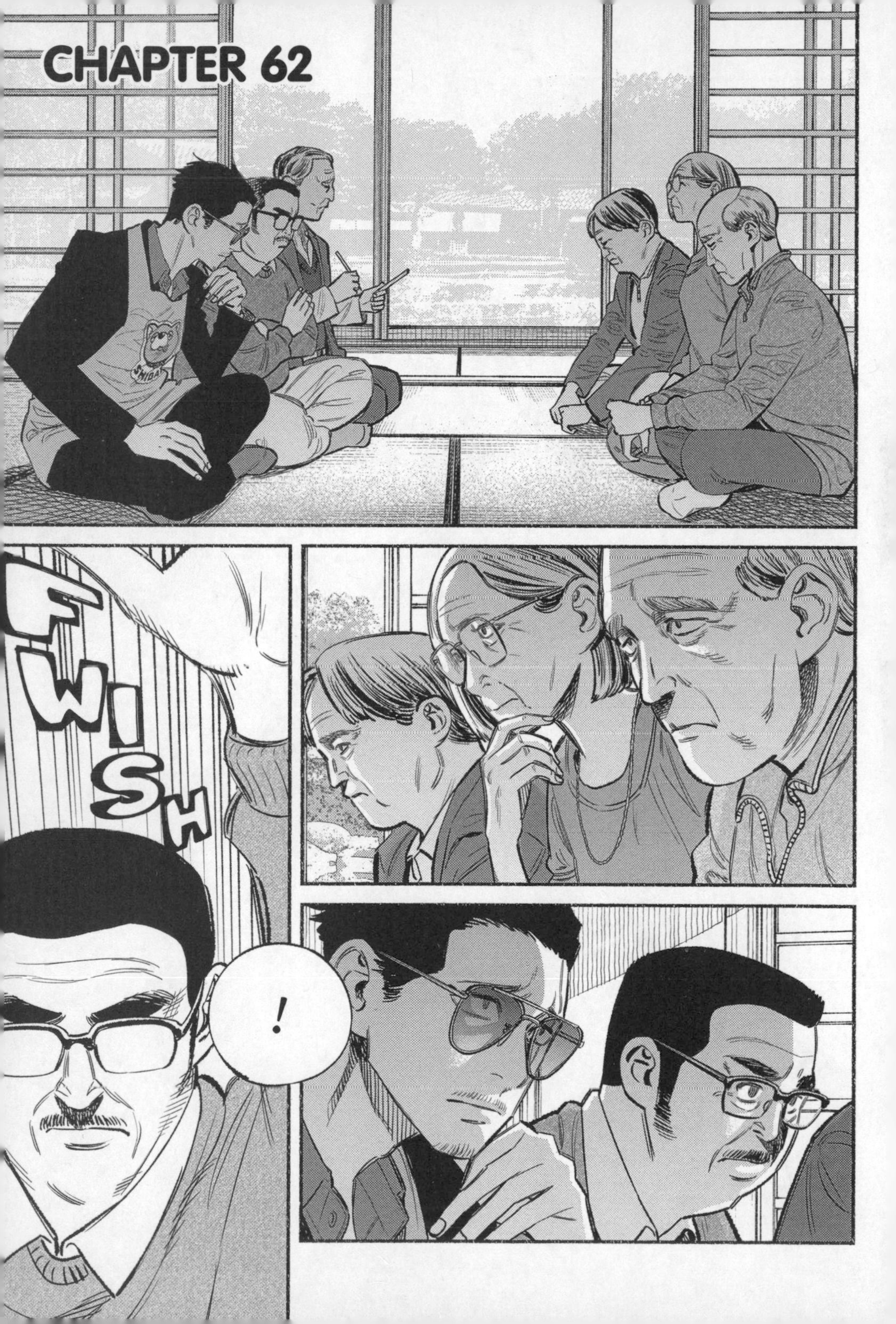
FWISH
!

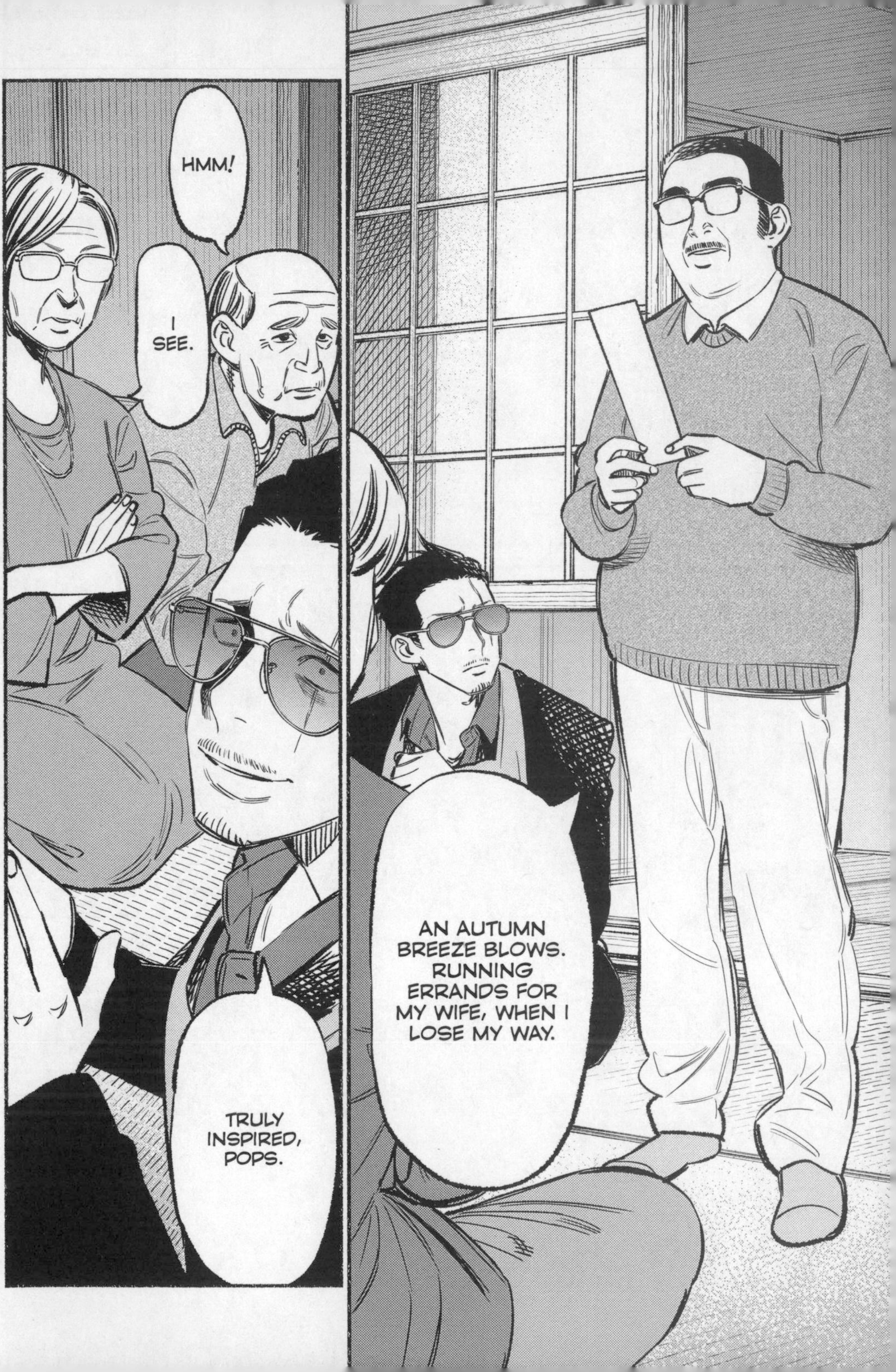
AN AUTUMN BREEZE BLOWS. RUNNING ERRANDS FOR MY WIFE, WHEN I LOSE MY WAY.
HMM!
I SEE.
TRULY INSPIRED, POPS.

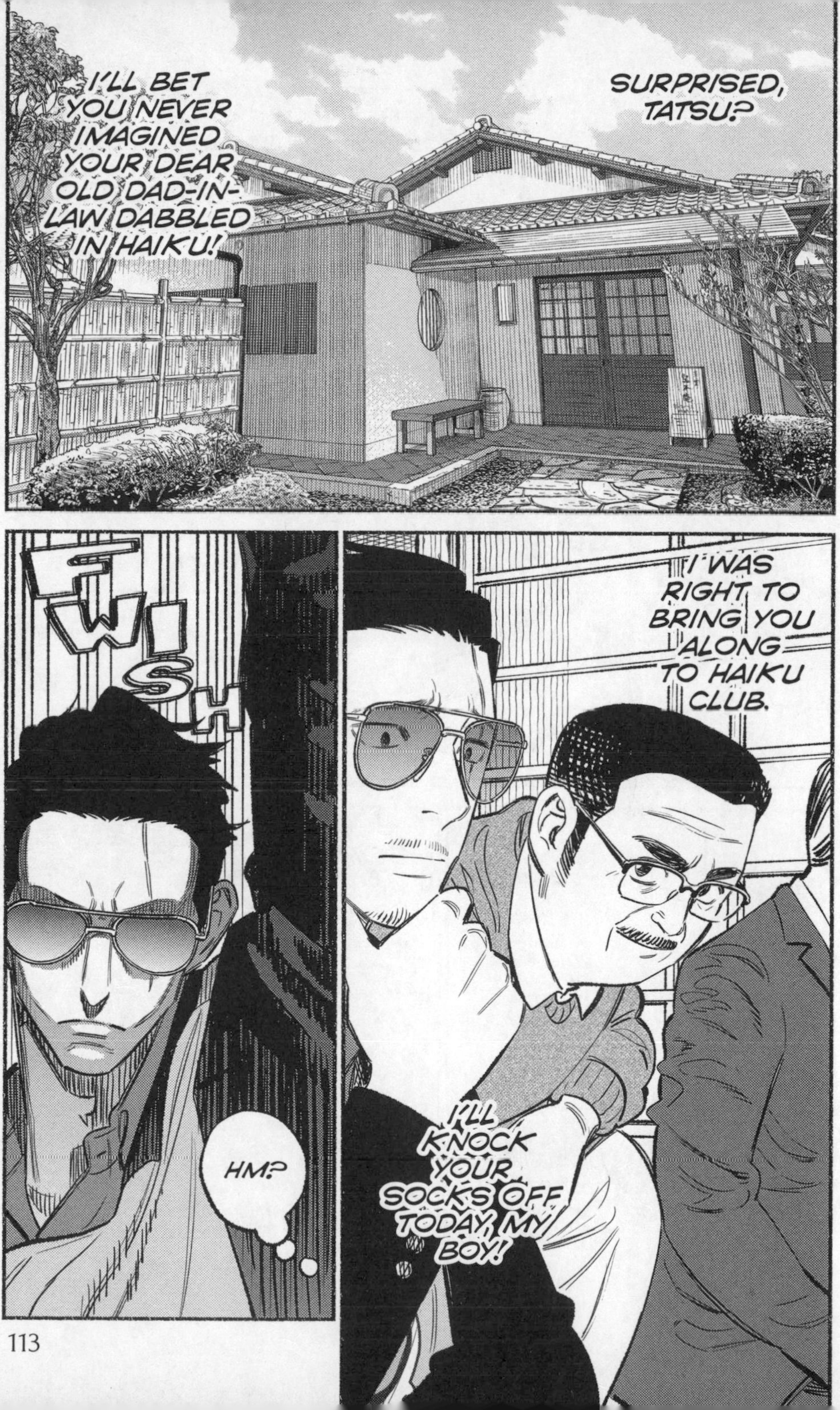
SURPRISED, TATSU?
I'LL BET YOU NEVER IMAGINED YOUR DEAR OLD DAD-IN-LAW DABBLED IN HAIKU!
I WAS RIGHT TO BRING YOU ALONG TO HAIKU CLUB.
I'LL KNOCK YOUR SOCKS OFF TODAY, MY BOY!
FWISH
HM?

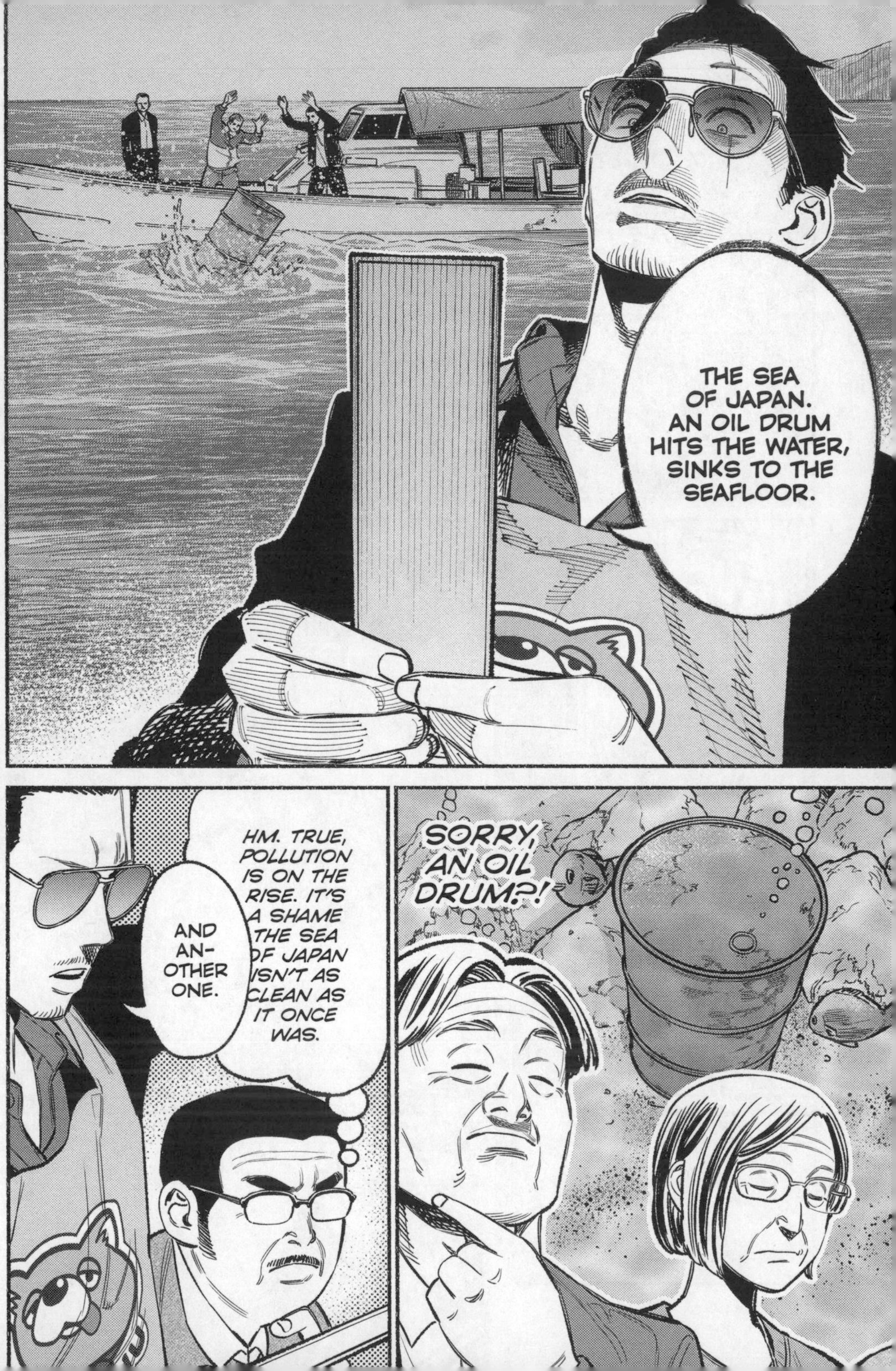
THE SEA OF JAPAN. AN OIL DRUM HITS THE WATER, SINKS TO THE SEAFLOOR.
SORRY, AN OIL DRUM?!
HM. TRUE, POLLUTION IS ON THE RISE. IT'S A SHAME THE SEA OF JAPAN ISN'T AS CLEAN AS IT ONCE WAS.
AND AN-OTHER ONE.

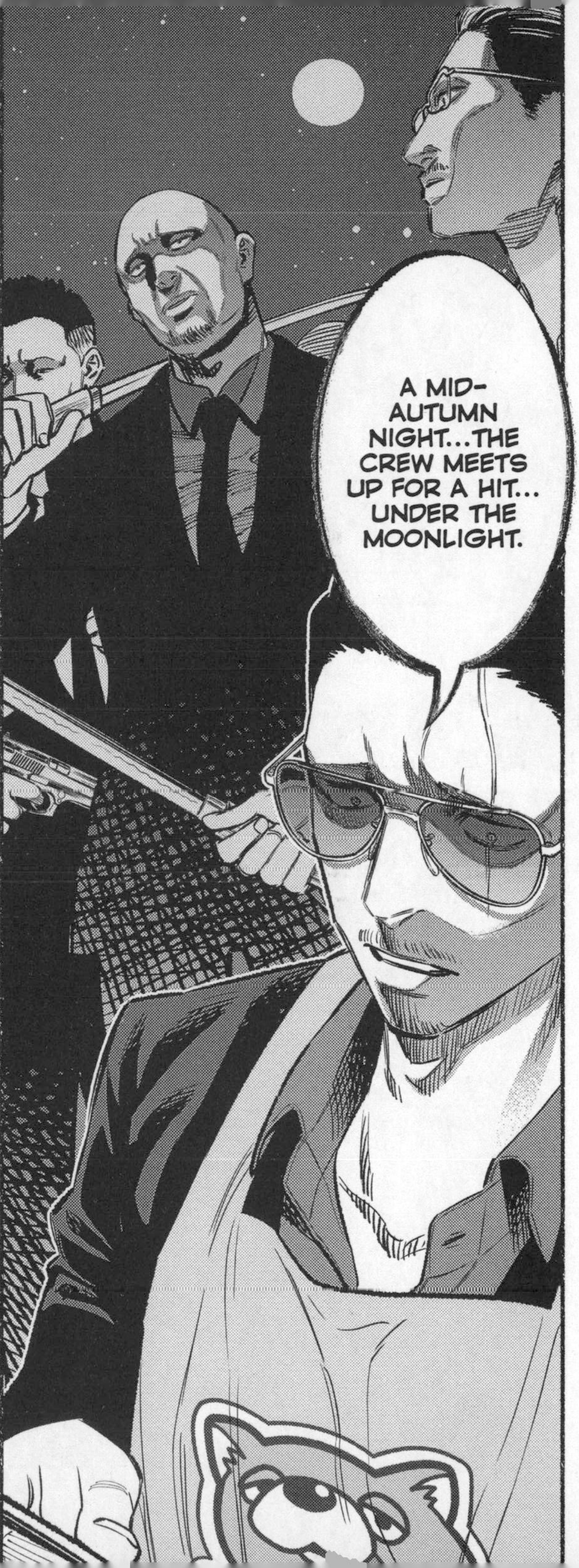
A MID-AUTUMN NIGHT...THE CREW MEETS UP FOR A HIT... UNDER THE MOONLIGHT.
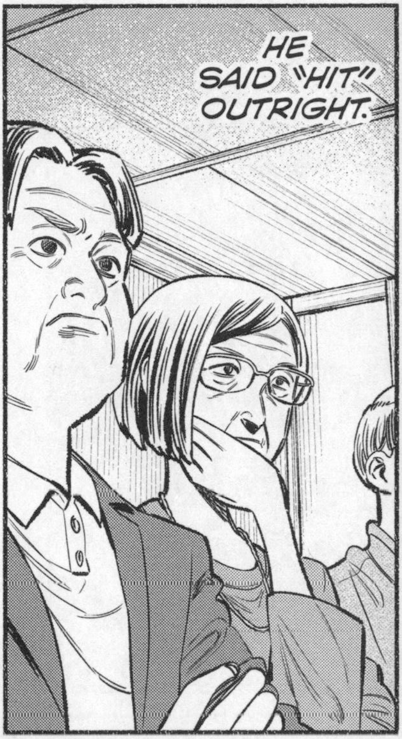
HE SAID "HIT" OUTRIGHT.
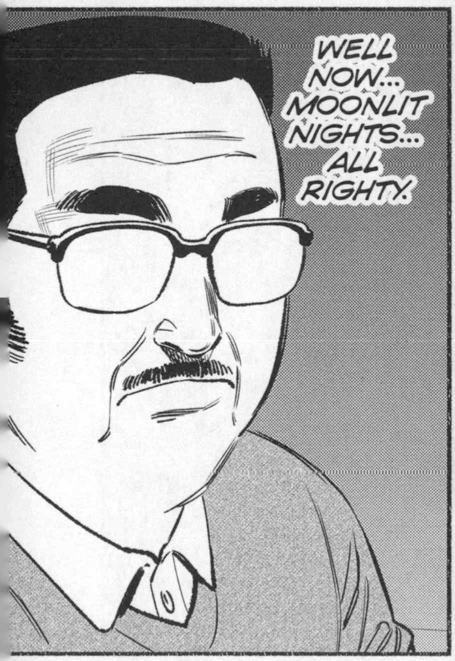
WELL NOW... MOONLIT NIGHTS... ALL RIGHTY.

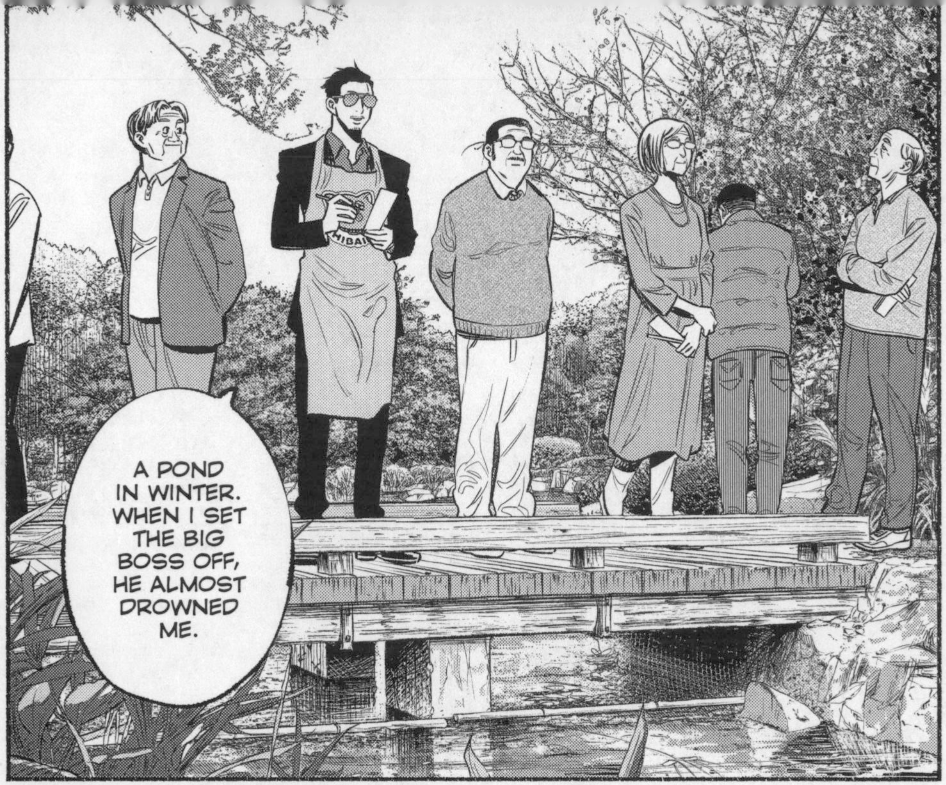
A POND IN WINTER. WHEN I SET THE BIG BOSS OFF, HE ALMOST DROWNED ME.

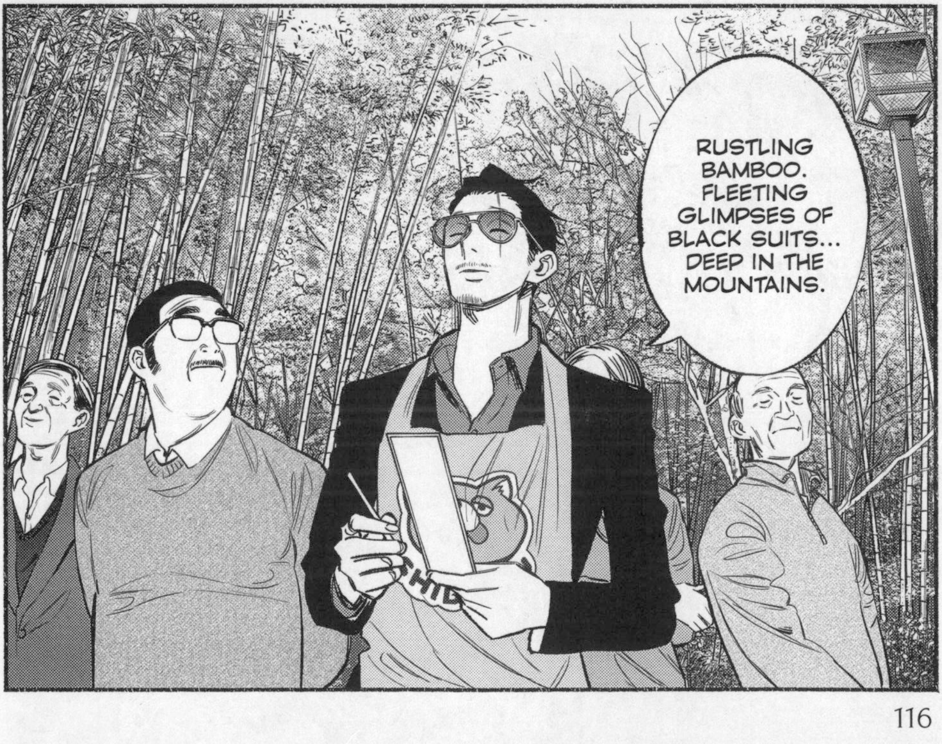
RUSTLING BAMBOO. FLEETING GLIMPSES OF BLACK SUITS... DEEP IN THE MOUNTAINS.

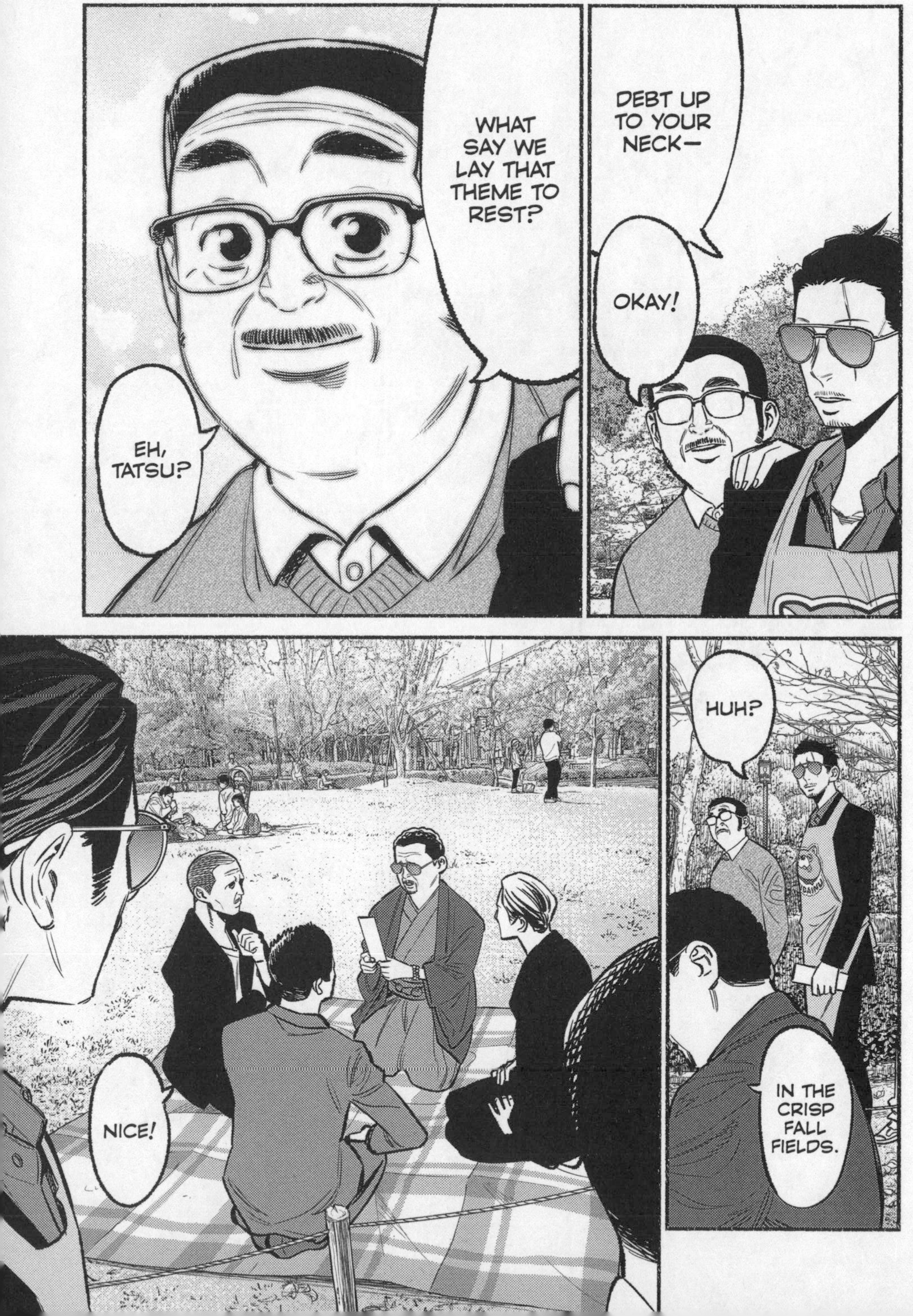
DEBT UP TO YOUR NECK—
OKAY!
WHAT SAY WE LAY THAT THEME TO REST?
EH, TATSU?
HUH?
IN THE CRISP FALL FIELDS.
NICE!

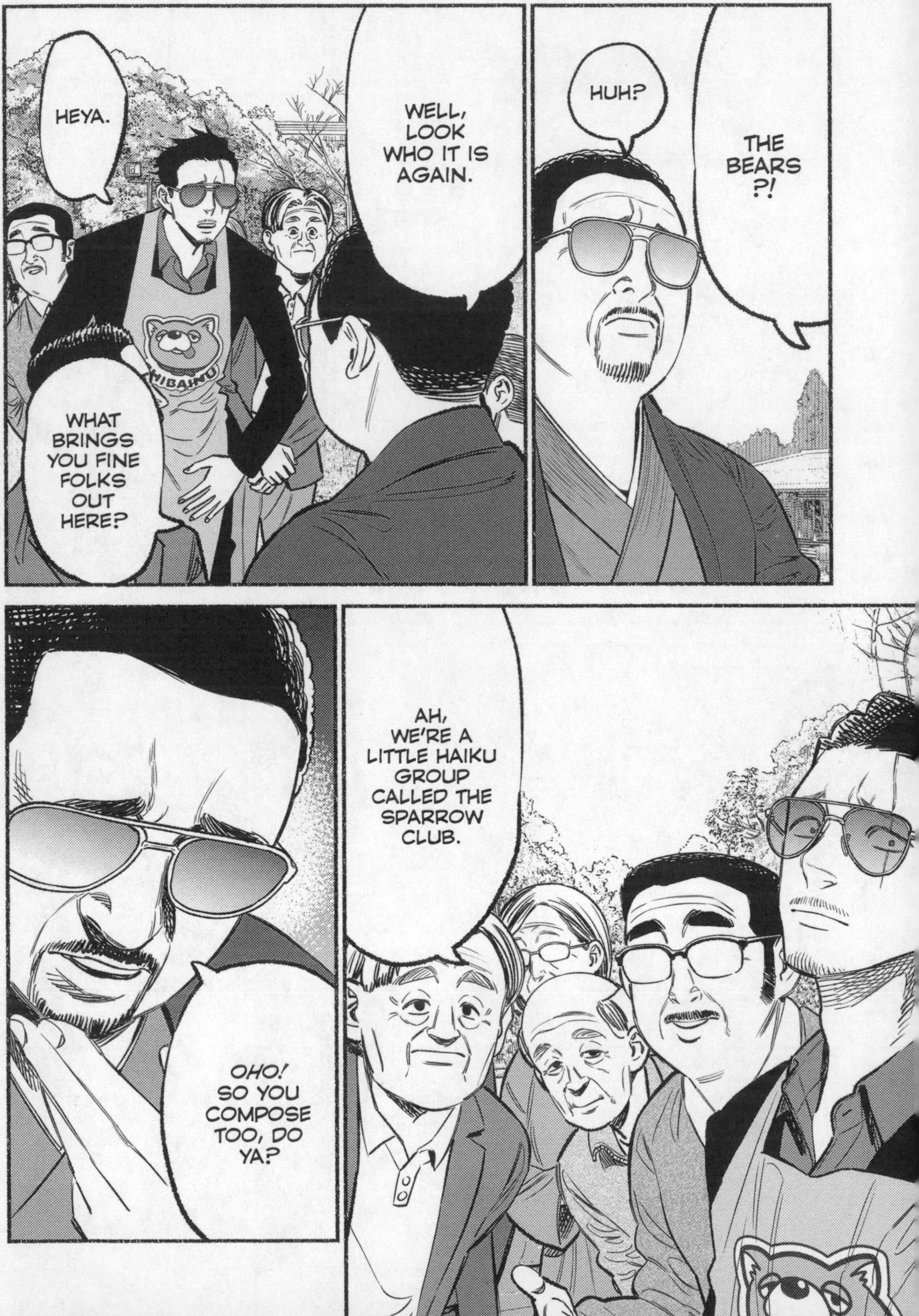
HUH?
THE BEARS?!
WELL, LOOK WHO IT IS AGAIN.
HEYA.
WHAT BRINGS YOU FINE FOLKS OUT HERE?
AH, WE'RE A LITTLE HAIKU GROUP CALLED THE SPARROW CLUB.
OHO! SO YOU COMPOSE TOO, DO YA?

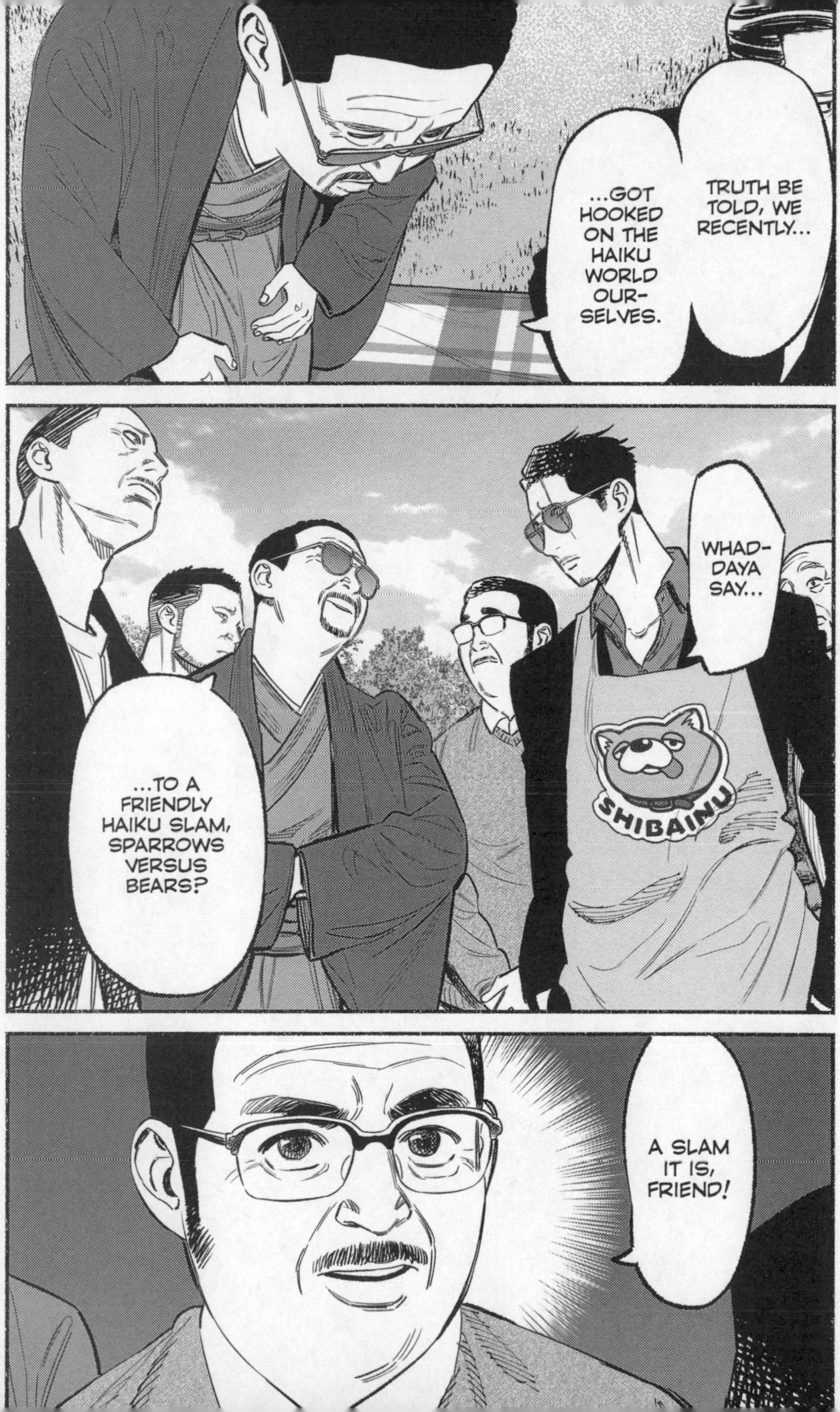
TRUTH BE TOLD, WE RECENTLY...
...GOT HOOKED ON THE HAIKU WORLD OUR-SELVES.
WHAD-DAYA SAY...
SHIBAINU
...TO A FRIENDLY HAIKU SLAM, SPARROWS VERSUS BEARS?
A SLAM IT IS, FRIEND!

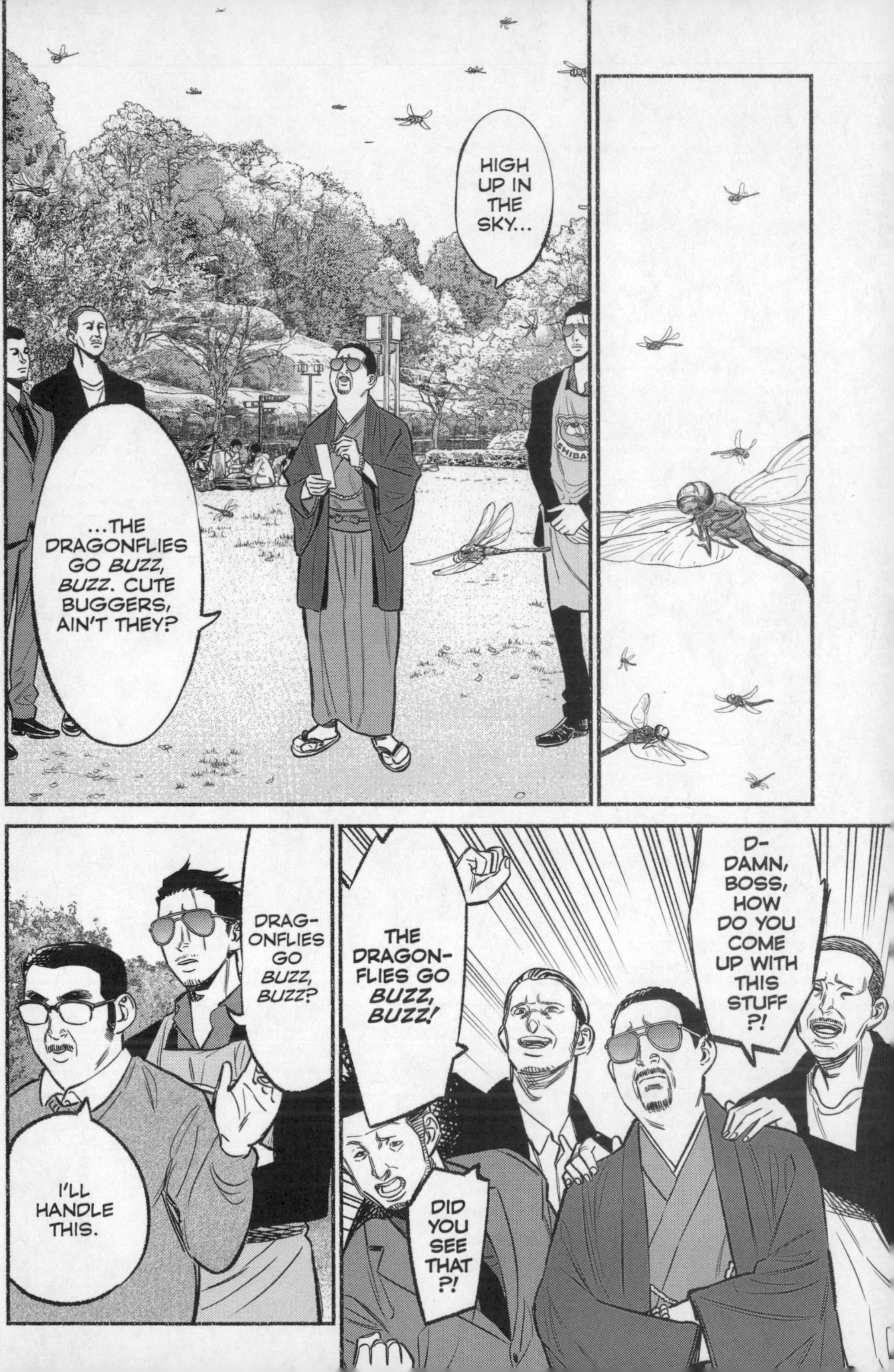
HIGH UP IN THE SKY...
...THE DRAGONFLIES GO *BUZZ, BUZZ*. CUTE BUGGERS, AIN'T THEY?
D-DAMN, BOSS, HOW DO YOU COME UP WITH THIS STUFF?!
THE DRAGONFLIES GO *BUZZ, BUZZ!*
DID YOU SEE THAT?!
DRAGONFLIES GO *BUZZ, BUZZ?*
I'LL HANDLE THIS.

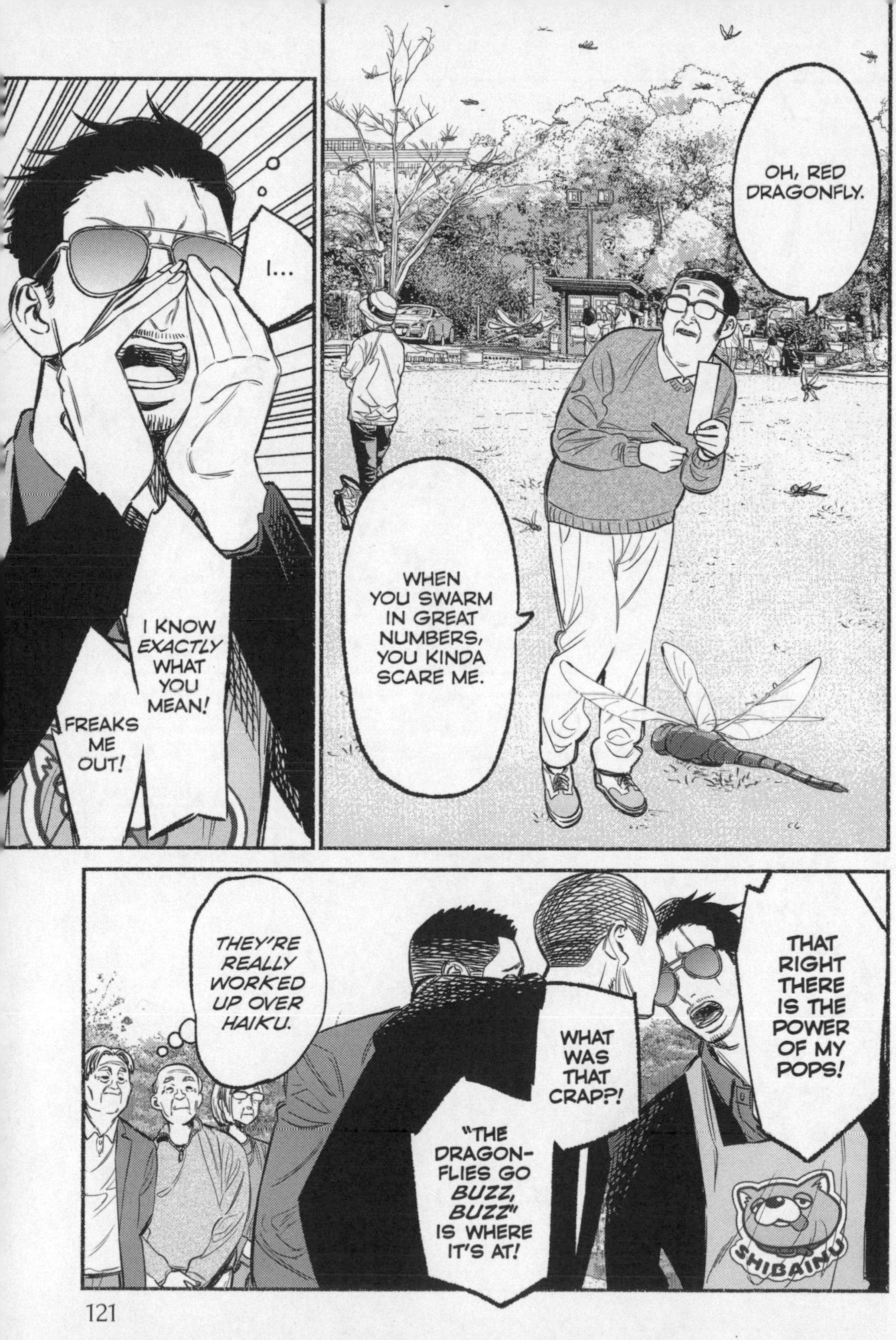
OH, RED DRAGONFLY.
WHEN YOU SWARM IN GREAT NUMBERS, YOU KINDA SCARE ME.
I...
I KNOW *EXACTLY* WHAT YOU MEAN!
FREAKS ME OUT!
THAT RIGHT THERE IS THE POWER OF MY POPS!
WHAT WAS THAT CRAP?!
"THE DRAGON-FLIES GO *BUZZ, BUZZ*" IS WHERE IT'S AT!
SHIBAINU
THEY'RE REALLY WORKED UP OVER HAIKU.

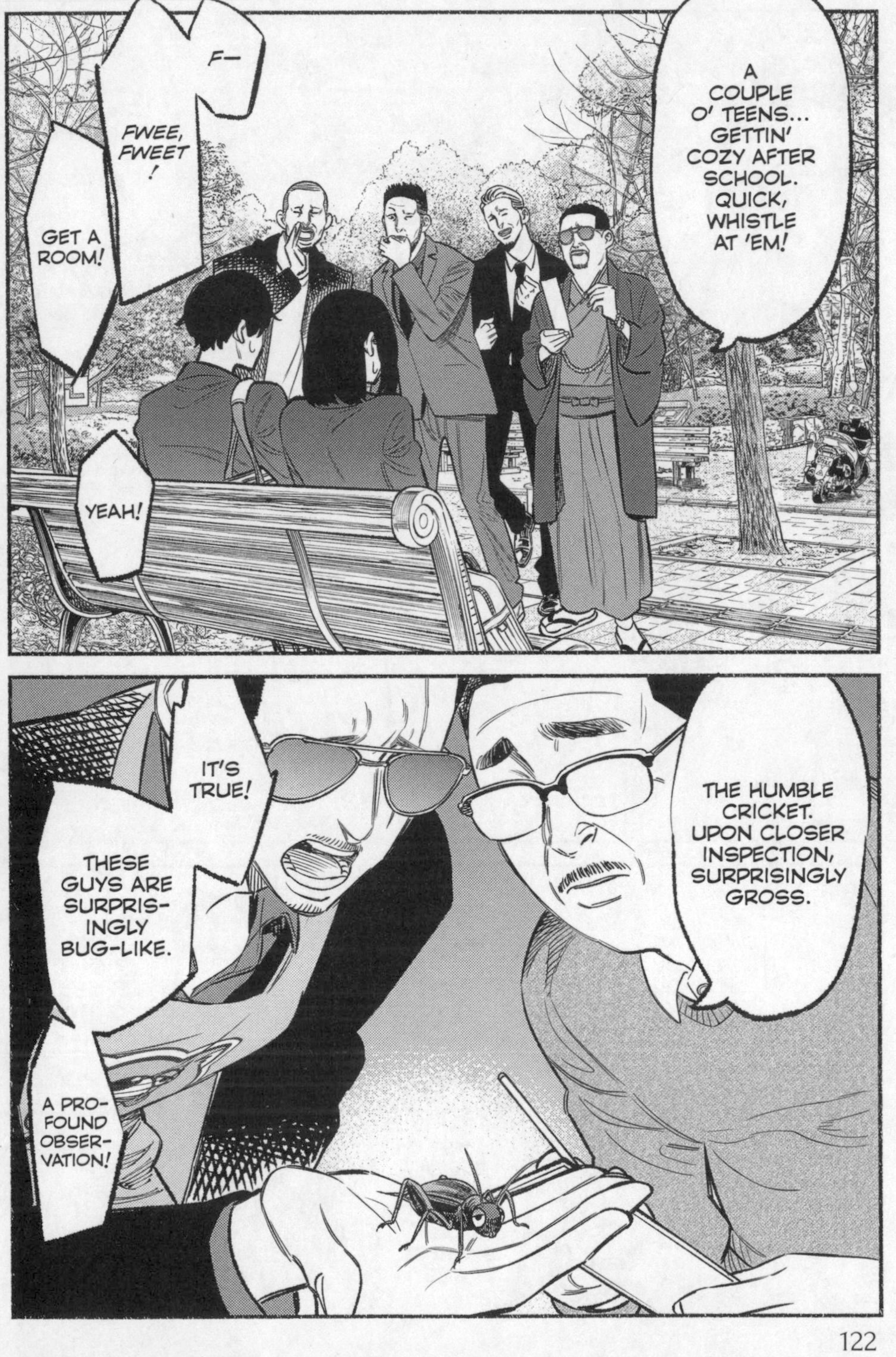
A COUPLE O' TEENS... GETTIN' COZY AFTER SCHOOL. QUICK, WHISTLE AT 'EM!
F—
FWEE, FWEET!
GET A ROOM!
YEAH!
THE HUMBLE CRICKET. UPON CLOSER INSPECTION, SURPRISINGLY GROSS.
IT'S TRUE!
THESE GUYS ARE SURPRIS-INGLY BUG-LIKE.
A PRO-FOUND OBSERVATION!

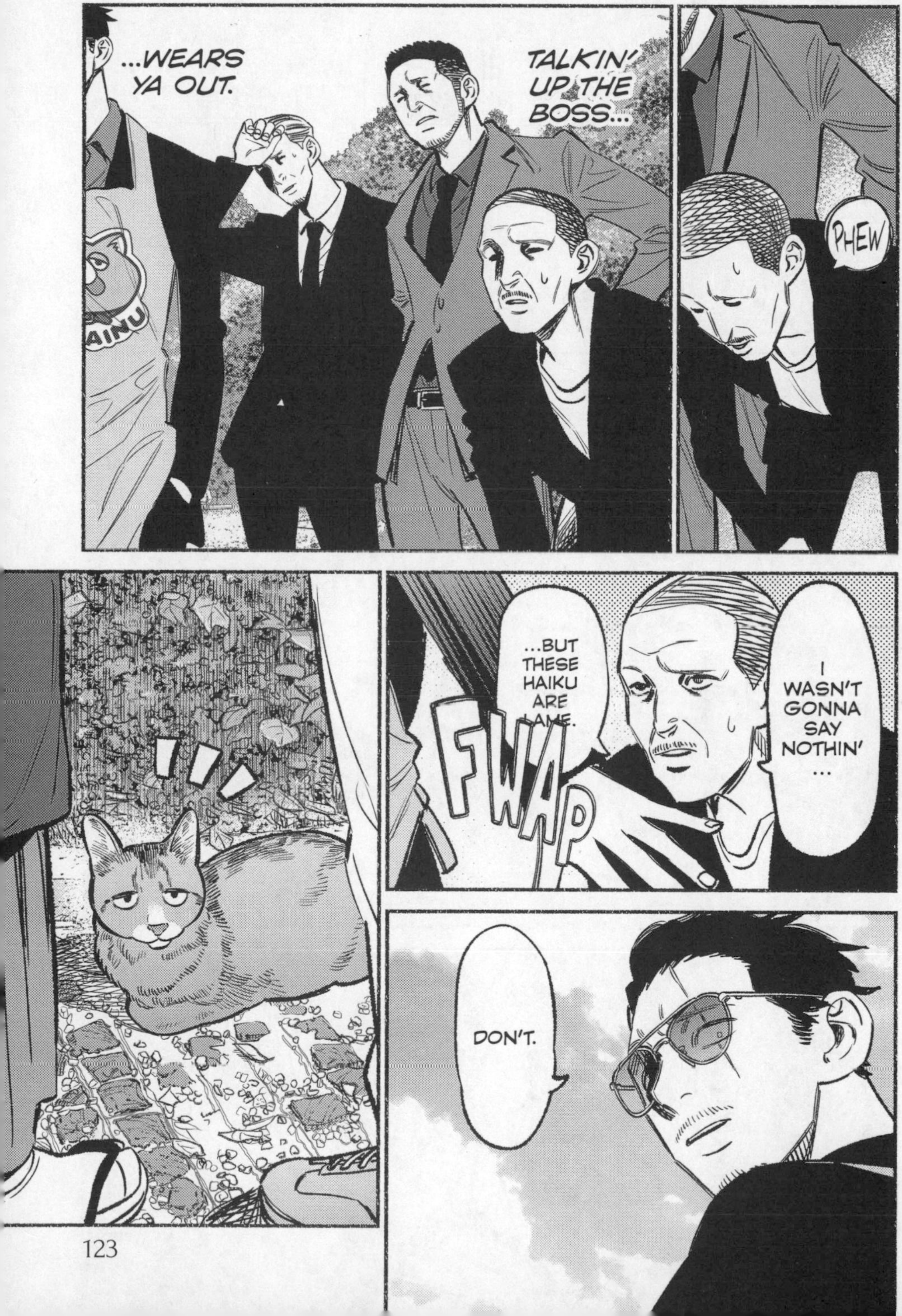
PHEW
TALKIN' UP THE BOSS...
...WEARS YA OUT.
I WASN'T GONNA SAY NOTHIN' ...
...BUT THESE HAIKU ARE LAME.
FWAP
DON'T.

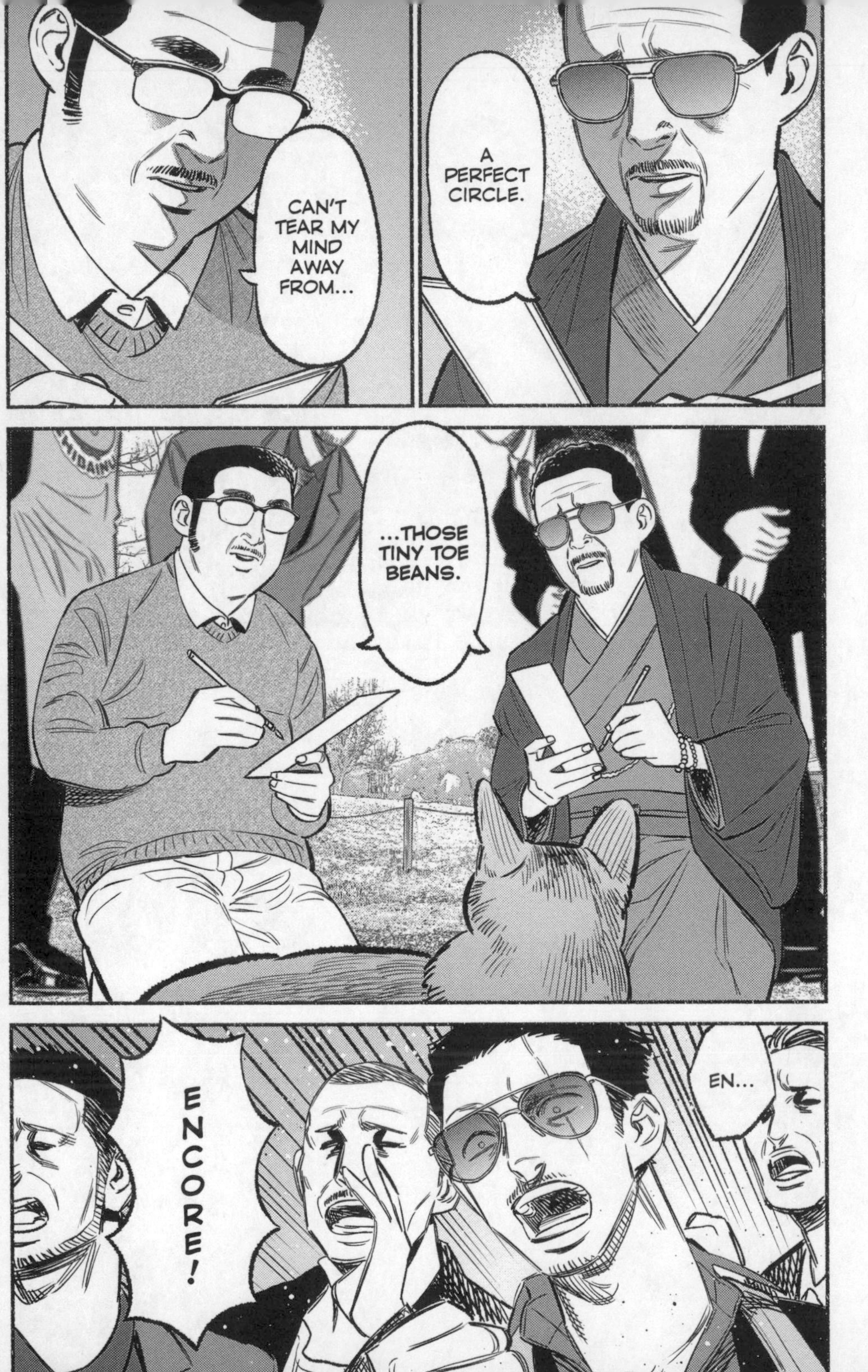
A PERFECT CIRCLE.
CAN'T TEAR MY MIND AWAY FROM...
...THOSE TINY TOE BEANS.
EN...
ENCORE!

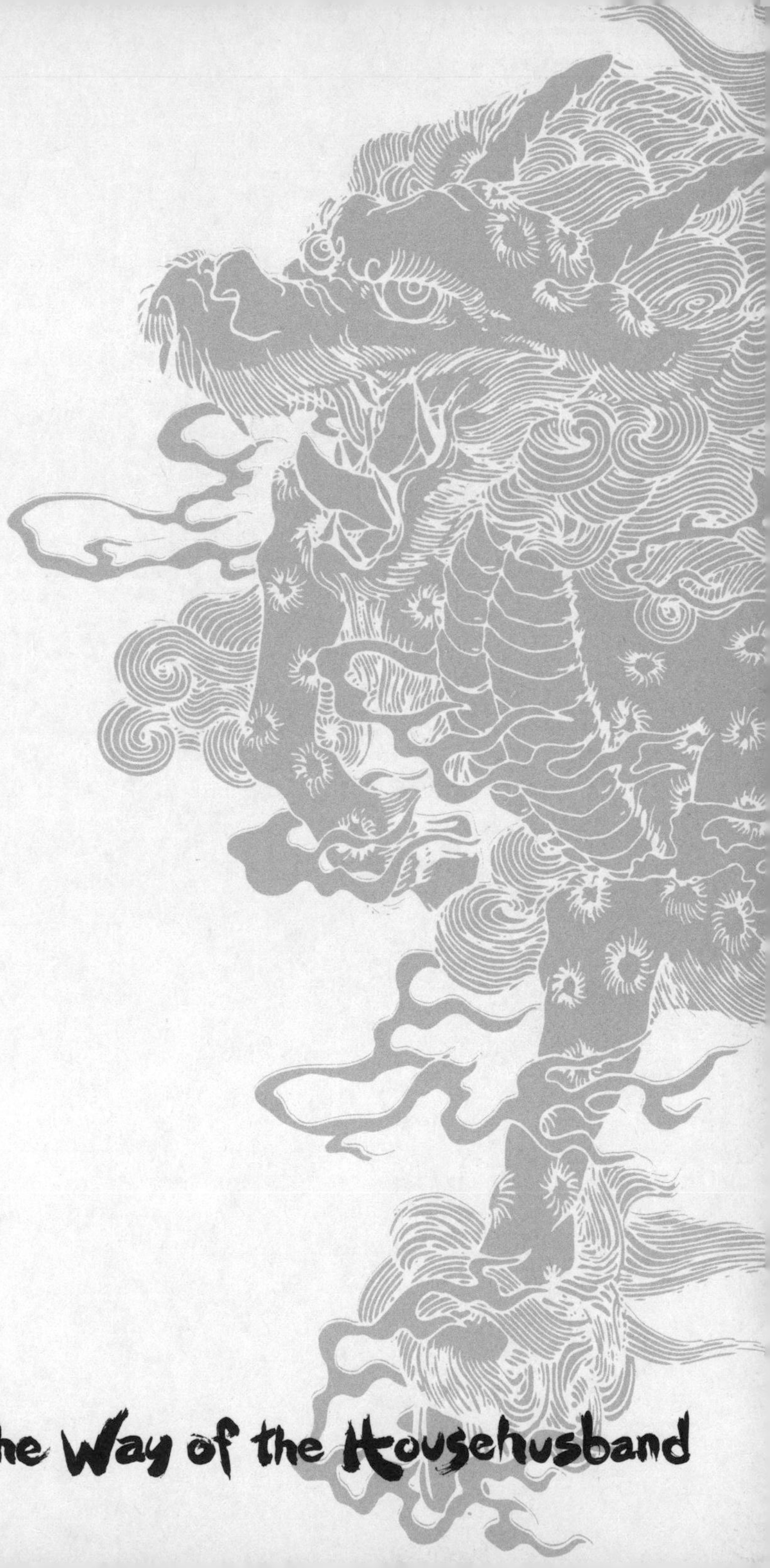

The Way of the Househusband

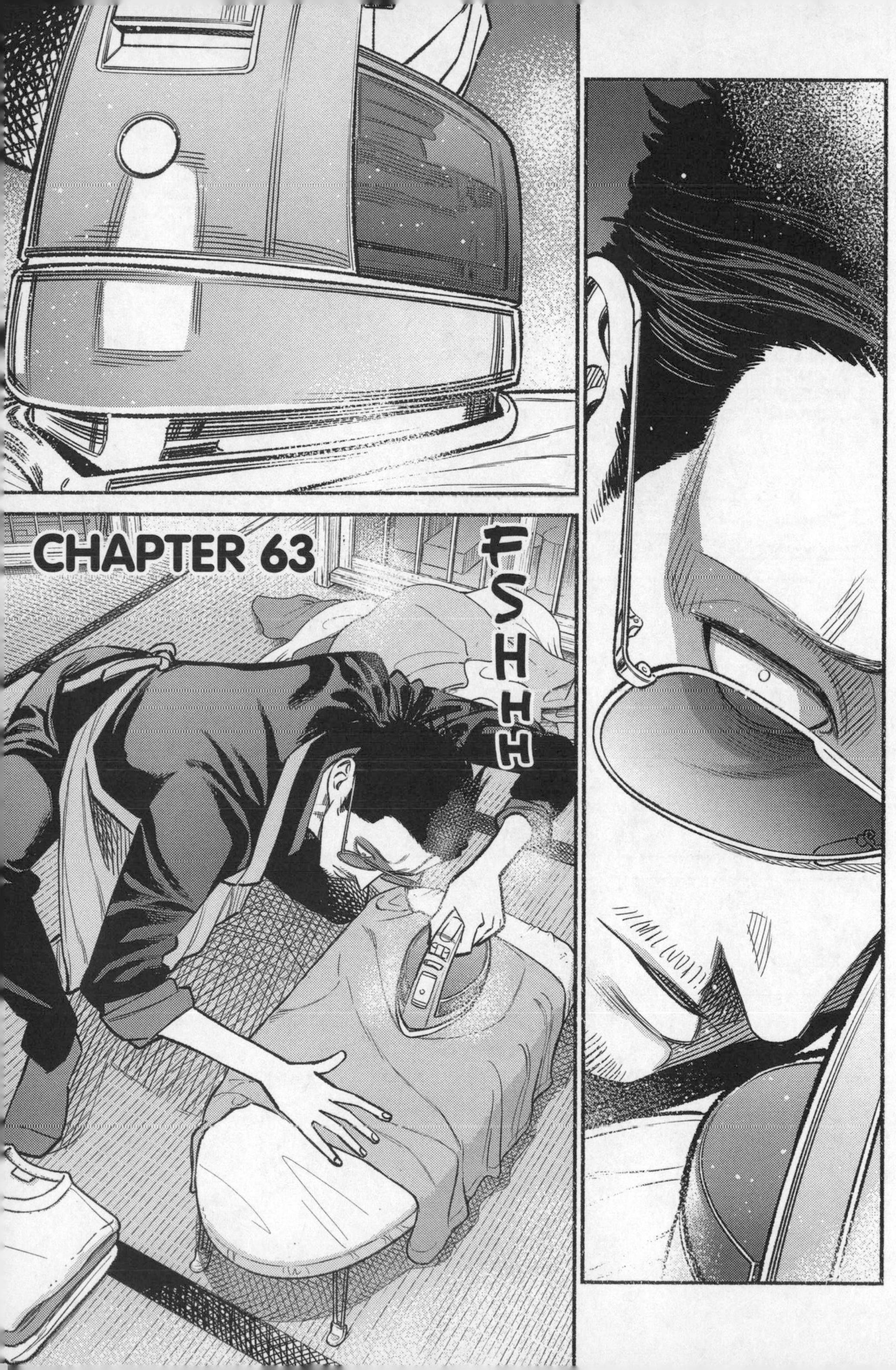
CHAPTER 63
FSHHH

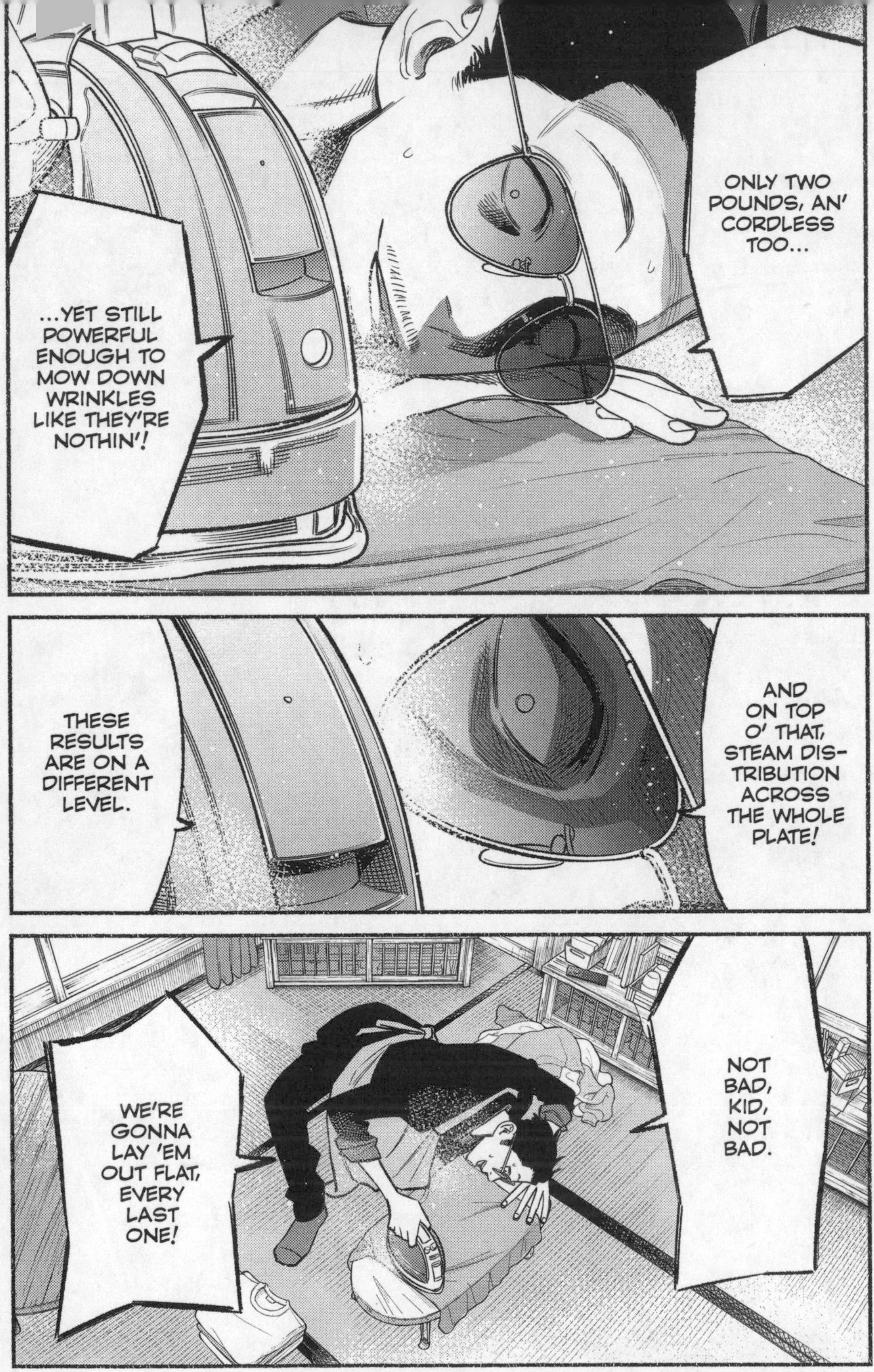
ONLY TWO POUNDS, AN' CORDLESS TOO...
...YET STILL POWERFUL ENOUGH TO MOW DOWN WRINKLES LIKE THEY'RE NOTHIN'!
AND ON TOP O' THAT, STEAM DIS-TRIBUTION ACROSS THE WHOLE PLATE!
THESE RESULTS ARE ON A DIFFERENT LEVEL.
NOT BAD, KID, NOT BAD.
WE'RE GONNA LAY 'EM OUT FLAT, EVERY LAST ONE!

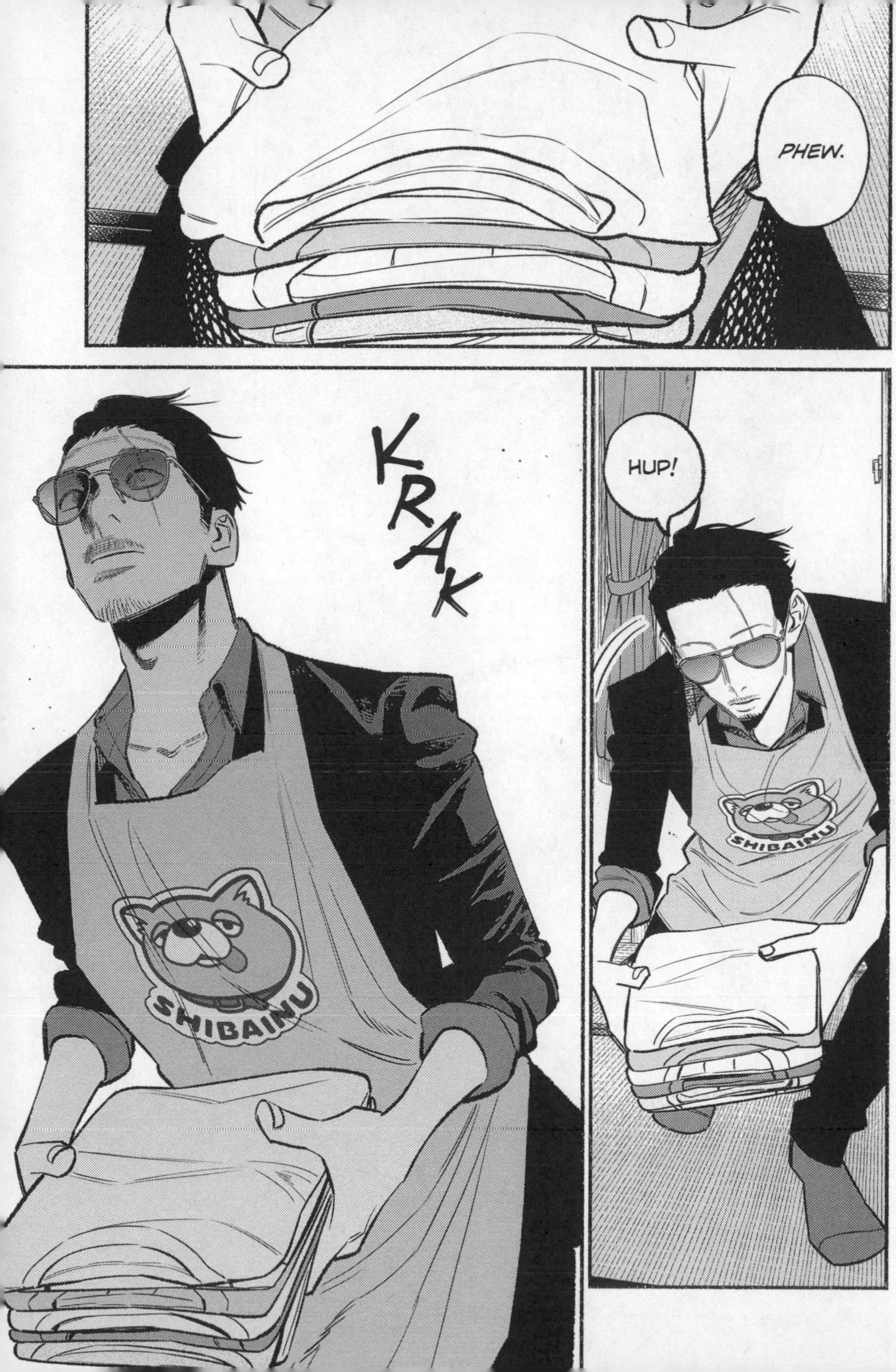
PHEW.
HUP!
SHIBAINU
KRAK
SHIBAINU

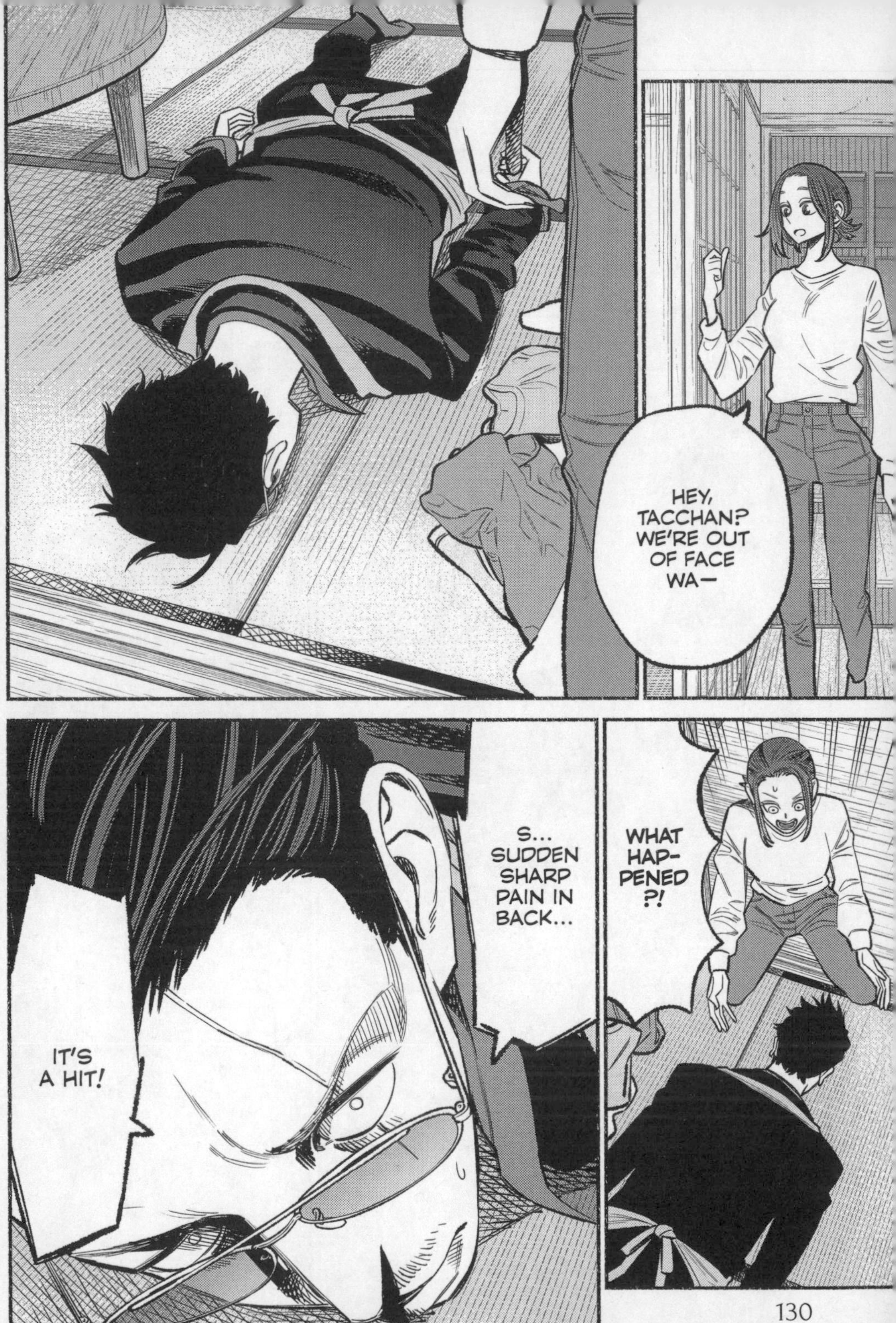
HEY, TACCHAN? WE'RE OUT OF FACE WA—
WHAT HAP-PENED?!
S... SUDDEN SHARP PAIN IN BACK...
IT'S A HIT!

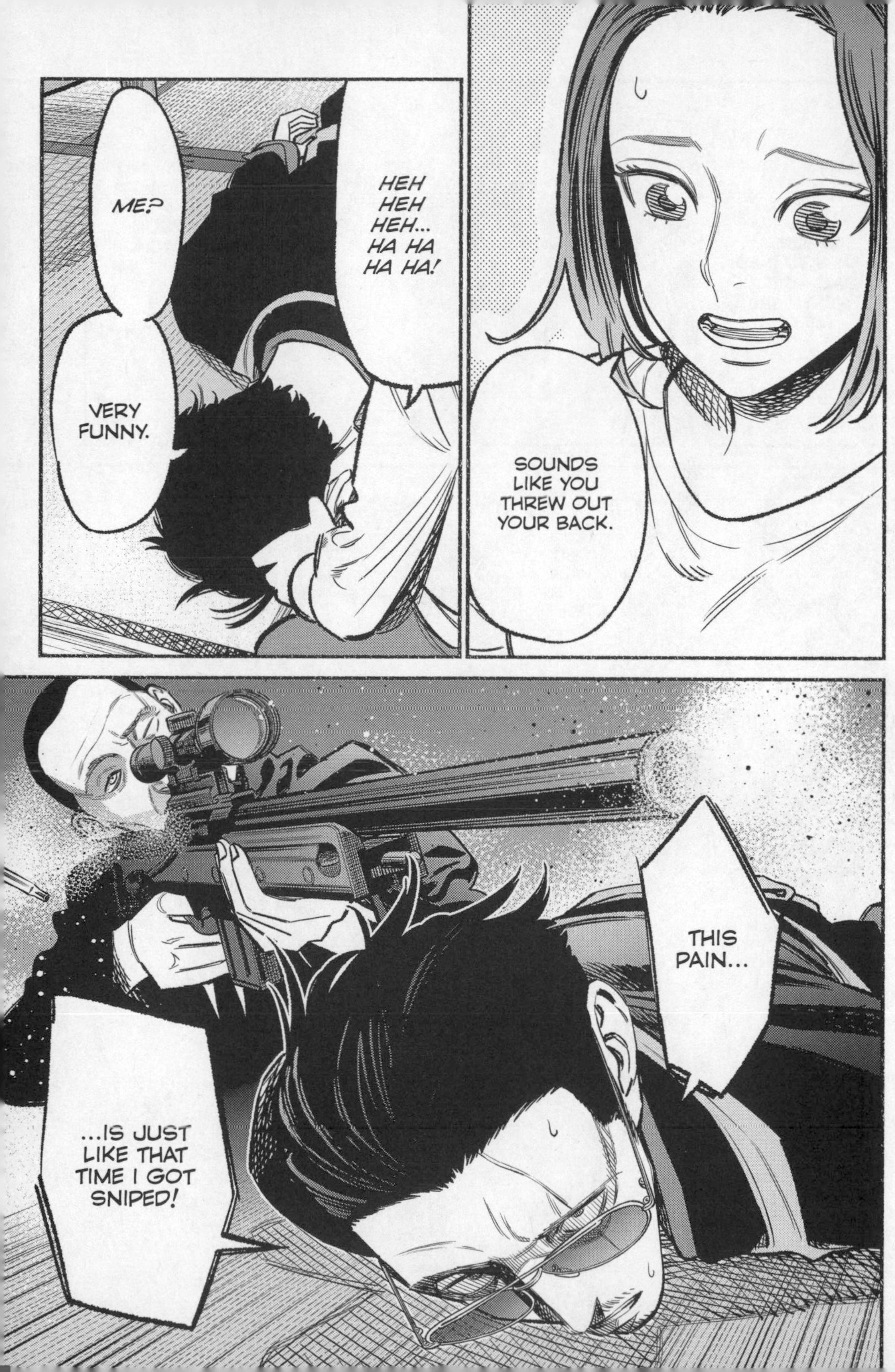
SOUNDS LIKE YOU THREW OUT YOUR BACK.
HEH HEH HEH... HA HA HA HA!
ME?
VERY FUNNY.
THIS PAIN...
...IS JUST LIKE THAT TIME I GOT SNIPED!

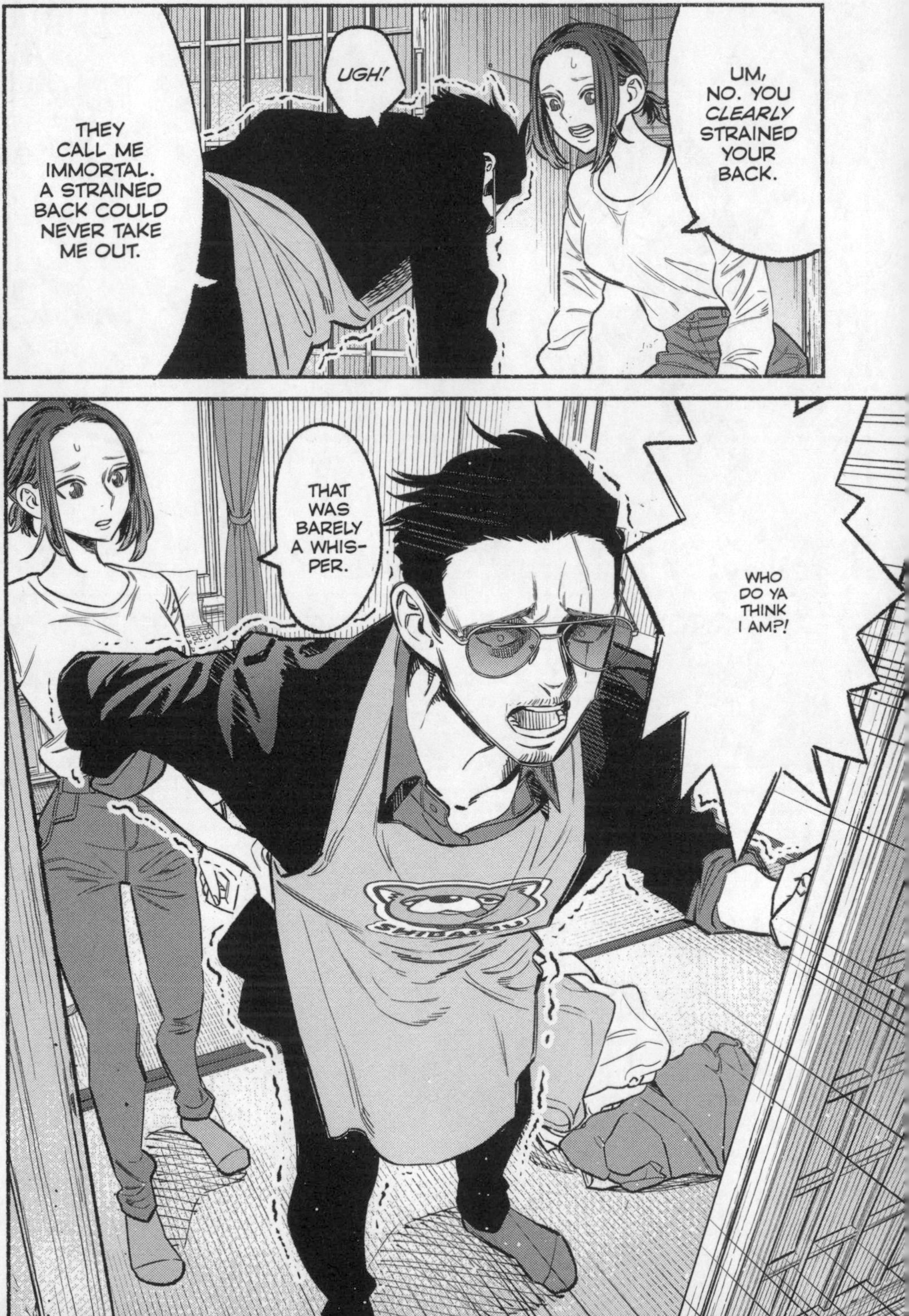
UM, NO. YOU *CLEARLY* STRAINED YOUR BACK.
UGH!
THEY CALL ME IMMORTAL. A STRAINED BACK COULD NEVER TAKE ME OUT.
WHO DO YA THINK I AM?!
THAT WAS BARELY A WHIS-PER.
SHIBAINU

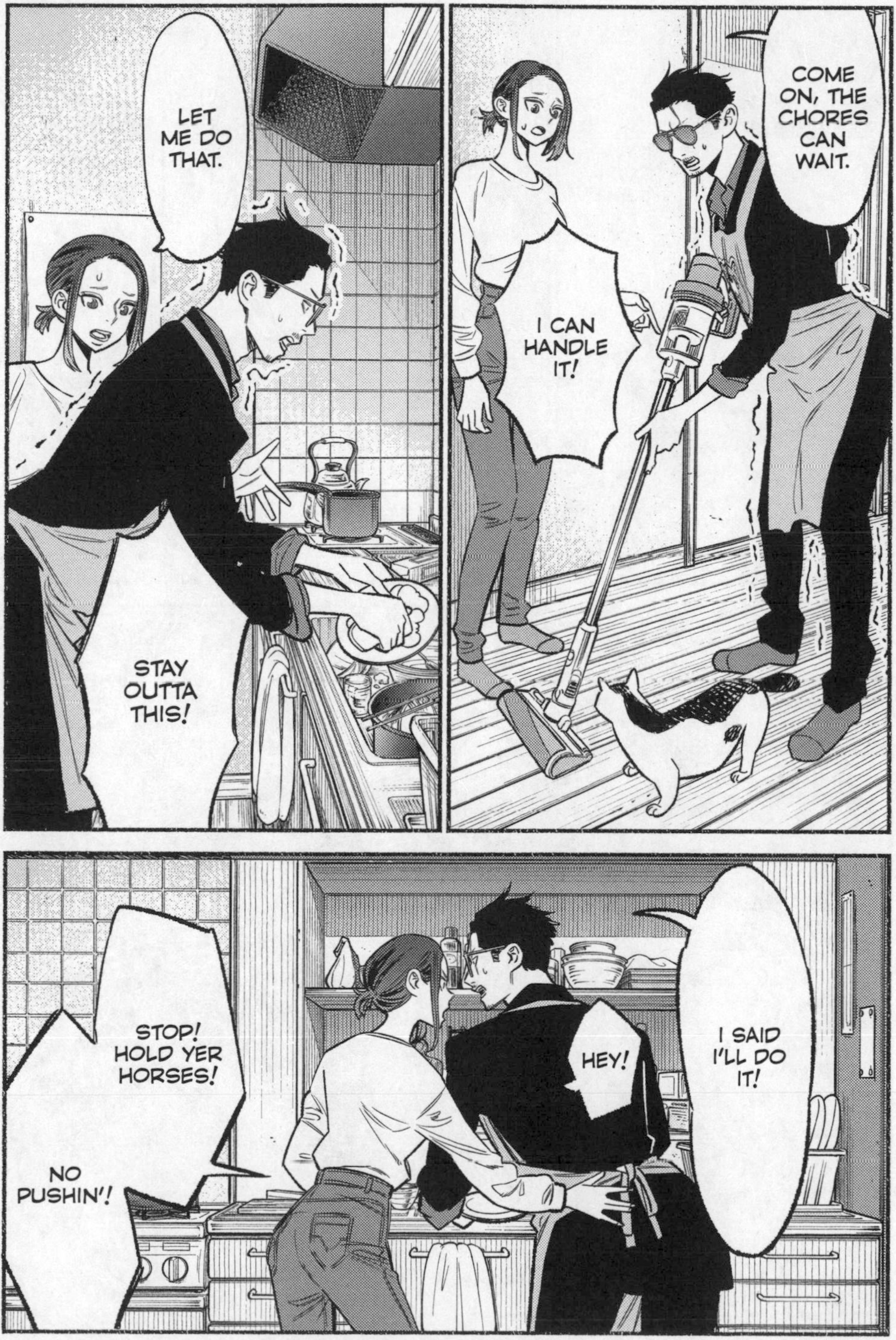
COME ON, THE CHORES CAN WAIT.
I CAN HANDLE IT!
LET ME DO THAT.
STAY OUTTA THIS!
I SAID I'LL DO IT!
HEY!
STOP! HOLD YER HORSES!
NO PUSHIN'!

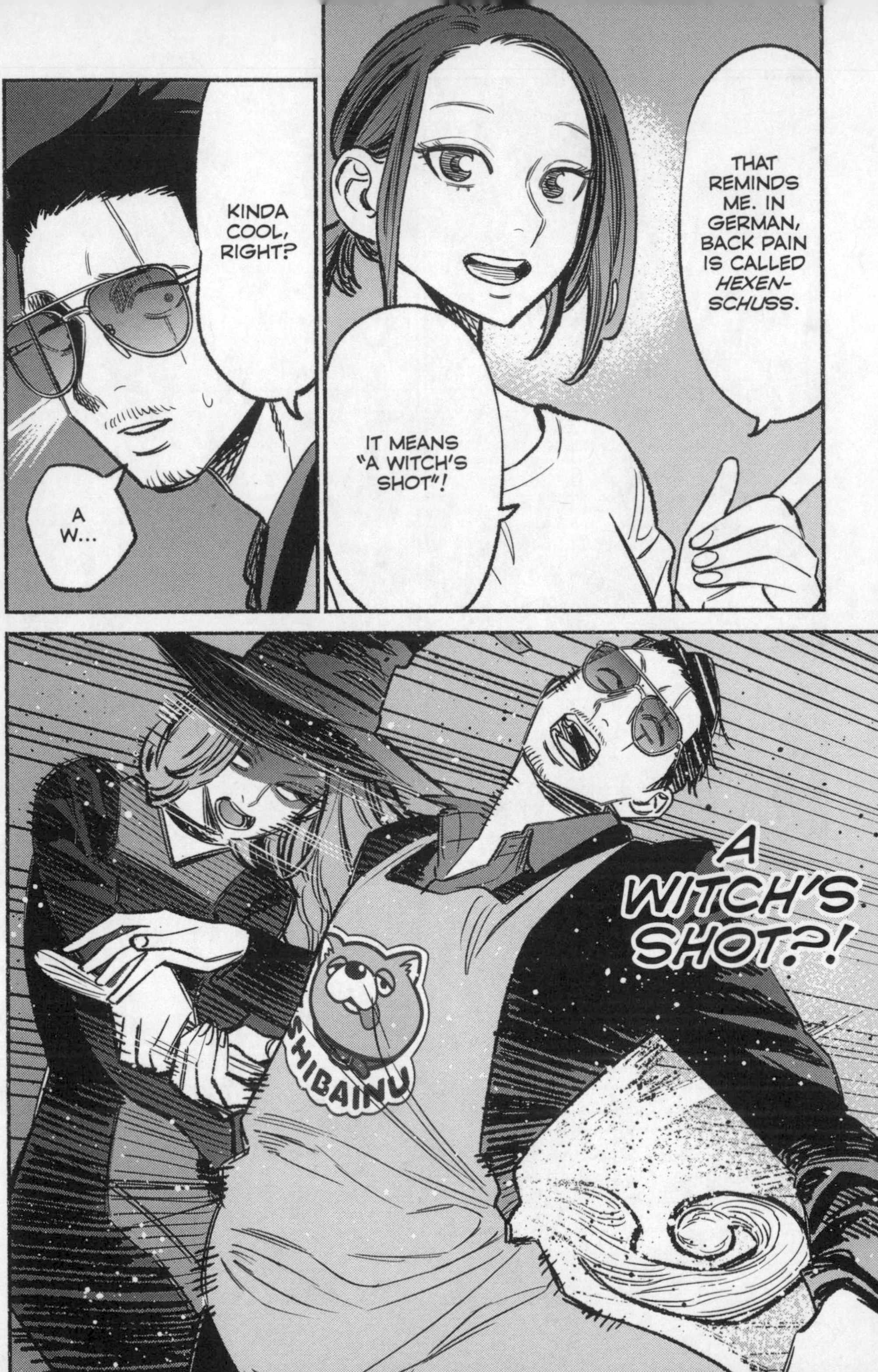
THAT REMINDS ME. IN GERMAN, BACK PAIN IS CALLED *HEXEN-SCHUSS*.
IT MEANS "A WITCH'S SHOT"!
KINDA COOL, RIGHT?
A W...
A WITCH'S SHOT?!
SHIBAINU

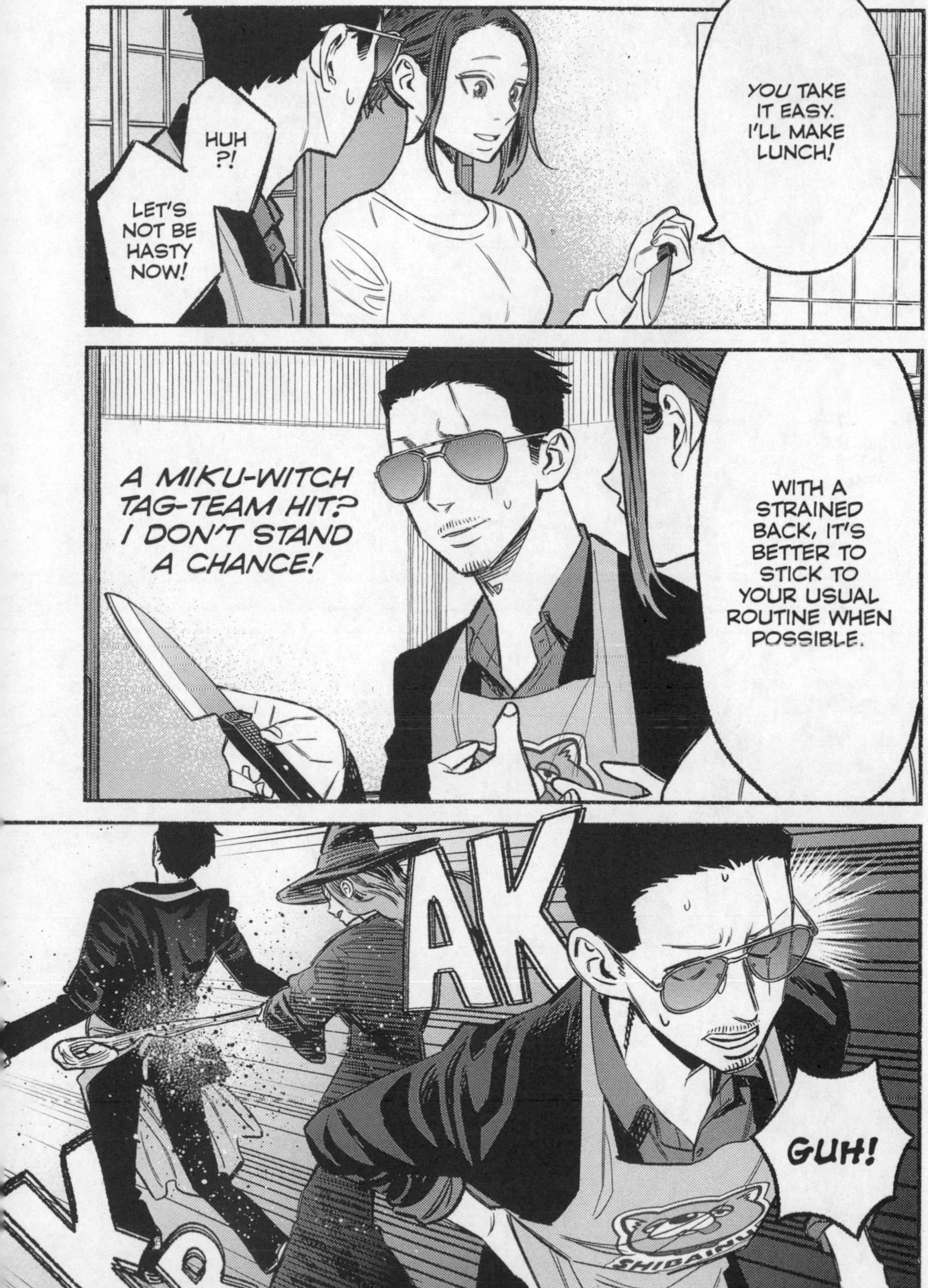
YOU TAKE IT EASY. I'LL MAKE LUNCH!
HUH ?!
LET'S NOT BE HASTY NOW!
WITH A STRAINED BACK, IT'S BETTER TO STICK TO YOUR USUAL ROUTINE WHEN POSSIBLE.
A MIKU-WITCH TAG-TEAM HIT? I DON'T STAND A CHANCE!
GUH!

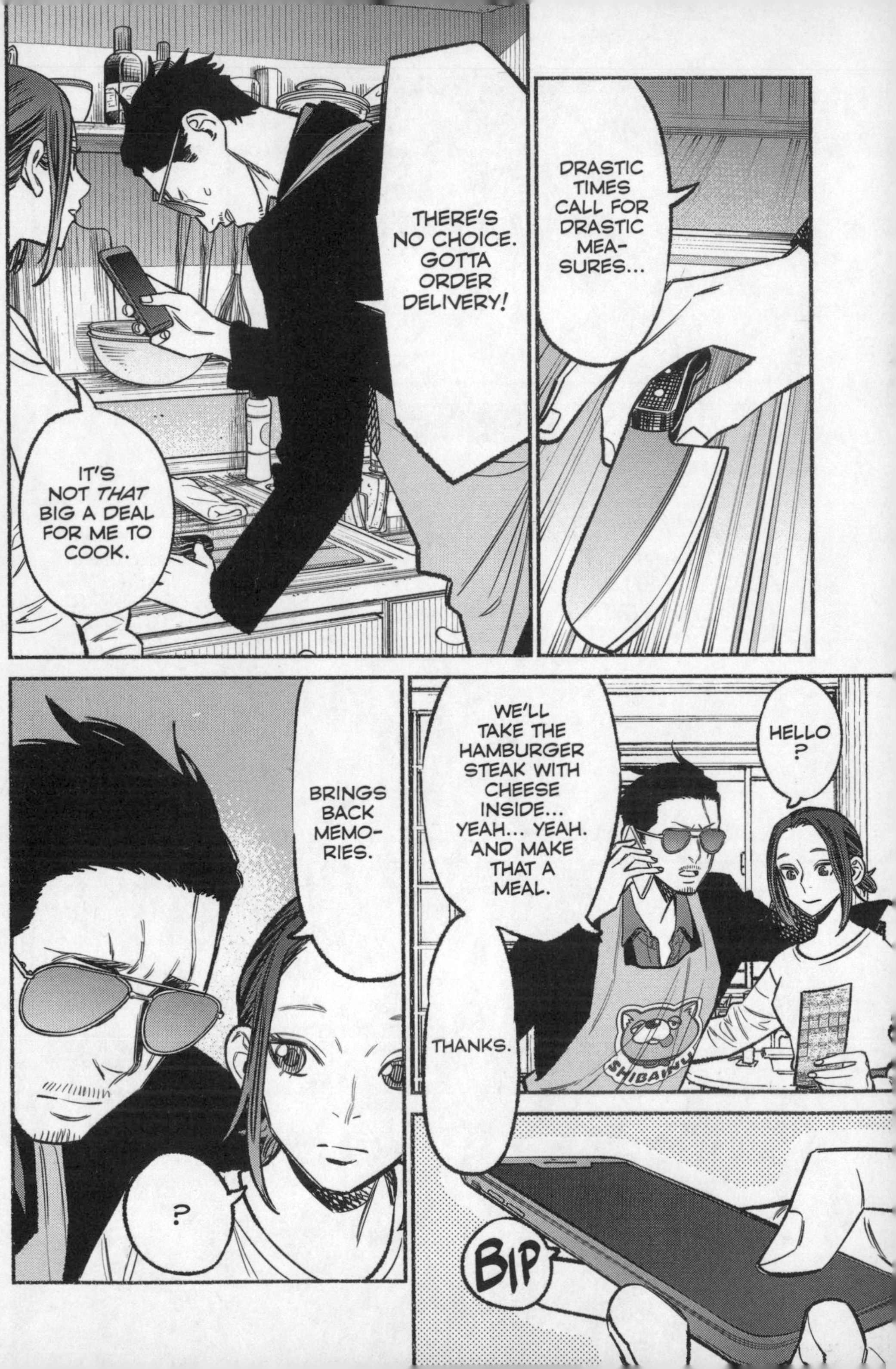
DRASTIC TIMES CALL FOR DRASTIC MEA-SURES...
THERE'S NO CHOICE. GOTTA ORDER DELIVERY!
IT'S NOT *THAT* BIG A DEAL FOR ME TO COOK.
HELLO?
WE'LL TAKE THE HAMBURGER STEAK WITH CHEESE INSIDE... YEAH... YEAH. AND MAKE THAT A MEAL.
THANKS.
SHIBAINU
BIP
BRINGS BACK MEMO-RIES.
?

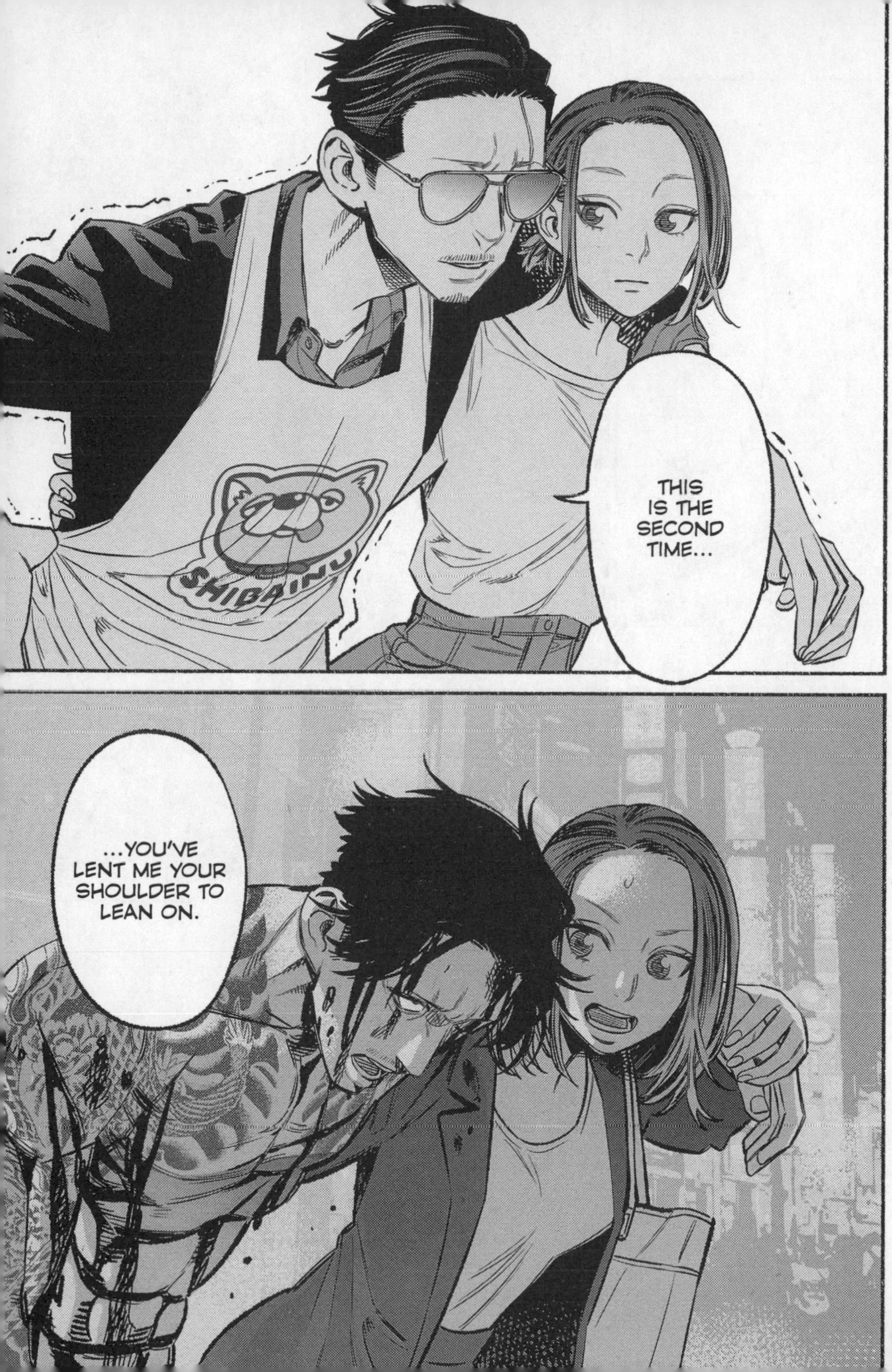
THIS IS THE SECOND TIME...
...YOU'VE LENT ME YOUR SHOULDER TO LEAN ON.
SHIBAINU

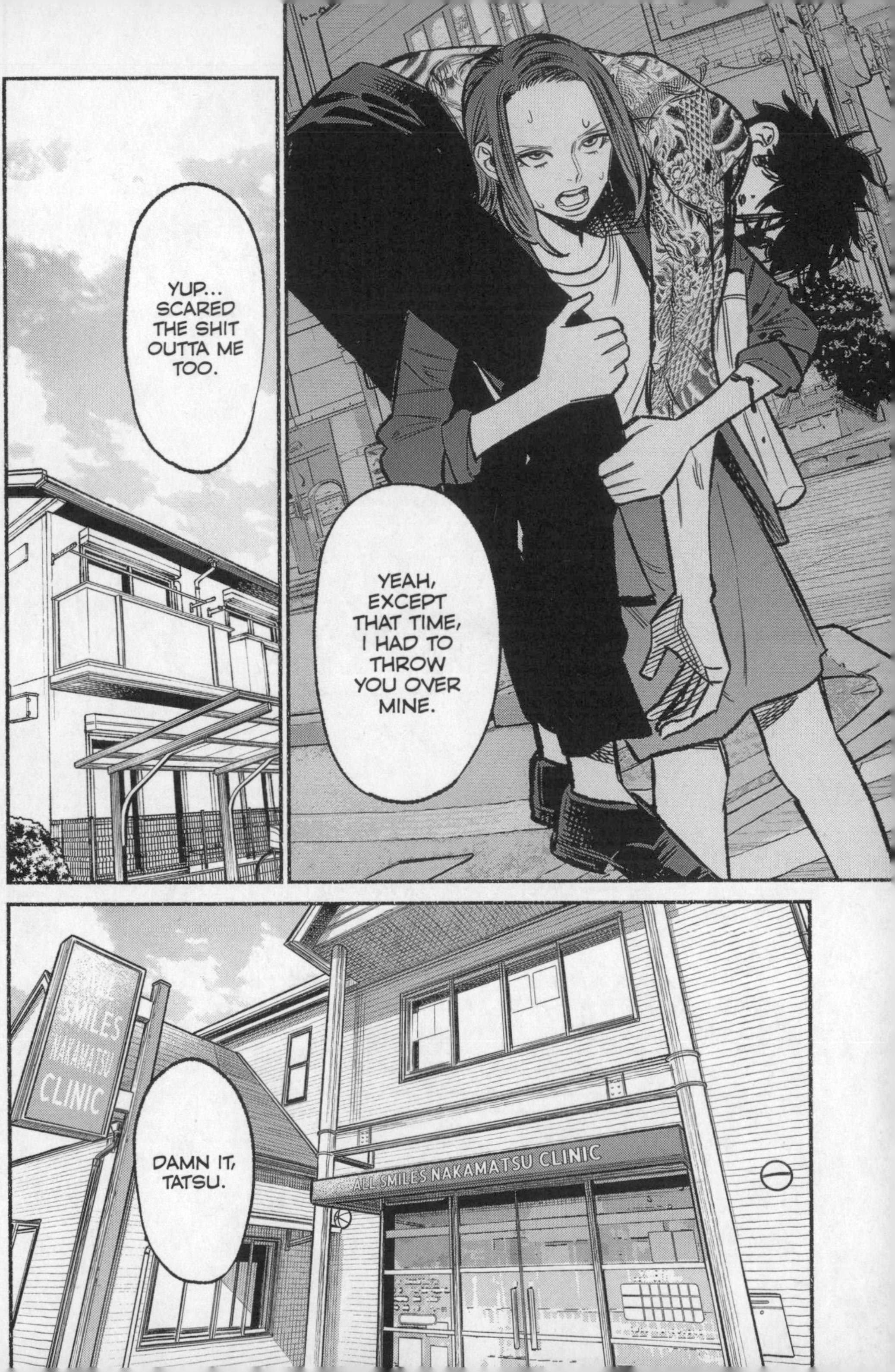
YEAH, EXCEPT THAT TIME, I HAD TO THROW YOU OVER MINE.
YUP... SCARED THE SHIT OUTTA ME TOO.
ALL SMILES NAKAMATSU CLINIC
SMILES NAKAMATSU CLINIC
DAMN IT, TATSU.

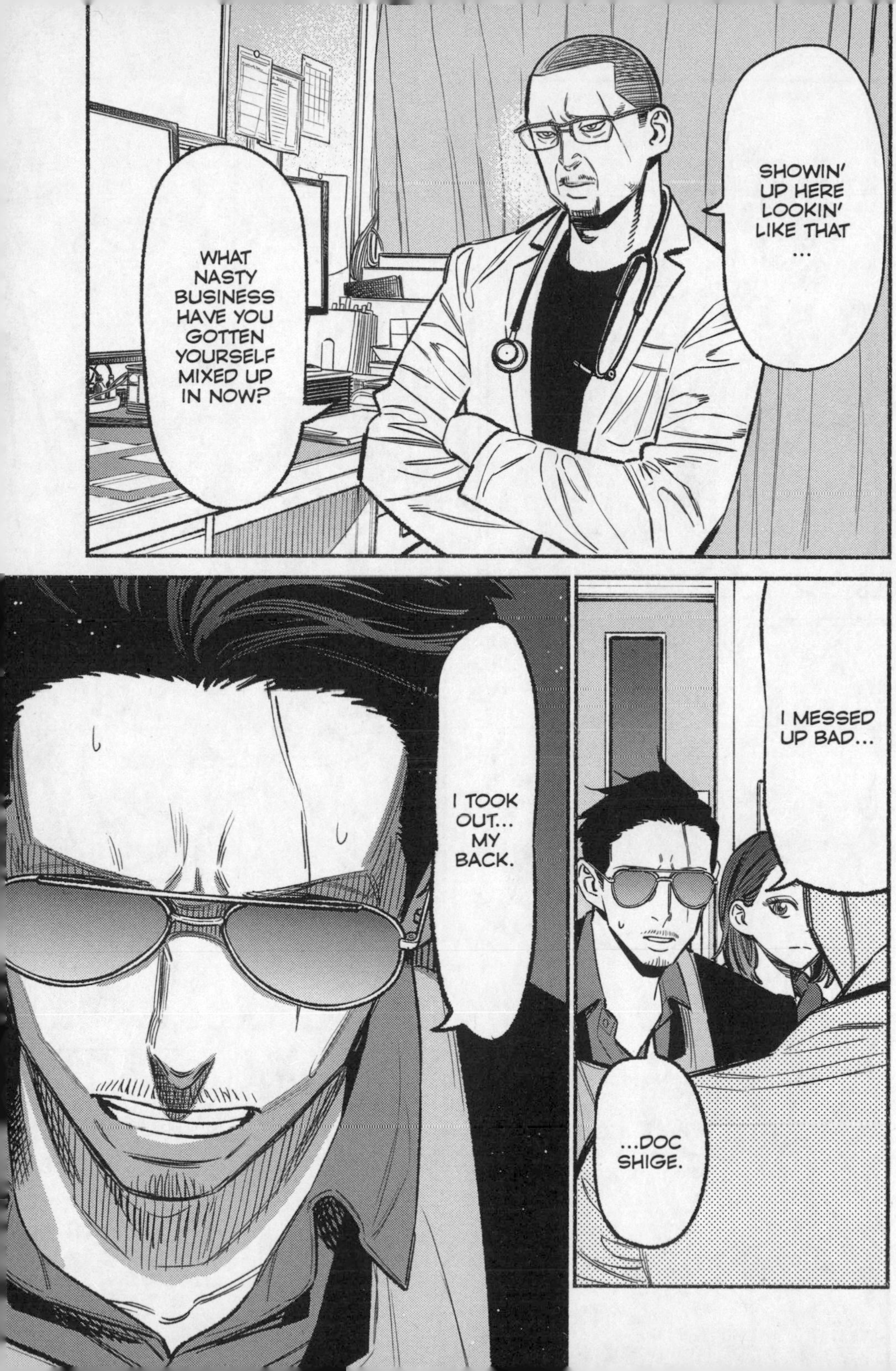
SHOWIN' UP HERE LOOKIN' LIKE THAT ...
WHAT NASTY BUSINESS HAVE YOU GOTTEN YOURSELF MIXED UP IN NOW?
I MESSED UP BAD...
...DOC SHIGE.
I TOOK OUT... MY BACK.

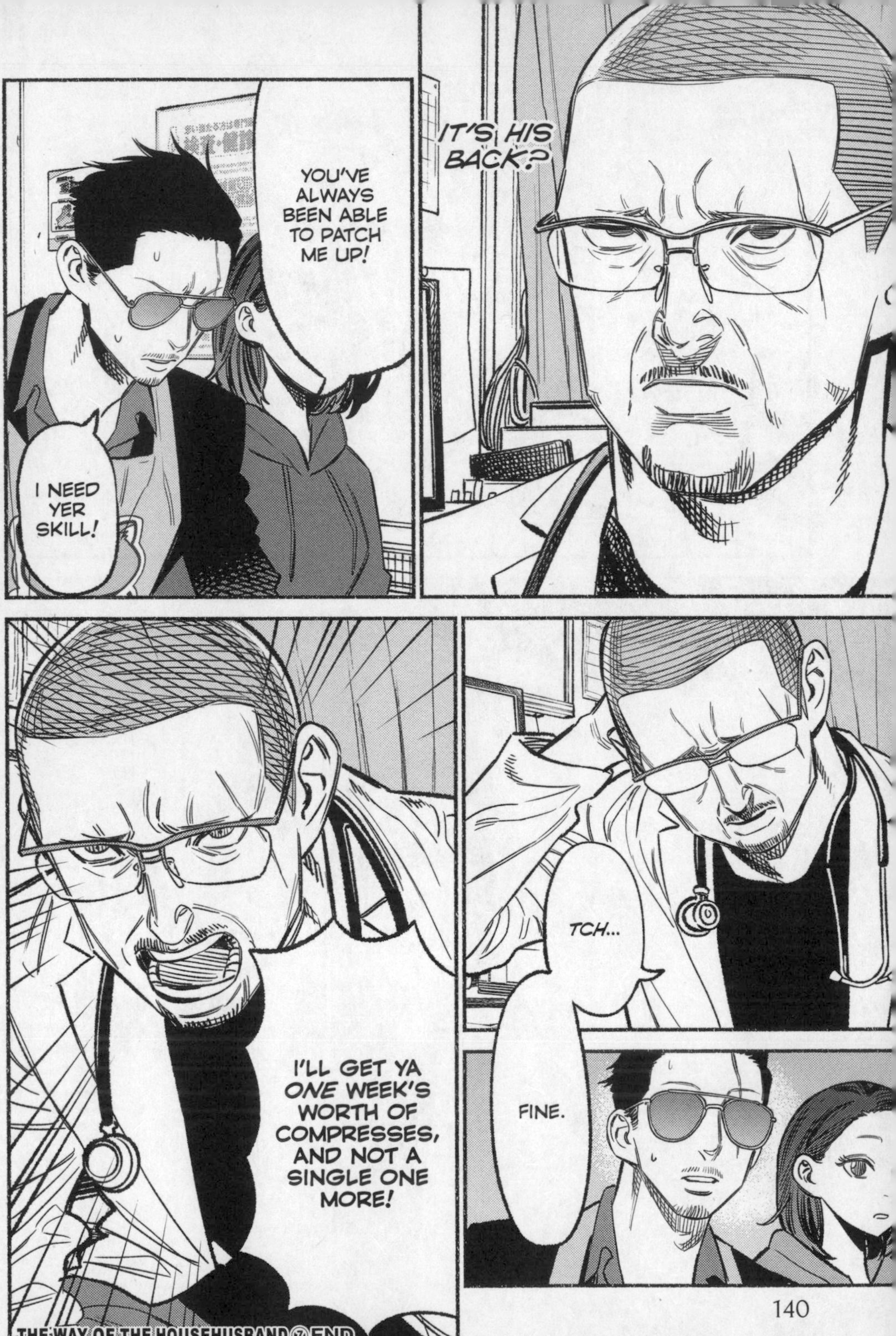
IT'S HIS BACK?
YOU'VE ALWAYS BEEN ABLE TO PATCH ME UP!
I NEED YER SKILL!
TCH...
FINE.
I'LL GET YA ONE WEEK'S WORTH OF COMPRESSES, AND NOT A SINGLE ONE MORE!

THE WAY OF THE HOUSEHUSBAND ⑦ END

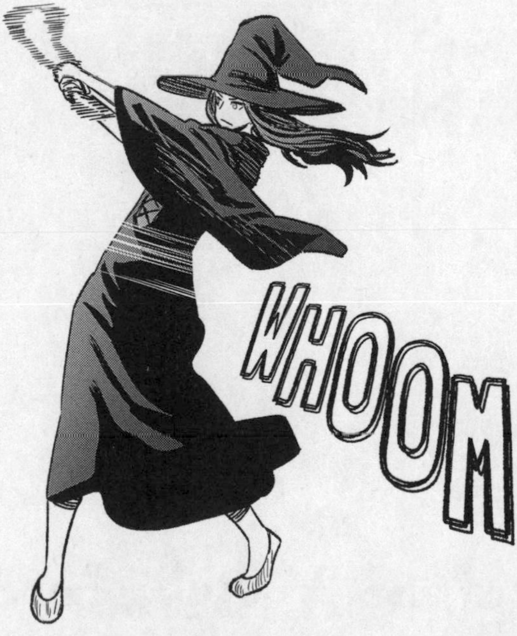
WHOOM

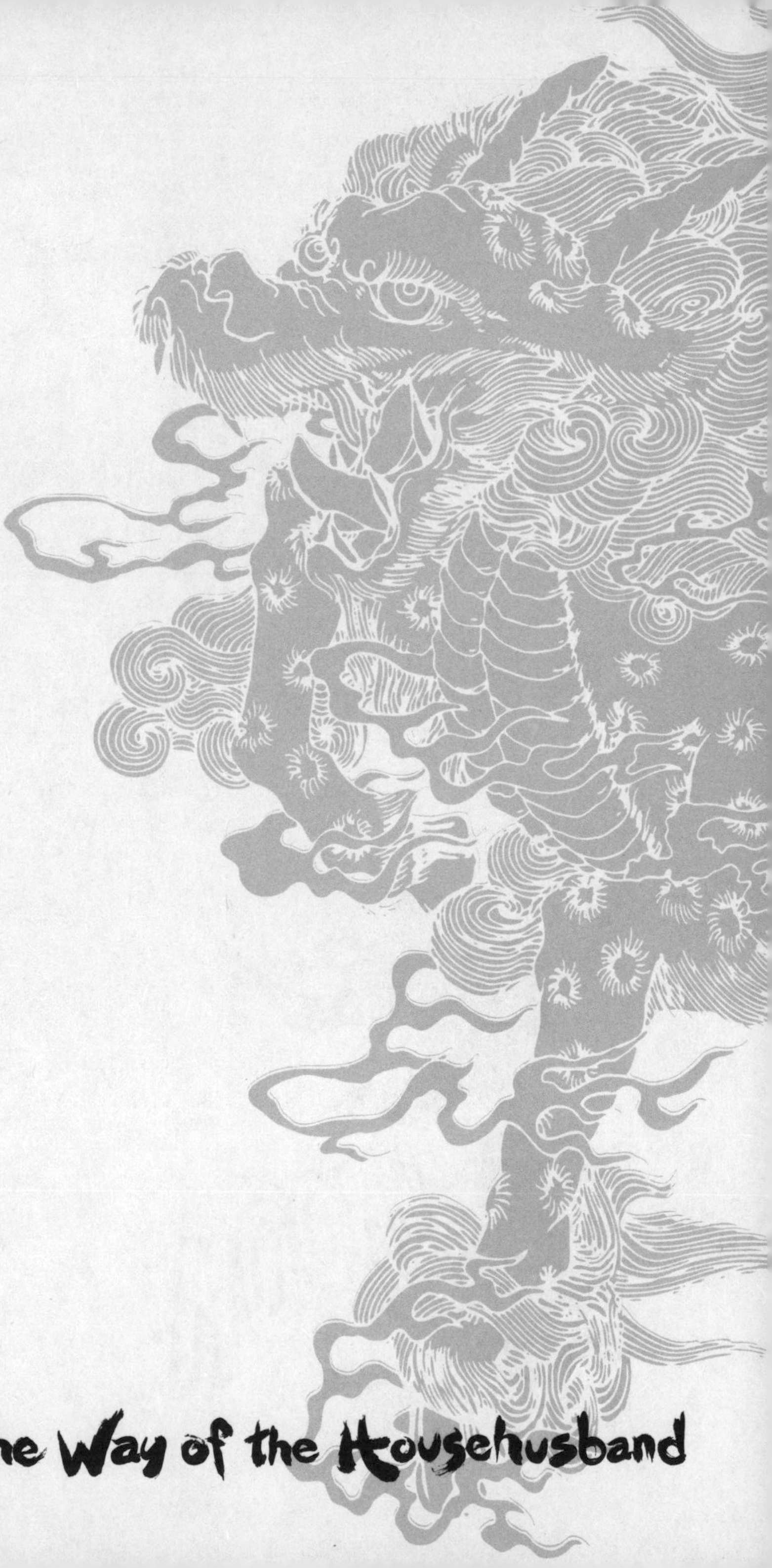

The Way of the Househusband

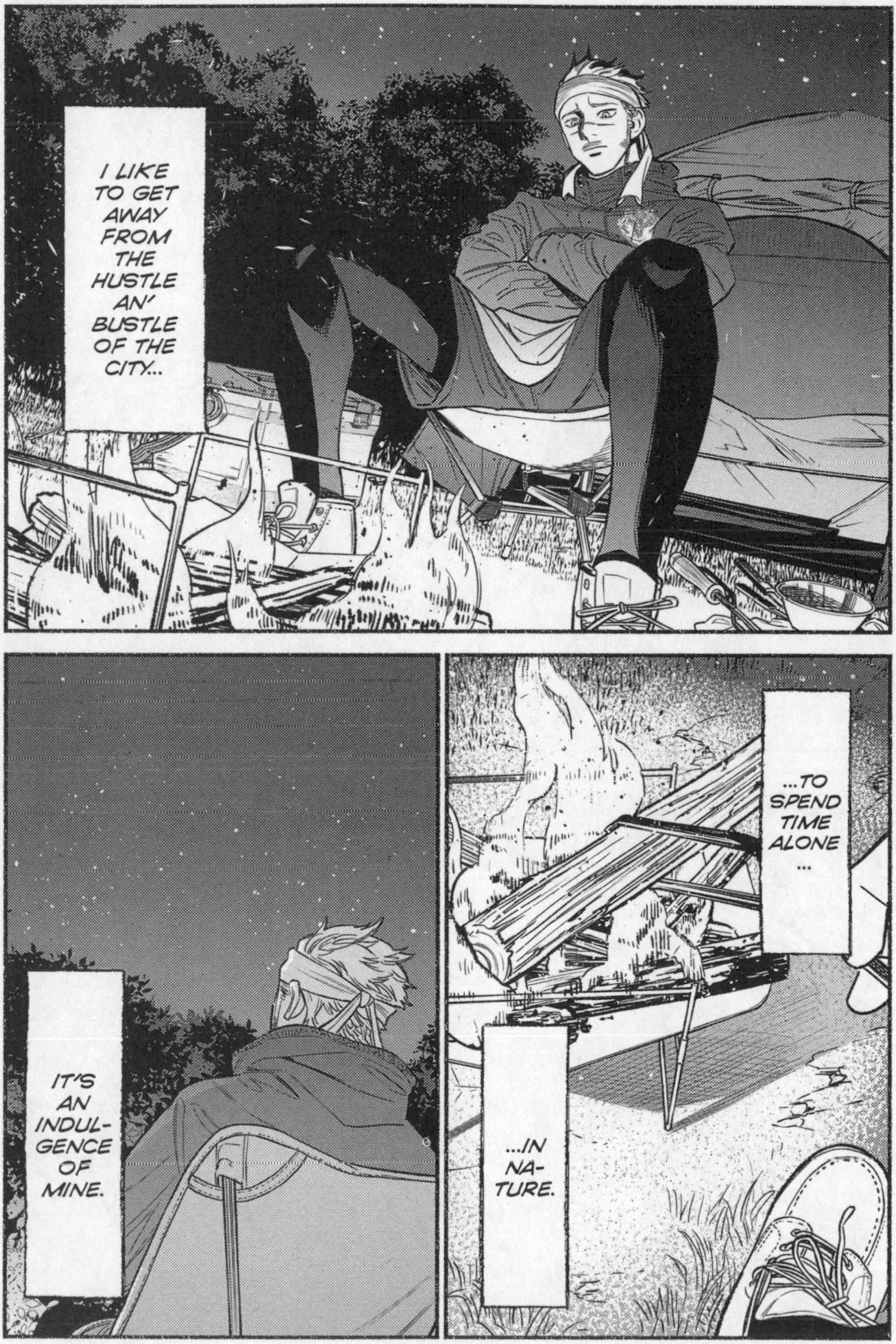
I LIKE TO GET AWAY FROM THE HUSTLE AN' BUSTLE OF THE CITY...
...TO SPEND TIME ALONE ...
...IN NATURE.
IT'S AN INDULGENCE OF MINE.

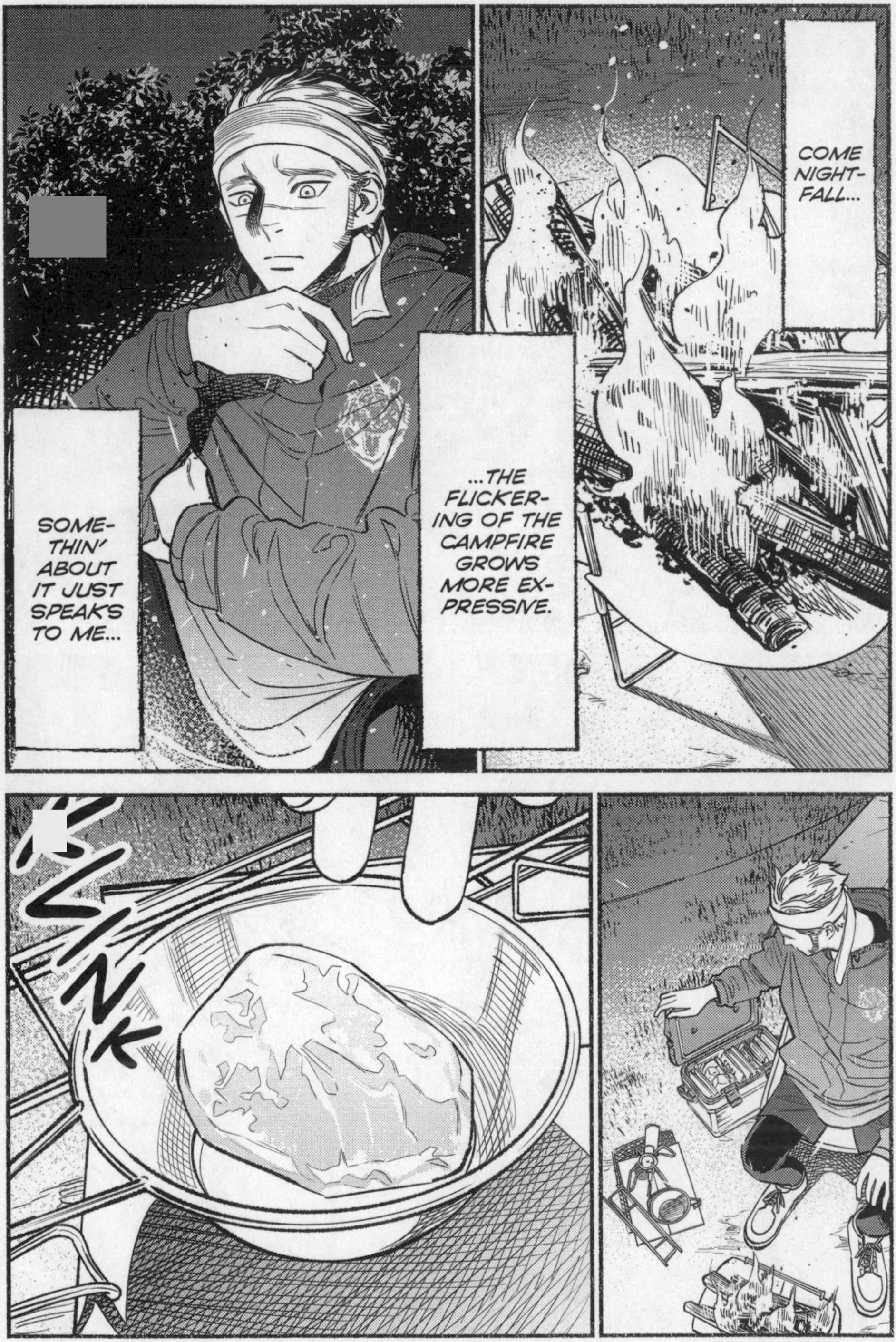
COME NIGHT-FALL...
...THE FLICKER-ING OF THE CAMPFIRE GROWS MORE EX-PRESSIVE.
SOME-THIN' ABOUT IT JUST SPEAKS TO ME...
KLINK

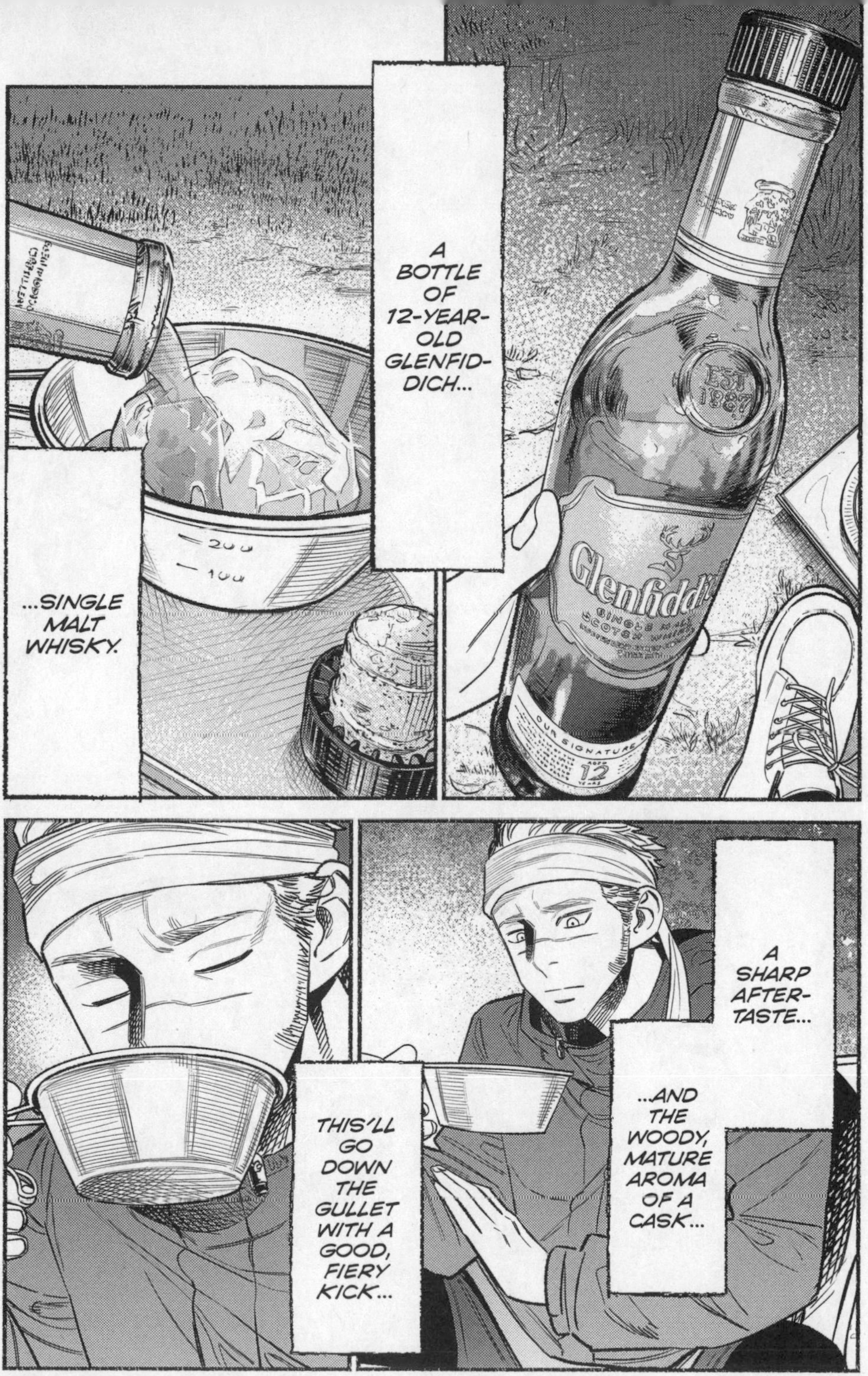
A BOTTLE OF 12-YEAR-OLD GLENFID-DICH...
EST 1887
SINGLE MALT SCOTCH WHISKY
OUR SIGNATURE
12
...SINGLE MALT WHISKY.
A SHARP AFTER-TASTE...
...AND THE WOODY, MATURE AROMA OF A CASK...
THIS'LL GO DOWN THE GULLET WITH A GOOD, FIERY KICK...

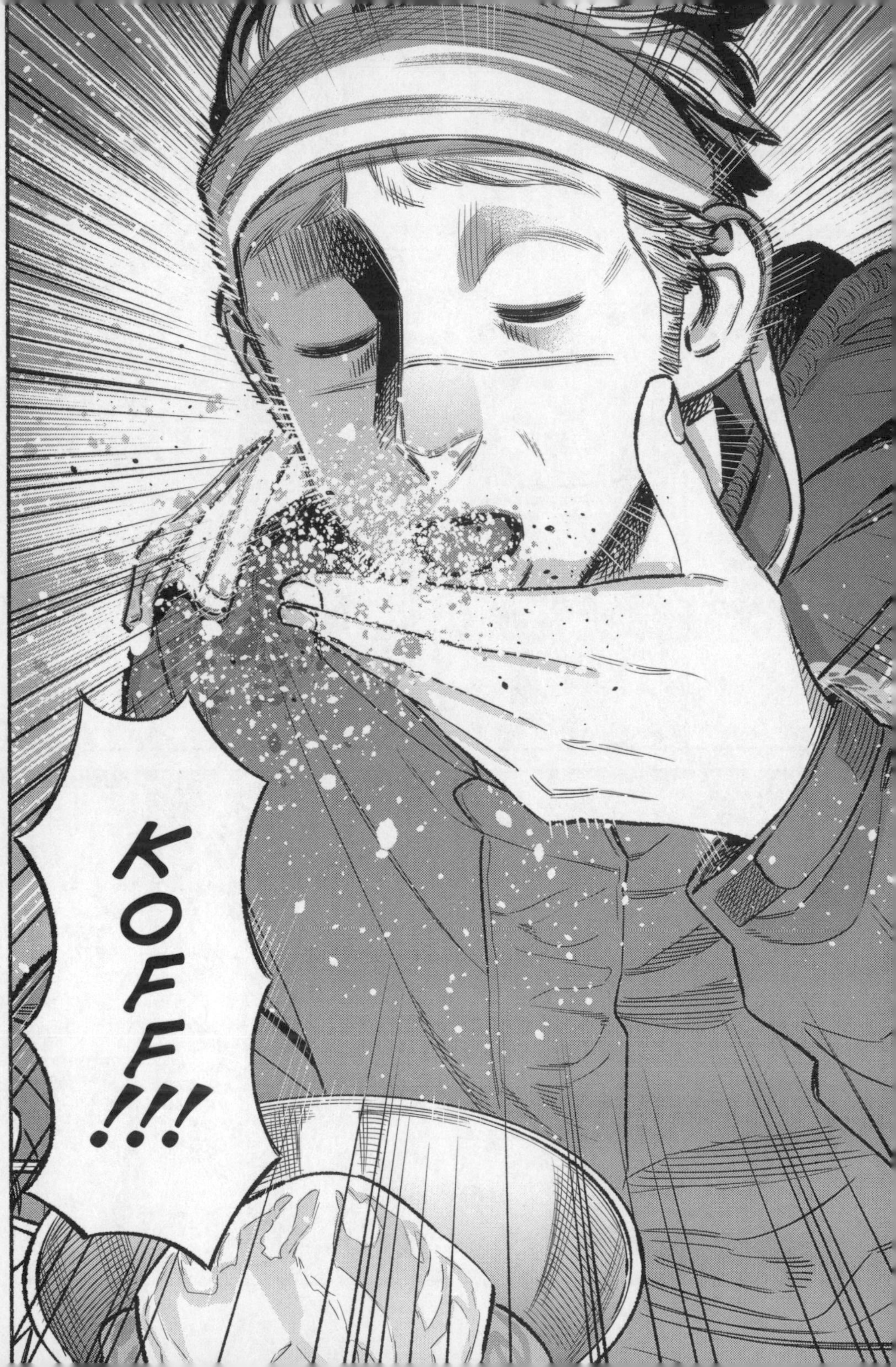
KOFF!!!

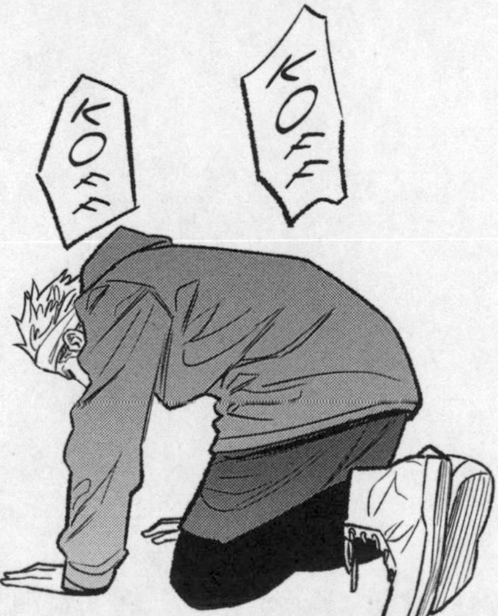
KOFF
KOFF

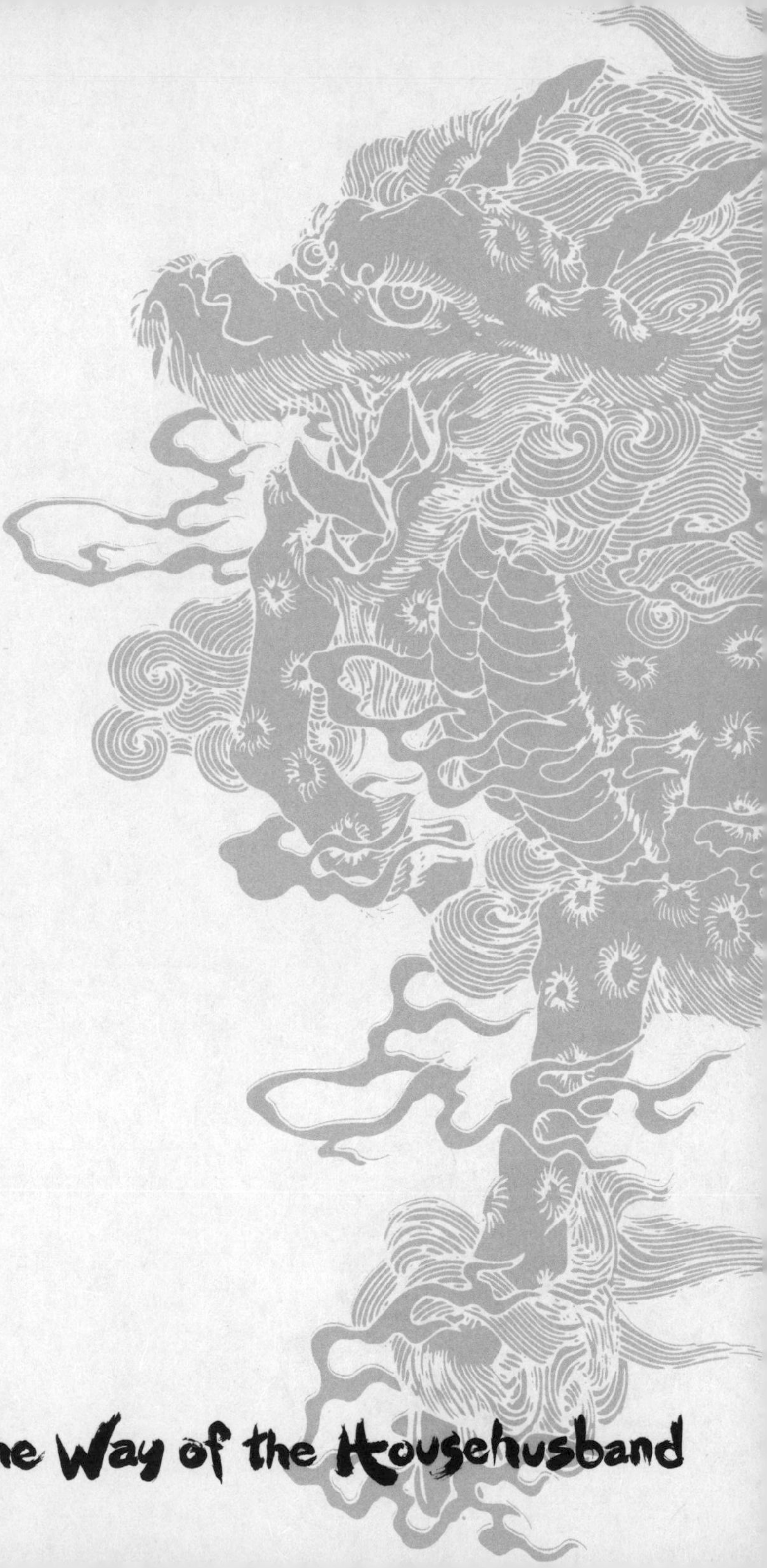

The Way of the Househusband

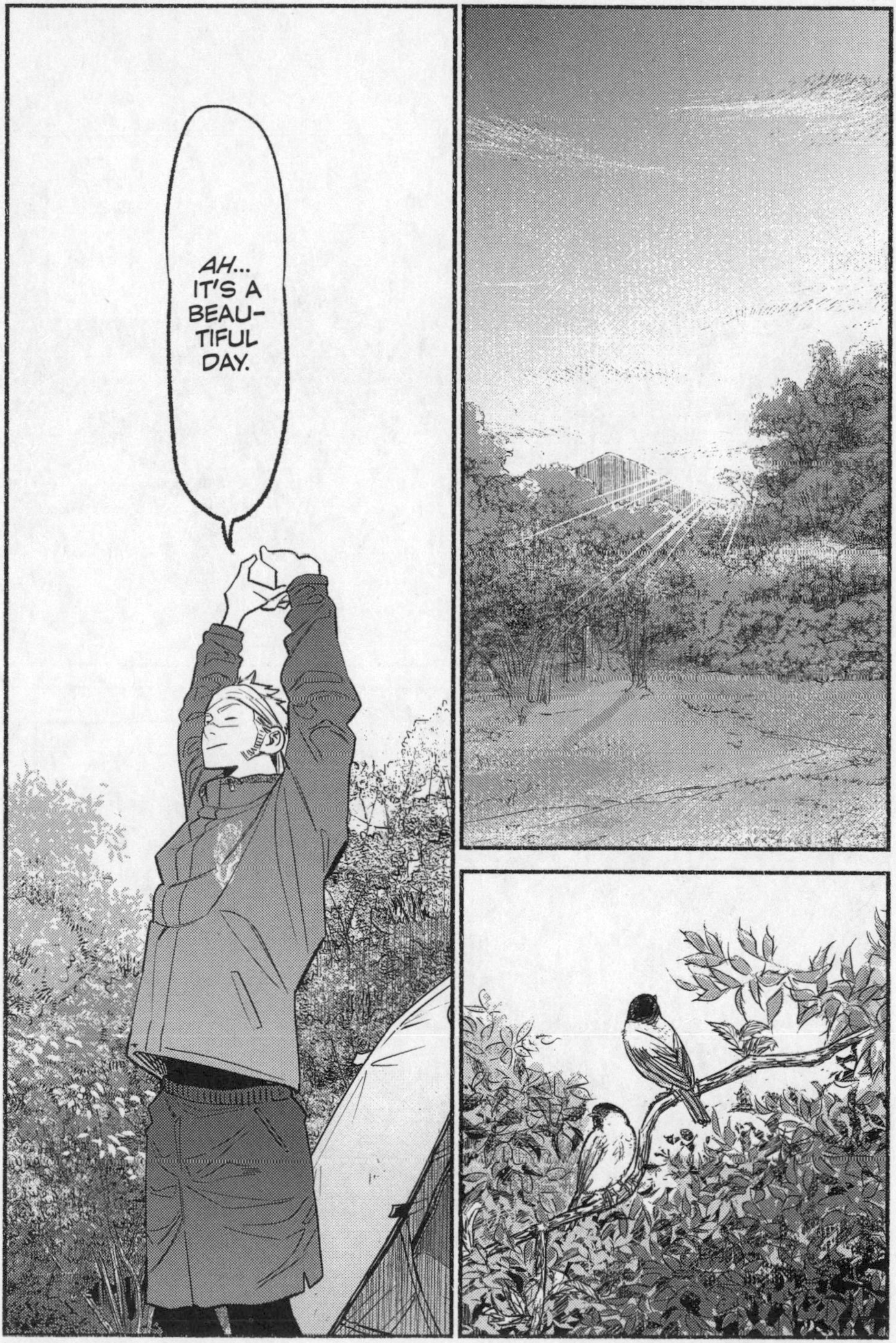
AH... IT'S A BEAU-TIFUL DAY.

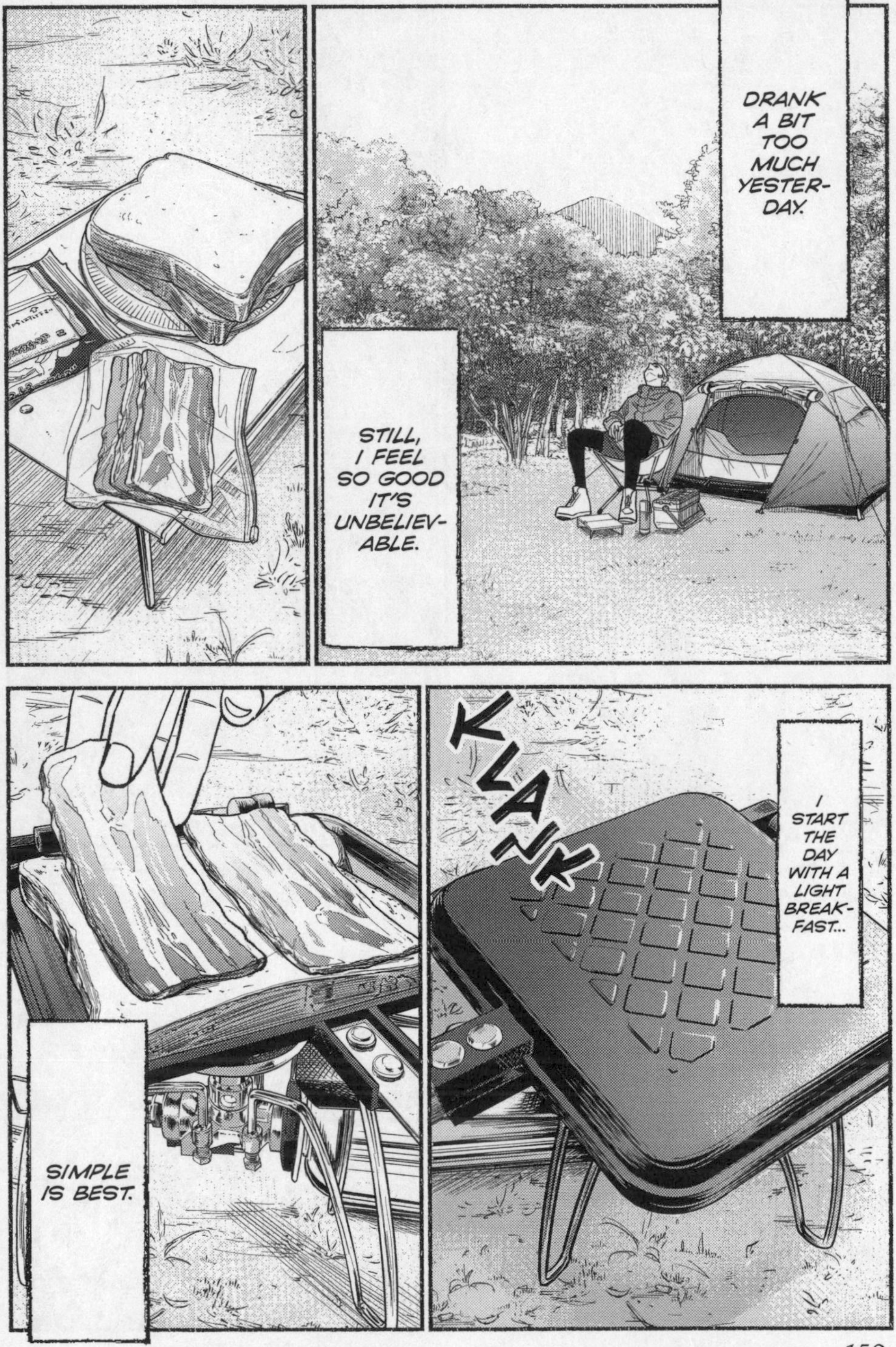
DRANK A BIT TOO MUCH YESTER-DAY.
STILL, I FEEL SO GOOD IT'S UNBELIEV-ABLE.
KLANK
I START THE DAY WITH A LIGHT BREAK-FAST...
SIMPLE IS BEST.

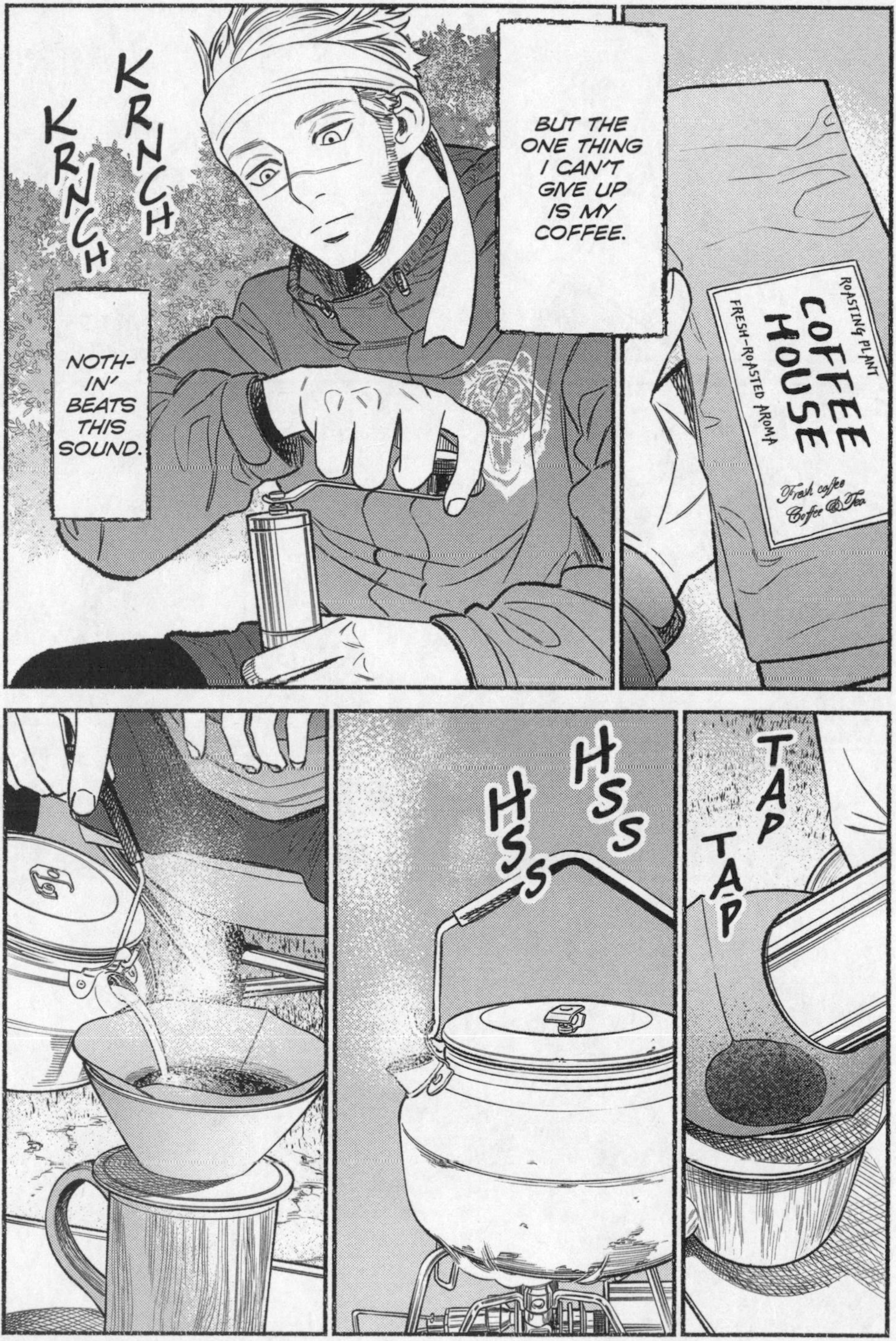
ROASTING PLANT
COFFEE HOUSE
FRESH-ROASTED AROMA
Fresh coffee
Coffee & Tea
BUT THE ONE THING I CAN'T GIVE UP IS MY COFFEE.
KRNCH
KRNCH
NOTH-IN' BEATS THIS SOUND.
TAP
TAP
HSS
HSS

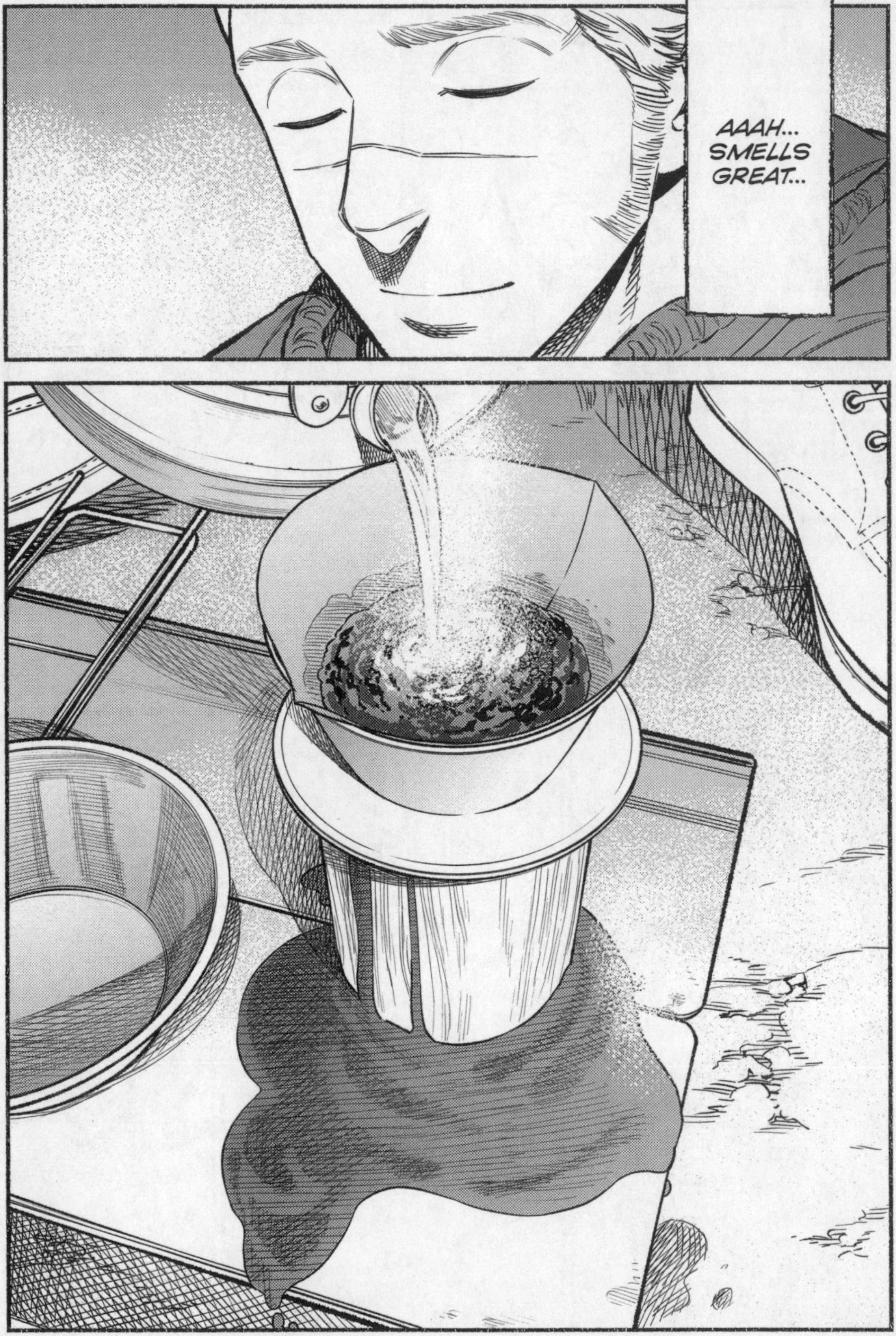
AAAH... SMELLS GREAT...

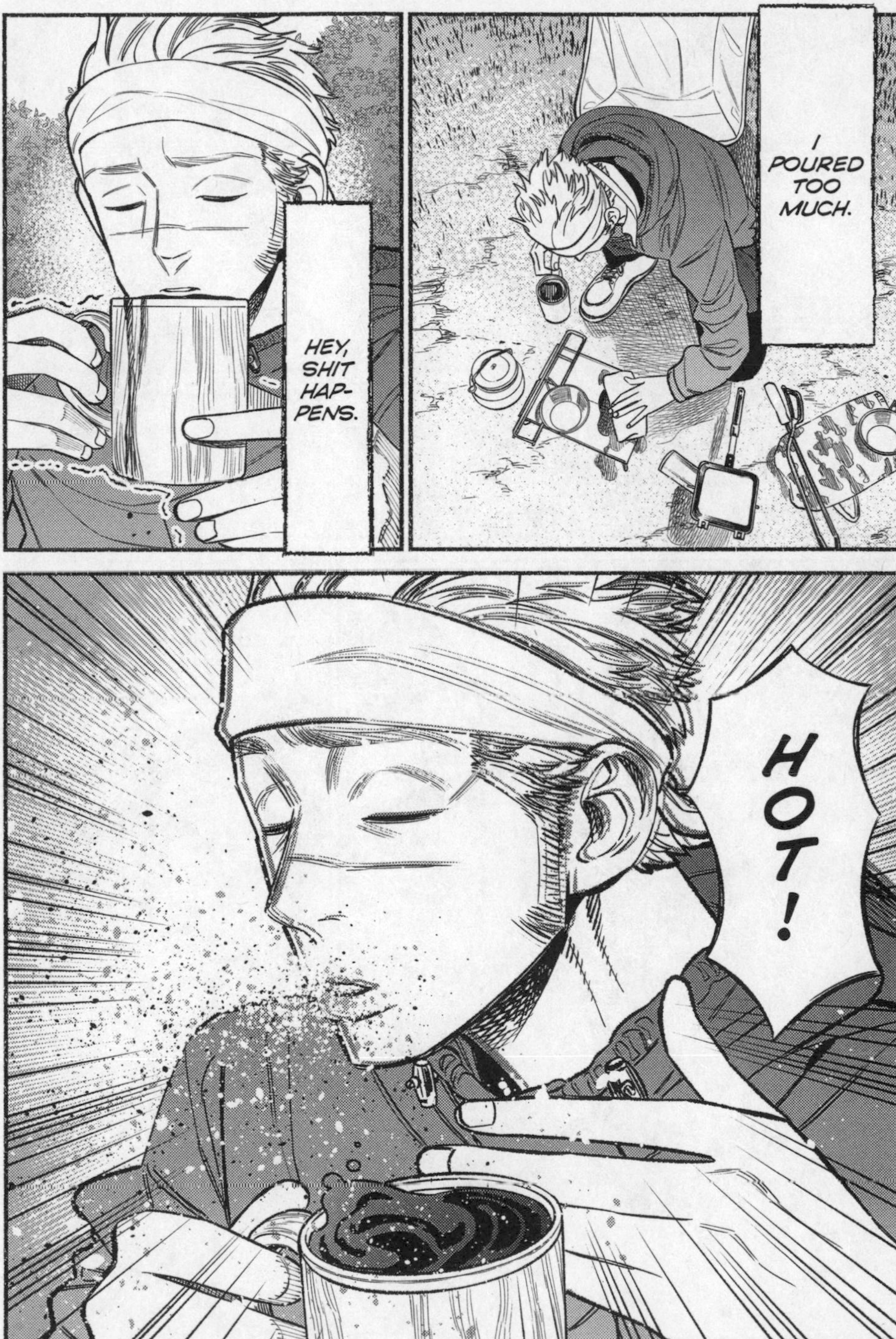
I POURED TOO MUCH.
HEY, SHIT HAP-PENS.
HOT!

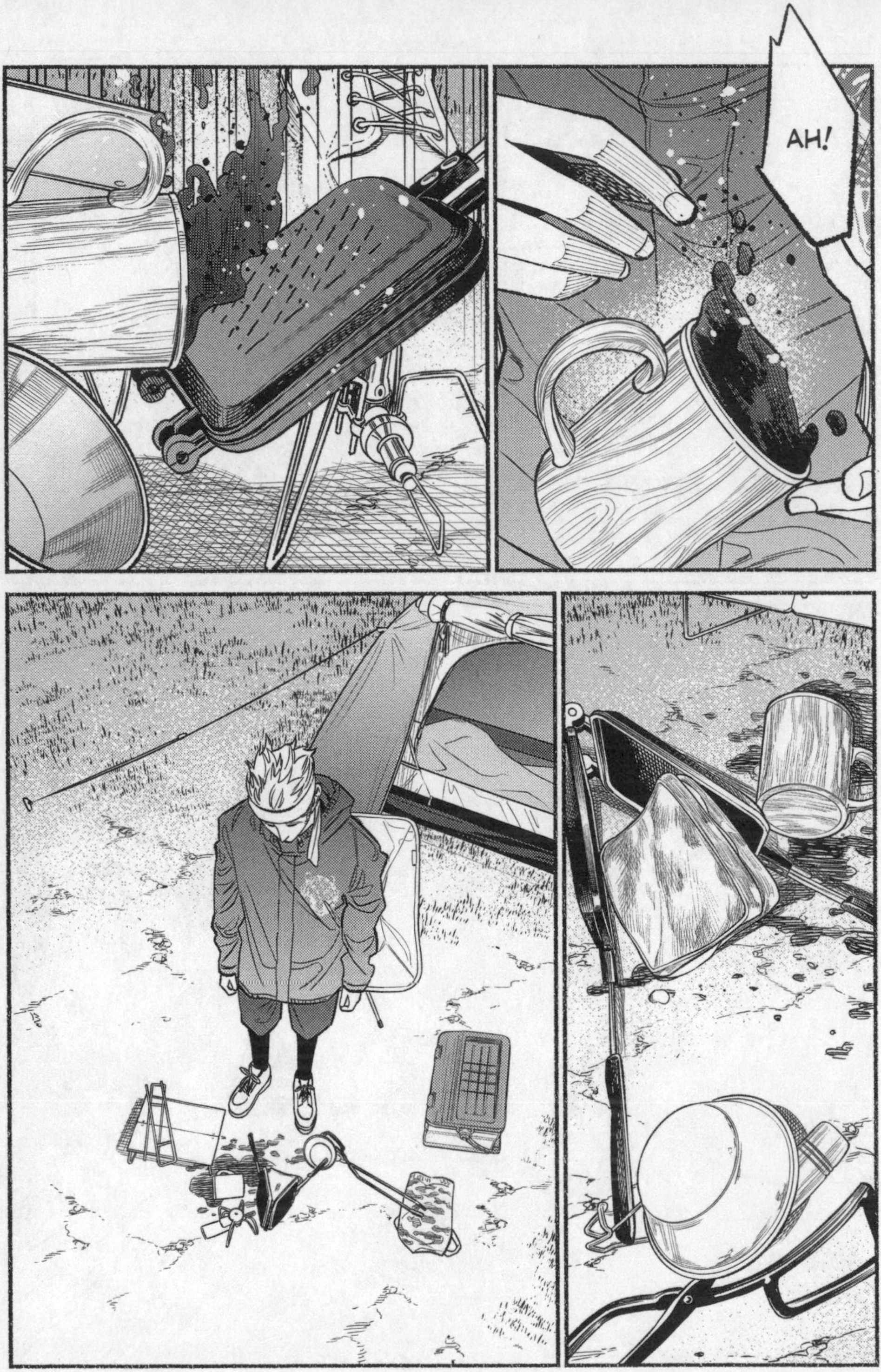
AH!

YOU GOTTA ROLL WITH THE PUNCHES.

THAT'S THE CAMPING WAY...

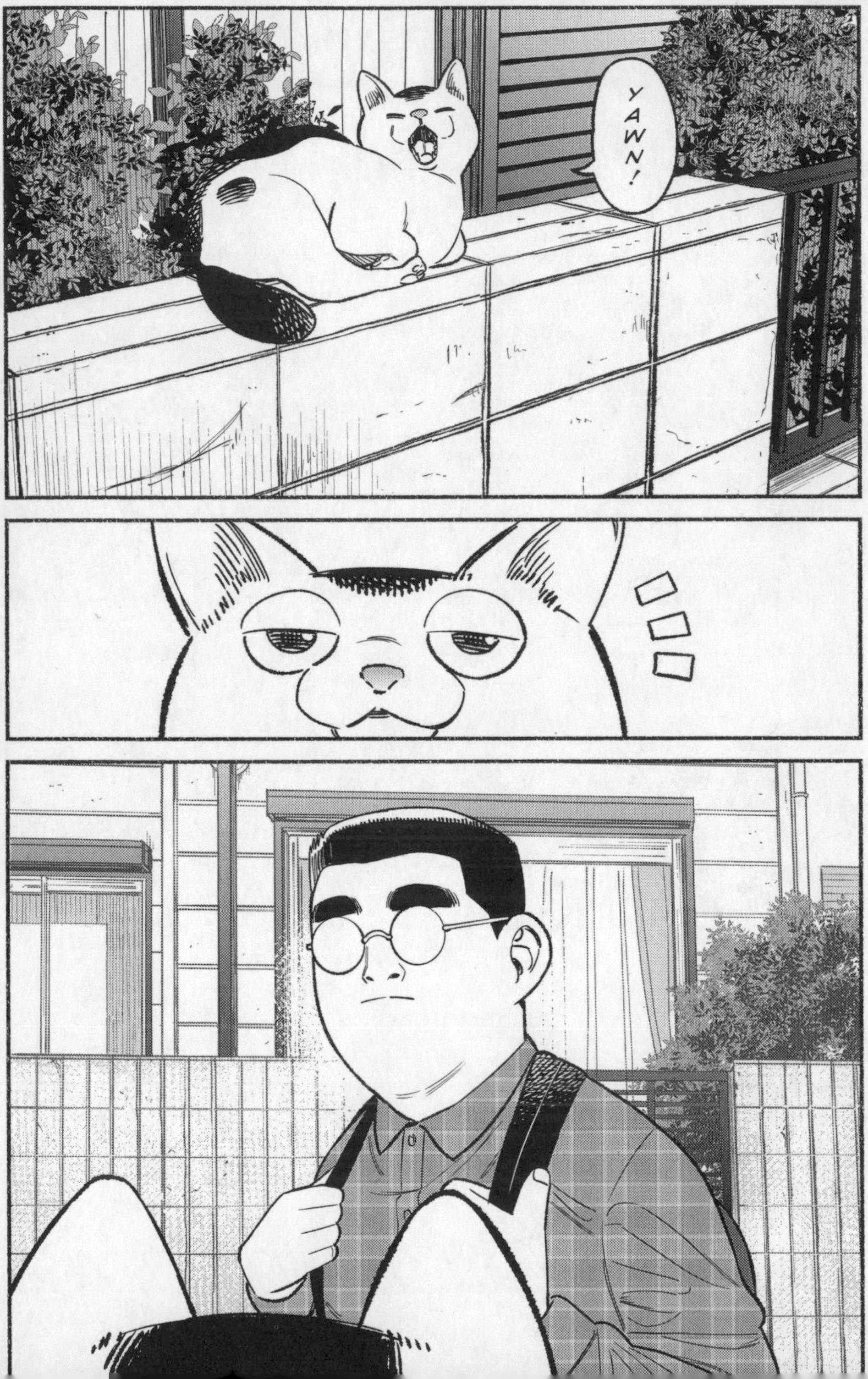
YAWN!

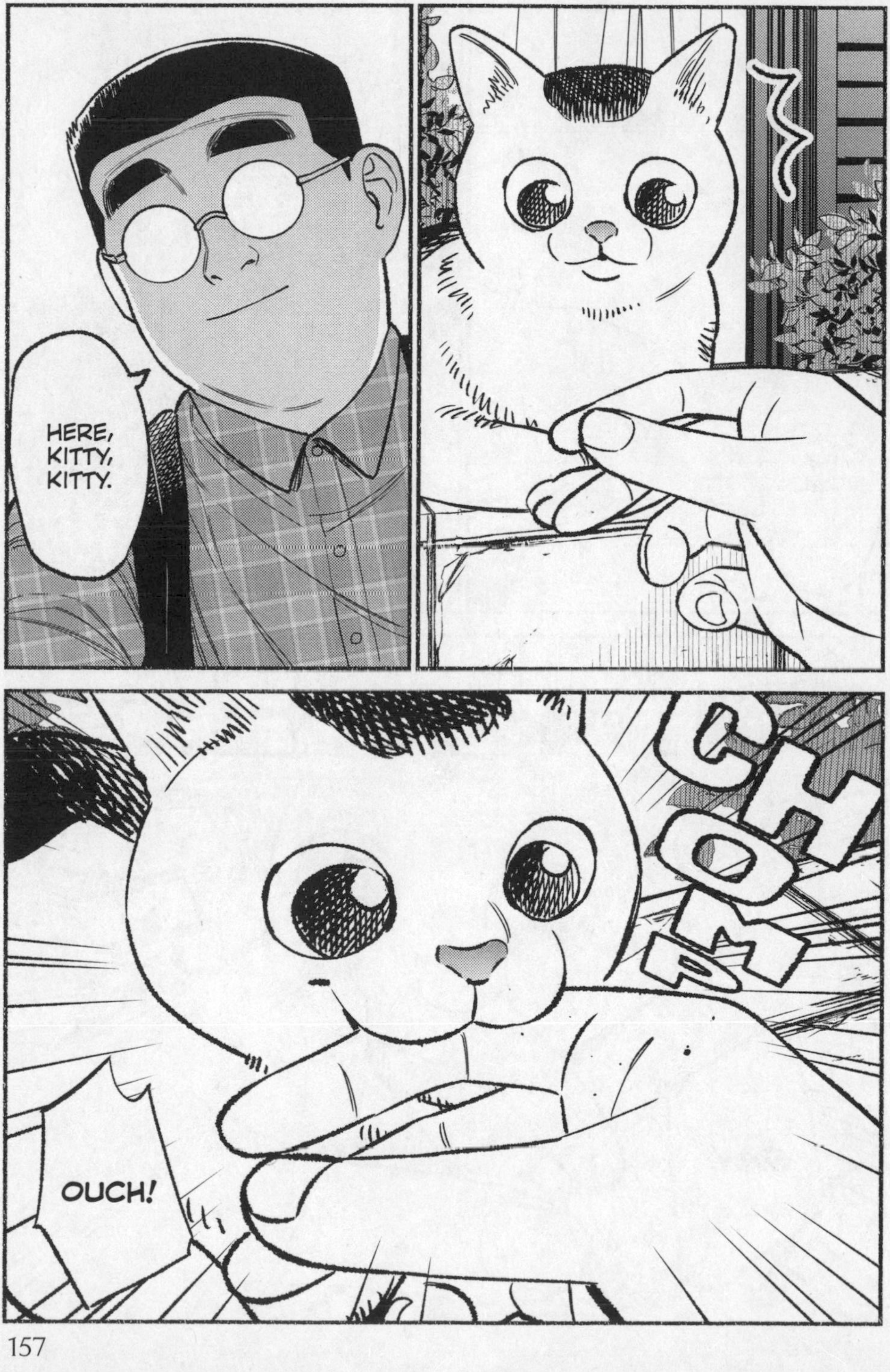
HERE, KITTY, KITTY.
CHOMP
OUCH!

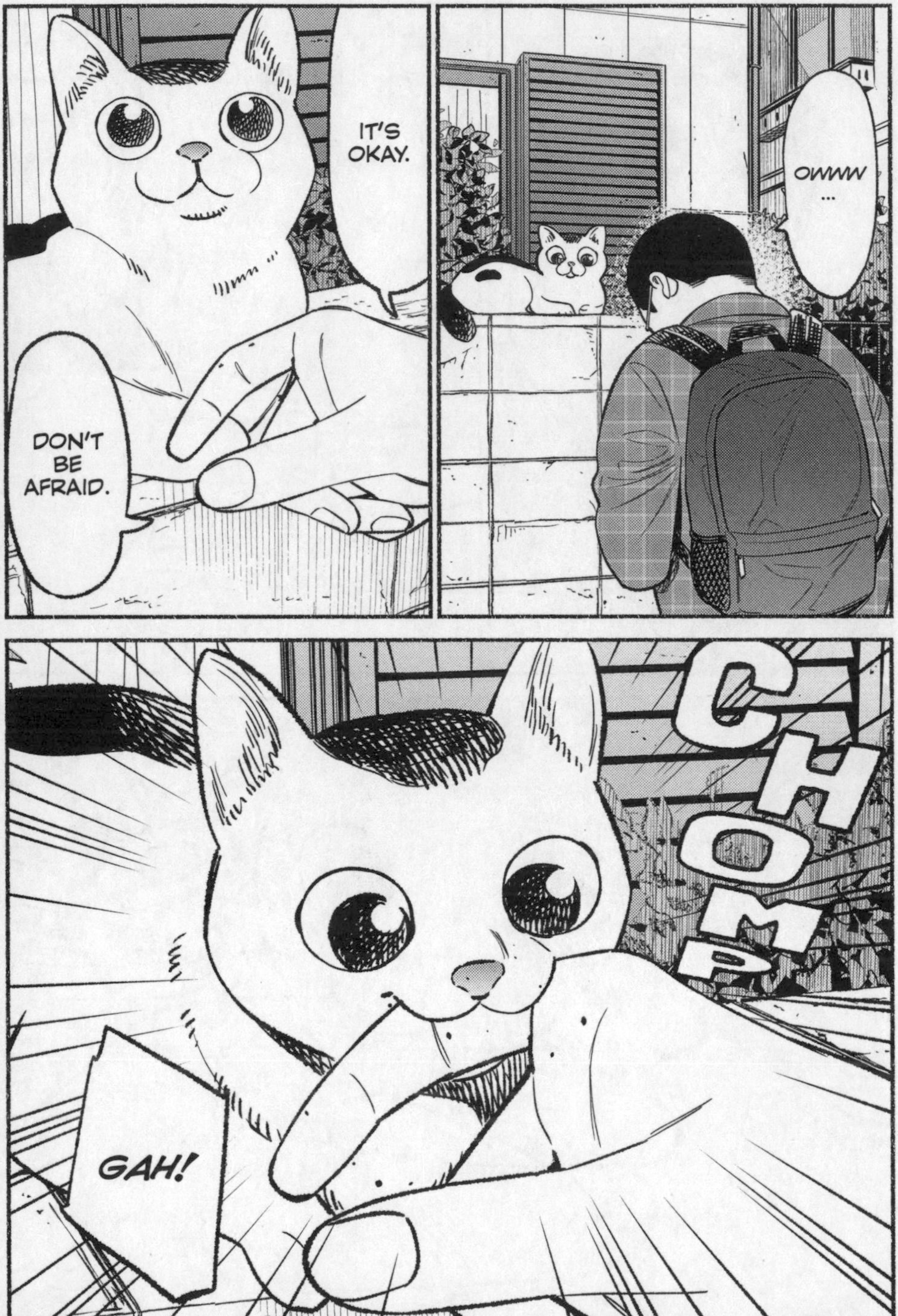
OWWW ...
IT'S OKAY.
DON'T BE AFRAID.
CHOMP
GAH!

I-I KNOW. YOU'RE JUST SCARED, THAT'S ALL.
HERE ...
LICK LICK
NOTHING TO BE AFRAID OF, SEE?
CHOMP

YOU SHOULD CALL IT QUITS AFTER THE FIRST BITE. SEE YOU AGAIN IN VOLUME 8.

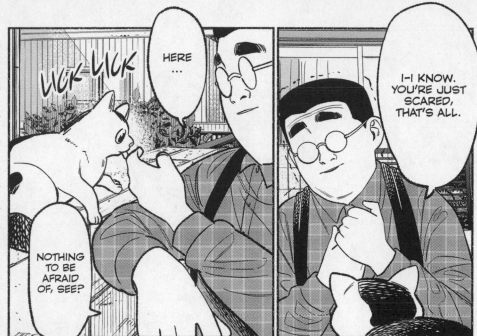

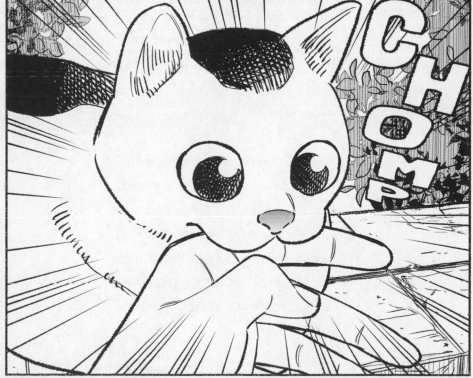

STAFF-MIDORINO HELP-KZK, KIMU BRO, YOSHIDA

I adopted a rescue cat
about a year ago. That might
explain why there are so
many cats in this volume.
My Shiba Inu is doing well too.

KOUSUKE OONO

Kousuke Oono began his professional
manga career in 2016 in the manga
magazine *Monthly Comics @ Bunch*
with the one-shot "Legend of Music."
Oono's follow-up series, *The Way of
the Househusband,* is the creator's first
serialization as well as his first English-
language release.

The Way of the House Husband

VOLUME 7

VIZ SIGNATURE EDITION

STORY AND ART BY
KOUSUKE OONO

TRANSLATION: Amanda Haley
ENGLISH ADAPTATION: Jennifer LeBlanc
TOUCH-UP ART & LETTERING: Bianca Pistillo
DESIGN: Alice Lewis
EDITOR: Jennifer LeBlanc

GOKUSHUFUDO volume 7
© Kousuke Oono 2018
All Rights Reserved
English translation rights arranged
with SHINCHOSHA PUBLISHING CO.
through Tuttle-Mori Agency, Inc, Tokyo

The stories, characters, and incidents mentioned
in this publication are entirely fictional.

No portion of this book may be reproduced or
transmitted in any form or by any means
without written permission from the copyright holders.

Printed in the U.S.A.

Published by VIZ Media, LLC
P.O. Box 77010
San Francisco, CA 94107

10 9 8 7 6 5 4 3 2 1
First printing, January 2022

PARENTAL ADVISORY
THE WAY OF THE HOUSEHUSBAND is rated T+
for Older Teen and is recommended for ages 16
and up. This volume contains violent situations.

VIZ MEDIA   VIZ SIGNATURE
viz.com   vizsignature.com

GANGSTER COOKING RECIPE vol. 2

RAINBOW TROUT ACQUA PAZZA

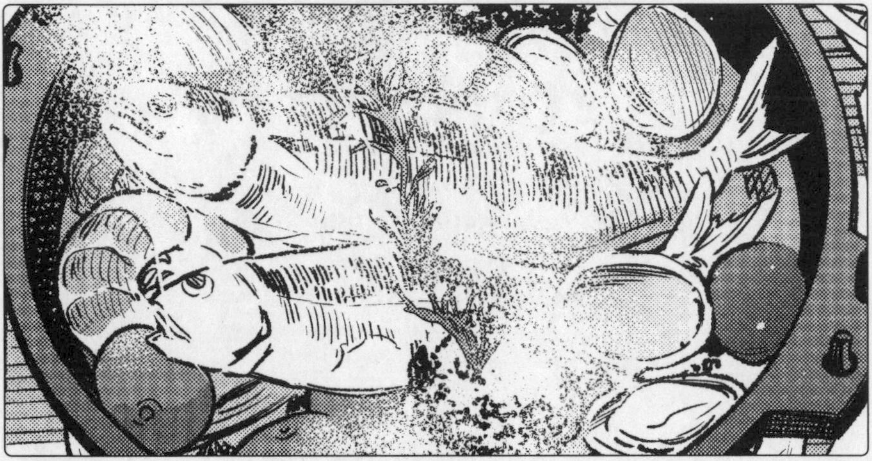

INGREDIENTS (SERVES 2)

- 2 rainbow trout
- 100 grams Manila clams
- 100 grams shrimp
- 80 grams broccoli
- 1/4 medium onion
- 4 cherry tomatoes
- 4 black olives (pitted)
- 1 clove garlic
- 2 tablespoons olive oil
- 1 sprig rosemary
- Salt and pepper to taste
- 50 milliliters white wine
- 150 milliliters water

DIRECTIONS

1. Gut fish, rinse, and pat dry. Deshell and devein shrimp. Soak clams in salt water to purge sand.
2. Wash cherry tomatoes and remove stems. Mince garlic. Cut onion into wedges.
3. Heat olive oil in a Dutch oven. Add garlic and cook until fragrant. Then add rainbow trout, lightly seasoned with salt. Once lightly browned, flip over and cook the other side.
4. Add clams, shrimp, broccoli, black olives, white wine, salt, and water. Put on lid, bring to a boil, and then reduce and simmer covered for about five minutes.
5. Turn off heat. Add cherry tomatoes and rosemary and steam for an additional five minutes.
6. For the finishing touch, add pepper, and then bring to the table, Dutch oven and all!

● Simple! ● Delicious! ● Torajiro's ● Special ● Recipe ●

Marshmallow, Chocolate, and Banana Sandwich

Torajiro
COOKING

A deluxe bind-up edition of Naoki Urasawa's award-winning epic of doomsday cults, giant robots and a group of friends trying to save the world from destruction!

20th Century Boys

THE PERFECT EDITION

NAOKI URASAWA

Humanity, having faced extinction at the end of the 20th century, would not have entered the new millennium if it weren't for them. In 1969, during their youth, they created a symbol. In 1997, as the coming disaster slowly starts to unfold, that symbol returns. This is the story of a group of boys who try to save the world.

20 SEIKI SHONEN KANZENBAN © 2016 Naoki URASAWA/Studio Nuts

VIZ

Cats *of the* Louvre

by TAIYO MATSUMOTO

A surreal tale of the secret world of the cats of the Louvre, told by Eisner Award winner Taiyo Matsumoto.

The world-renowned Louvre museum in Paris contains more than just the most famous works of art in history. At night, within its darkened galleries, an unseen and surreal world comes alive— a world witnessed only by the small family of cats that lives in the attic. Until now…

Translated by *Tekkonkinkreet* film director Michael Arias.

LOUVRE NO NEKO © 2017 Taiyou MATSUMOTO/Futuropolis/Musée du Louvre éditions, Paris

BEASTARS

Story & Art by Paru Itagaki

At this high school, instead of jocks and nerds, the students are divided into carnivores and herbivores.

At a high school where the students are literally divided into predators and prey, friendships maintain the fragile peace. Who among them will become a Beastar—a hero destined to lead in a society naturally rife with mistrust?

© 2017 PARU ITAGAKI (AKITASHOTEN)

 VIZ

CHILDREN OF THE WHALES

In this postapocalyptic fantasy, a sea of sand swallows everything but the past.

In an endless sea of sand drifts the Mud Whale, a floating island city of clay and magic. In its chambers a small community clings to survival, cut off from its own history by the shadows of the past.

VIZ
viz.com

RATED T+ OLDER TEEN

© 2013 ABI UMEDA (AKITASHOTEN)

THE DRIFTING CLASSROOM

PERFECT EDITION

by KAZUO UMEZZ

Out of nowhere, an entire school vanishes, leaving nothing but a hole in the ground. While parents mourn and authorities investigate, the students and teachers find themselves not dead but stranded in a terrifying wasteland where they must fight to survive.

COMPLETE IN 3 VOLUMES

RATED T+ OLDER TEEN

UMEZZ PERFECTION! 8 HYORYU KYOSHITSU © 2007 Kazuo UMEZZ/SHOGAKUKAN